WHO SPEAKS FOR MAN?

THE MACMILLAN COMPANY
NEW YORK · CHICAGO
DALLAS · ATLANTA · SAN FRANCISCO

THE MACMILLAN COMPANY
OF CANADA, LIMITED
TORONTO

WHO SPEAKS

FOR MAN?

by NORMAN COUSINS

The Macmillan Company . New York 1953

To
Ellen
and the
Four Girls

ACKNOWLEDGMENTS

Literary indebtedness is a curious and troublous thing. One never knows whether an acknowledgment discharges a debt or incurs one. What is sent as a garland may be received as a contaminant. Perhaps the acknowledgment page, like the formal engagement announcement, ought be attempted only on the basis of mutual consent. But even this brooks the dangers that go with placing gratitude in a display case. One ought to avoid, if possible, being put in the category reserved by Mark Twain for those who discharge their obligations in such a way that the report is heard for miles around.

Another hazard of the acknowledgment page is that the most important creditors are seldom listed; indeed, the author himself may be hardly conscious of his primary sources. Just as every man is "an omnibus in which his ancestors ride," as Dr. Holmes observed, so every book is the progeny and common property of a community of ideas in which there are no real owners, only contributors and custodians. My primary and overriding acknowledgment then, must be to every writer I have ever read, directly or indirectly, for the things a man reads, even though he may not remember them, work on him and provide him with nutriment or catharsis, essential inspiration or equally essential irritation, forcing him to act or react. To those writers who have given rough treatment to my own ideas, I am especially grateful. Goldsmith used to like a silent argument because he could not recall ever having lost one; perhaps I was more fortunate. I can't say that I relished defeat when it came, but at least it compelled me to bring up reinforcements for the next battle. Fun with books generally begins with an argument, for the pursuit of an effective rebuttal is often the best way of making a bookshelf come alive.

In a more explicit sense, I am indebted to my colleagues at *The Saturday Review* for having so graciously and patiently carried the workload of the editor during the too-frequent absences that made this book possible. I am no less grateful to them for their encouragement in developing this book out of editorials and articles appearing in the magazine. My thanks to Mr. Richard J. Walsh, of the John Day Company, for permission to draw upon the published transcript of *Talks with Nehru;* to Mr. Edward Mills, of Longmans, Green, for permission to adapt an essay written for *Years of the Modern;* to Mr. Frederick Lewis Allen, of *Harpers Magazine,* and Ambassador Chester Bowles for permission to draw upon an article answering the principal arguments against world federation, written in collaboration with Mr. Bowles. Because of their possible pertinency, several passages are used or adapted from the book, *The Good Inheritance* and the essay, *Modern Man Is Obsolete.*

Most explicitly of all, I am grateful to my wife, Ellen, for her extraordinary understanding of the anatomy of pre-occupation as it concerns a typewriter-husband, and for her boundless encouragement. For his specific help and continuing inspiration, I acknowledge my debt to Mr. Antonio Iglesias. Mrs. Charlotte Munger and Miss Julia Roche, alternately, kept me from making a wilderness out of my notes and papers and suffered the dozen retypings of the manuscript before the final version was turned over to the publisher who, in the pre-publication phase at least of a book, is inevitably the author's best friend.

CONTENTS

PART II: IDEAS AND DECISIONS

WHO SPEAKS FOR MAN?

"If I be right, I pretend not to have made any mighty discovery. And if I be wrong, I must acknowledge myself to be indeed a very backward scholar . . ."

—DAVID HUME

* * *

"If men can be found who revolt against the spirit of thoughtlessness, and who are personalities sound enough and profound enough to let the ideals of ethical progress radiate from them as a force, there will start an activity of the spirit which will be strong enough to evoke a new mental and spiritual disposition in mankind."

—ALBERT SCHWEITZER

* * *

"Politics and philosophy are alike. Socrates neither set out benches for his students, nor sat on a platform, nor set hours for his lectures. He was philosophizing all the time—while he was joking, while he was drinking, while he was soldiering, whenever he met you on the street, and at the end when he was in prison and drinking the poison. He was the first to show that all your life, all the time, in everything you do, whatever you are doing, is the time for philosophy. And so also it is of politics."

—PLUTARCH

* * *

"Unlike other nations, we regard the person who takes no direct interest in the affairs of his government as a useless, rather than an unambitious person. Instead of regarding public discussion as a stumbling block to effective action, we regard it as an indispensable preliminary to any wise action at all."

—PERICLES

* * *

"The great advantage of the Americans consists in their being able to commit faults which they may afterward repair."

—ALEXIS DE TOCQUEVILLE

* * *

"The fault of others is easily perceived, but that of oneself is difficult to perceive. A man winnows his neighbor's faults like chaff, but his own fault he hides, as a cheat hides the false die from the gambler."

—THE TEACHINGS OF BUDDHA

Who Speaks for Man?

PERSONAL AND PRELIMINARY

The reader is entitled to know something about the author.

No man can, or perhaps should, attempt to climb far enough outside his own skin and psyche to know whether he is a representative product of his times. And yet, typical or otherwise, two-thirds of my chronological existence coincides squarely with the period that historians may refer to as that of the Protest Generation that became the Violent Generation before it was through.

From the moment we were born, history laid siege to our times and our affairs. Our earliest memories were of World War I, of brothers or fathers or uncles who said goodbye and never came back, of lowered voices in the other rooms reading and rereading letters from overseas until they were leveled into rote. When we were old enough to think creatively about politics and philosophy, the depression laid strong hands on our ideas, and the old and accepted systems of thought and politics seemed feeble and irrelevant, fit for museums or textbooks but not for the throbbing issues of the day. By the time we got out of school, the word "career" had become a painful anachronism, and grimly we counted the physical and moral casualties among our friends.

We were being propelled into a world which was as reluctant and unprepared to receive us as we were to become a part of it. We groped for economic footing and for intellectual anchorage. When the New Deal came along, the more conservative among us took hope and root in it, for which we were damned as timid experimentalists by our more politically adventurous contemporaries, and as irresponsible revolutionaries by our elders.

The books we read and the plays we saw and the things we talked about added up to a sort of philosophy of orphanism; to paraphrase Mr. Housman and Mr. Farrell, we were in a world we never made and there was nothing to indicate that it would ever be any different. We didn't belong, nor was there anything we really felt we wanted to belong to.

When we surveyed the future, it was like looking out over a frozen tundra; if the thaw ever came, we were certain it would be in some far-off age. To be sure, there was excitement over the Oxford pledge and over Marxism and over the economic interpretation of history and over the debunking of the hero. But all these were flurries and not the real thing. For the fact was that we were going through the motions of being interested and being part of something when actually we ourselves lacked any real adhering surface to which ideas might stick.

Archibald MacLeish some years later summed it up in the word "irresponsibles." It was the irresponsibility of default rather than of design. How did you go about being responsible when you weren't sure what responsibility meant?

The paradox, of course, was that we were being intellectually static in a politically dynamic world. This is not to say that we were unaware of, or uninterested in, the bulging and threatening shape of things to come. But these were things without impact; we could see them and take note of them, but they were outside us. It was like blinking at the size and speed of an oncoming locomotive while standing on the track.

Such was the curious sense of unreality and wasted motion, the sense of separation from our times, that was the dominant mood in our college years and through most of the thirties.

It didn't last—it couldn't. But the circumstances of the awakening weren't the same in every case. Some of us emerged gradually, moved along by the momentum of events; others had to be blasted out of it by the war; still others by the continuing crisis following the war. And some of us, apparently, haven't come out of it yet.

In my own case, at least, the winds that blew from the East helped to ventilate my thinking and to clear off the foggy negativism that was the fashion of the time. I remember reading in 1937 about

Gandhi for the first time in a form more substantial than scattered newspaper accounts. It was a book by Romain Rolland. It combined a short, highlight biography of Gandhi with an account of his spiritual and political development. The final chapters contrasted the ideas of Gandhi with those of Tagore, dramatizing the importance of this dualism in awakening India. In some respects it was like the Hamilton-Jefferson controversy, with important elements of the philosophy of each coming together to create a vital blend. Gandhi approached mankind through India; Tagore approached India through mankind.

What impressed me most about Gandhi was not only his philosophy, impressive though it was under the special conditions in India, or the effectiveness of non-violence, for the technique was frequently at odds with the philosophy behind it. What impressed me most was the dramatic proof that the individual need not be helpless against massed power—that he need not be overwhelmed by any supposed inexorabilism or fatalism, that there was scope for free will and conviction in the shaping of society, that history could be fluid, not fixed, if men were willing to transcend their egos in order to merge themselves with the larger body of mankind.

It is difficult to describe adequately my sense of wonder at all this, for an idea that until then seemed beyond debate or even speculation was the utter domination of individual man by his times. Since you had never questioned it, you never had to think about it. History was the ocean—alternately calm and turbulent—and the individual was the rudderless vessel. As for the great leaders and commanding figures of history, you had been in the habit of seeing them as products rather than as architects of their times. But Gandhi didn't fit into the conventional role of the historical leader. He was in no position of power, nor did he seek power. He exercised leadership without being an official leader. He was a person, Anyman, demonstrating the practical value of ethics as applied to political problems. The response of the Indian people is one of the most stirring chapters in history. Little wonder that, when our government asked me in 1950 to accept an assignment to India, described in a later chapter, I jumped at the chance.

In reading Rolland, it was clear that Gandhi's teaching and his non-cooperation movement were enriched and invigorated as the result of Tagore's ceaseless prodding in behalf of universalism.

Tagore recognized the danger to the world of yet another purely nationalist movement. He could see that the Gandhi movement might get beyond Gandhi; that the heat generated by non-cooperation could become the fever of a national authoritarianism. India's problem, as Tagore saw it, was inseparable from the world problem. "No nation can find its own salvation by breaking away from the others. The awakening of India is bound up in the awakening of the world." I can recall now the thrill I felt in reading Tagore's poetic definition of universalism:

> Where the mind is without fear and the head is held high;
> Where knowledge is free;
> Where the world has not been broken up into fragments by
>   narrow domestic walls;
> Where words come out from the depth of truth;
> Where tireless striving stretches its arms towards perfection;
> Where the clear stream of reason has not lost its way into
>   the dreary desert sand of dead habit;
> Where the mind is led forward by thee into ever-widening
>   thought and action—
> Into that heaven of freedom, my Father, let my country
>   awake.

What was happening in India made me feel foolish for having been mired so long in the futility that was the fashion of my generation. Compared to India's, our problems were as wisps of smoke alongside a thunderhead. And yet, India was moving toward freedom precisely because a philosophy compounded of affirmation, action, compassion, and universalism was giving inspiration and direction to countless millions who were learning to think about the idea of freedom for the first time.

It was natural that the momentum generated by Gandhi and Tagore should carry me back to a reappraisal of the American philosophers, and even more natural, perhaps, that I should begin with Emerson, with whom the Indian thinkers seemed to have such a rich affinity. What formerly had seemed to me in Emerson to be a collection of bland philosophical truisms somewhat in the lavender tradition now came alive with force and distinction. As in Gandhi and Tagore, there was the rigorous assertion of individual integrity and purpose as a foundation for service to the general welfare. There was the Gandhian disdain in Emerson for conformity and convention: "Every true man is a cause, a country, and an age; requires infinite spaces and numbers and time fully to accomplish his design; and posterity seems to follow his steps as a train of clients." Then, in a one-line distillation of the Gandhi philosophy, Emerson wrote, "Nothing can bring you peace but the triumph of principles." Dozens of others had said it before Emerson; he brought it into rich focus.

It was Emerson's discussion of political philosophy that drove the final nail into the coffin for my disillusion; he defined both the power and responsibility of the individual in a complex society. He saw a wide and fertile field for individual action in advancing the general welfare. He didn't believe that man, collectively or individually, need feel he was incarcerated by history. The individual did belong. No state, no custom, no convention, could alter or destroy that fact. Then, almost as though he were anticipating one of the great debates of the twentieth century—the debate over inevitability and the "wave of the future"—Emerson wrote that we were not at the "mercy of any waves of chance. . . . In dealing with the state, we ought to remember that its institutions are not aboriginal, that they are not superior to the citizen, that one of them was once the act of a single man, that every law and usage was a man's expedient to meet a particular case, that they are all limitable, all alterable."

Apart from the impact of such ideas after almost a decade of saturating cynicism, the rereading of Emerson had an important by-effect; it convinced me that what I had read up to then had largely been misread or underread. Why, I asked myself, should there have been such a gap between the Emerson I read at eighteen and the Emerson I read at twenty-four?

The answer was simple but not pleasant: I had never really learned how to read. What had happened was that the books I had read had become ends in themselves, instead of means to ends beyond the books. I had read the things young people were supposed to have read by the time they got out of school. It was survey-course stuff —titles to check off on a long list that by actual measurements took up five feet or so on a bookshelf. To be sure, as I thought back about these books, each title called forth certain standardized associations, and I knew that with a little brushing up I could probably get by on an examination. And yet, how much of it had I really read? How much of it bristled with meaning? How much of it had given me vital insight into the author's purpose—insight essential to truly creative reading?

This led to an even more disturbing, although related, series of questions. If my reading had wound up in literary bankruptcy, what about my education in general? What, after all, was education without the understanding of books? How much of my formal education truly met my essential needs? Hadn't I been as uncreative in absorbing and making use of knowledge as I had in my general reading?

Before I could attempt to ponder the answers to these questions, or even be sure I had the right questions, I first had to define what it was I had expected education to do. As I thought about it, I realized that no single definition could possibly have enough elasticity to be all-inclusive.

Basically, I knew education had to narrow the gap between the individual and society, bringing individual capacity as close as possible to collective needs. In an ideal sense, education should produce the rounded man. It should enlarge the ability to think and the capacity for thought. It should be helpful in creating constructive attitudes—both on an individual and on a group level. It should impart basic and essential general knowledge for balanced living, and basic and essential specialized knowledge for specific careers. It should develop ethical values. It should furnish the individual with the necessary intellectual, moral, and technical clothing for a presentable appearance in the world community.

When I surveyed myself in terms of the ideal education, I could see that the clothing didn't fit; indeed, that it was thin and embarrassingly scanty. I was overexposed and underdeveloped. How much did I know about the most important science of all—the science of interrelationships—that critical area beyond compartmentalization where knowledge must be integrated in order to have proper meaning? Nothing. Did I have sufficient knowledge and understanding for vital participation in the world community? Hardly. Did I have any vital understanding of, or feeling for, cultures other than my own? Not enough to show. Was I able to see events against the broad historical flow? Only vaguely.

My feeling of inadequacy was not softened by the knowledge that I was not unique, nor by the fact that I was but a single unit among countless thousands turned out by the obsolescent assembly belt of "higher education." "Higher education" had indeed become a misnomer in the light of the new needs. What seemed adequate at the turn of the century for the purposes of top-level education now fulfilled only an intermediate function at best. The danger described so well by Whitehead—that events might outrun man and leave him a panting and helpless anachronism—was rapidly becoming more than a figure of speech.

On the level of educational techniques, as apart from purposes, what had been missing, at least in my case, now seemed clear: reasons. I had been educated in everything except the meaning and purpose of education itself. It was like a wheel with beautiful spokes but no rim. If there was real direction or destination, it was never convincingly explained. If there was real integration to all the educational compartments in which the various studies were located and isolated, I was never apprised of it.

I had no reason to suppose that I could ever catch up with, or even remotely approach, any of the definitions I tried to rough out as to what constituted an educated person in our time. But at least I had found the motive power for re-examining and re-appraising my knowledge of history and philosophy. Every book I reread was as though I had never come across it before. Every idea I explored had its own chain reaction.

What I was doing, of course, was attempting to seek the vital connections between ideas instead of viewing ideas as sovereign entities, which was the direction my formal reading had taken. You might call it the difference between the vertical and the lateral approach to history.

The vertical, or conventional, approach was to begin at a designated place and time in history, and then climb the chronological ladder until you reached the present. For example, if you were studying American history, you would start either with Columbus or with the Pilgrims or with the background of the Revolution, and then climb up in a straight line, event by event, until you arrived at, let us say, World War II. The same was true of the approach to French history or English history or European history in general. Whatever the philosophy behind it, the effect of this method was to emphasize the nationalistic interpretation of history at the expense of a rounded view of the general development of man—politically, socially, culturally.

The lateral method, however, could break down this compartmentalization and enable you to observe the interaction of events and ideas. You would use time as your principal frame of reference, selecting a certain period and then searching in many lands for common elements of common problems, and, most important, the interconnections that affected mankind as a whole. If, for example, you took periods surrounding such key years as 400 B.C. or after Christ, 350 or 1492 or 1789 or 1873 or 1914 or 1945, and used those years as arenas for the study of *world* history, with your emphasis on peoples rather than on nations, you could discover surprising mutualities—mutualities of experience, of philosophies and attitudes, of aspirations. You would discover, too, cross-fertilization of ideas among peoples that were otherwise obscured in the national or vertical study and interpretation of history.

In terms of a working philosophy, out of this expedition in ideas and morals came the confirmation and enlargement of the doctrine not only of natural liberty but of natural scope in creating liberty. I had come a long way from the cynicism and disillusion which had soured so much of my earlier thinking. And little by little, I could see the evidence growing all around me that many others of my generation were re-examining their beliefs against the background of an accelerating history. Nazism and nihilism were joined and mobilized and people were being killed; it dawned on many of us that notions of futility were an intellectual luxury, that the threat was alive and real, and that decisions might have to be made that we had thought need never be made again.

It was at this point that the second step or challenge in the general design of my re-education asserted itself. Admitting that there was no retreat for the individual and that he could find no refuge in fatalism or determinism, what kind of world was he trying to build—assuming the world could be saved for the rebuilding? T. S. Eliot said it about Munich: "The feeling which was new and unexpected was a feeling of humiliation, which seemed to demand an act of personal contrition, of humility, repentance and amendment; what had happened was something in which one was deeply implicated and responsible. . . . Was our society, which had always been so assured of its superiority and rectitude, so confident of its unexamined premises, assembled round anything more permanent than a congeries of banks, insurance companies and industries, and had it any beliefs more essential than a belief in compound interest and the maintenance of dividends?"

Once again, our society was in the process of calling upon the individual to offer himself in sacrifice in order to perpetuate the group; but the individual didn't always define the bond that connected him to the group in the same terms that society did. If the individual believed that society, no less than the individual, was obligated to live the life of virtue, could he justly say that virtue was at stake? The evil and the power of Nazism were quite clear; and there could be no doubt that the threat would have to be turned back. But was it enough just to fight *against* something? Why couldn't we fight *for* something?

Just as earlier I re-examined my own place in society, and the potentiality of the individual for effective ethical action, so now I re-examined my ideas on the nature of society, on the potentialities within the group for ethical ideas and action, and, in general, on government as an organism with a metabolism rate of its own, a conscience of its own, and a life cycle of its own. Unlike the previous search, which began with Gandhi and went weaving in and out, with no fixed pattern and stretching over the entire history of ideas, this search came to rest in two areas: classical Greece and late eighteenth century America.

Greece offered the example of a civilization that, on the basis of the evidence, seemed to have passed into decay, not because it had become moribund, but primarily because of sheer human error. In the case of America, you had a nation designed on a drawing board, the architects of which understood error in government as did no other group assembled before or since. With Greece, you had a golden age that was abruptly terminated precisely because the city-states themselves, in their dealings with one another, lacked a mechanism for dealing with error, and so became its victims. With America, the concept of the inevitability of error, and the specific means provided to deal with it, represented one of the chief building blocks of the new government.

In each case, what I was interested in primarily was the anatomy of error. I use the word "error" not only in the familiar sense of blunder or mistake, but in the broader sense of avoidable failure. For history can be viewed as an accumulation of error; the nature of the error and the thought proceeding out of error often determine the rate of progress and the type of progress. Indeed, the story of men and nations is largely the story of their attitude toward error. The less democratic a society, the smaller the margin for error of its subjects and the greater the margin for error of its rulers. The more arbitrary the definition of error, the less important the machinery of justice. The more protection error receives in high places, the less scope for public opinion and an ungoverned press.

Apart from the errors committed by the highly privileged citizens of Greece under the double standard of virtue and morality that existed between themselves and their slaves, there was the endless series of errors in the dealings among the Greek city-states themselves. The great similarities among the peoples were no bar to war; indeed, it almost seemed as though their mutualities lubricated their antagonisms. What was missing was the means of bringing order into their collective life—the life of the city-states in their relations with one another. They made the mistake of attempting to seek national security through military coalitions or balance-of-power arrangements, or through conspiracy with sympathetic elements in the other city-states. They made the error of not facing up to the need of federation among themselves and the need for a rule of law which federation alone might have provided. Their leaders were unwilling to effect a larger junction except on their own terms, which is to say, domination of all others. Besides, as Madison later observed, the last place in the world to look for the basic motive power of federation is officialdom, for it is unreasonable to expect rulers voluntarily to turn in their seals of office and accept a lesser role; the psychology of power and leadership has little margin for subordination. The motive power for larger law would have to be supplied by the people themselves. But this, too, was lacking.

Generally speaking, the frictions between the Athenian coalition in the north of Greece and the Spartan coalition in the south fell into two broad categories. In the first category, there were the ideological differences growing out of the contrast between an outgoing, culturally vibrant, liberal-aristocratic Athens, and an ingrown, inbred, militaristic, oligarchic Sparta. Along with this was the inevitable commercial rivalry between the two leading powers in Greece—one a maritime empire, the other the leading land power.

In the second and more important category were the frictions that grew out of the competition for physical security. For the ideological and economic differences, great as they were, did not figure as prominently in the causes of war as the fact that neither state had any real basis for confidence in the short-range or long-range intentions of the other. Each state felt insecure in the absence of any higher agency with power to protect it against attack. Thus, each prepared against the other—and the preparation took the form not only of military measures, but of jockeying for position and power in building up influence in other states that were needed as possible allies.

It was the old story—old even 2,400 years ago—of the lack of specific machinery of law and law enforcement to eliminate at least that aspect of the danger that grew out of the need to be secure. And law machinery in this case meant federation. Federation might not have resolved all the ideological and economic differences, but at least it might have made unnecessary and impossible the measures leading to war that each state took as the only means of protecting itself.

This failure made a profound impression on the American federalists. The function of the Constitution makers, as Hamilton and Madison saw it, was to build "monuments" to experience. Again, the key to good government was in the approach to error. There were two broad groups of error. The first grew out of the neglect or violation of principles. The second was on the operational or functional level, and proceeded out of the fallibility of man. As they saw it, then, theirs was a dual responsibility. They had to establish a framework of principle within which states could live side by side on a fairly rational basis. Next, they had to provide the people with the means of coping with error—inevitable error—by their elected and appointed officials.

On the level of principle, this meant that states within a geographic unit must have binding obligations among themselves for the great safety of all. But these obligations were to be limited only to those matters affecting the common security and welfare. In all matters pertaining to the relationships of the states to one another, particularly when and where there were disputes, the central government was to have jurisdiction.

On the operational level error was to be taken for granted. For no man was deemed wise enough to be free of error. The important thing was to limit the effect of those errors by depriving their makers of the natural secrecy in which errors breed and multiply. The dictator enjoys the privilege of enshrouding his errors; a democracy's chance for progress exists in direct proportion to its ability to keep errors out in the open. If one branch of the government makes the error of attempting to arrogate too much power to itself, another branch of the government should be able to correct it, or at least to call public attention to it. The head of the government, for example, must remain within reach of free and open criticism. If any of the military services acts too arbitrarily, even though the action may seem natural according to military lights, it must subject itself to public scrutiny and judgment. The general term for all this was "checks and balances"; more accurately, perhaps, it is the error theory of government. In short, there must not only be an accounting *of* error, but an accounting *for* error.

The history of early Greece and the Constitutional period of American history had a profound effect on my development into a world federalist. It gave a deeper sense of purpose and usefulness to my fast-developing interest in, and concern with, the philosophy of universalism. It added political form to ideological substance. Another important result of the Greek-American laboratories was that it deepened and reinforced my conviction against historical determinism. Greek civilization died, not because of any natural laws or life cycles affecting nations, but because the Greek peoples were unable to deal with the final error of war. It was only a matter of time before they would fight the one war from which they could not recover. Nor did historical determinism operate in the founding of the United States. Here was a magnificent example of the scope and power of free will and decision in the affairs of man. Here was the bold validation of the long-challenged theory of human progress. And here, finally, was the specific application of historical experience and principle to the deliberate creation of a structure of government possessing the form of law and the substance of justice.

It was natural that I should attempt to apply these lessons of federalism to my own time. In observing the decline and fall of the

League of Nations, it seemed clear that the failure to invest it with a sovereignty of its own and with effective powers had doomed it from the start, in precisely the way that the Articles of Confederation were doomed and the Amphictyonic League in early Greece was doomed. This was not to say that there was any strict historical analogy between the League and the American states under the Articles. The process of federation would have been immeasurably more difficult for all the states of the world in 1938 than it was for the states of the east coast of America in 1787. But the basic principle was precisely the same; states within a geographic unit must unite or fight. Such differences and difficulties as existed in the way of federation actually defined the challenge. For these were the differences that spelled out the threat of conflict and made it critically essential to find some way to keep them from breaking out in open war.

But when I thought about federalism in 1938, I did so against the background of impending war. There was no doubt that the nations were now part of a single geographic unit. The only real doubts concerned the auspices under which the attempt to co-ordinate the unit would be made—whether it would be done under democratic or totalitarian leadership. In short, whose world government would it be? Would it be brought about through organization or subjugation?

By the summer of 1939, these questions had a razor edge, for Germany seemed well on the way to hammering out a world unity according to her own design. Even without open warfare, Germany was bringing the entire continent of Europe under her dominion; indeed, the attempt was being made to have the entire world revolve on the Rome-Berlin-Tokyo axis. The effect of all this was to give a cold chill to world-government enthusiasts, who now knew the absurdity and the danger of talking about world government without also defining exactly what such a world government was to be, and how it was to operate, if it was to deserve the support of the world's peoples who would have to establish it. In any event, we had a long way to go before we would be prepared to advance ideas for a world organization with enforceable powers. At the moment, the critical problem was staying alive.

When the war did break out, we received another jolt, for we were even less prepared to face it intellectually and politically than we were militarily. There was a good deal we had to unlearn; we had been brought up on the vested-interest theory of war. Wars happened, we had been taught—in and out of school—because armament manufacturers had to keep their factories going. The common people were the innocent dupes, according to this theory; therefore, the way to deal with war was to spurn the call. The only trouble with the theory, of course, is that it didn't tell you what to do if the common peoples of the enemy, far from spurning the call, actually seemed to relish the kill and the conquest.

The curious air of unreality that existed during the first winter of war, when very little happened and when there was talk of "certain accommodations" being made between the opposing governments at the expense of the peoples, did little to bring about the necessary intellectual reconditioning for what was in truth a fight for sheer survival. Indeed, it was not until Dunkirk that things snapped into place. The change was as quick as it was deep. In just a few weeks or so, we had learned more about what we wanted to do, and where we were going, and what there was worth saving, than we had once thought it was within our ken to learn in a lifetime. We had come of age almost overnight; we weren't afraid to think or talk about values. If there were any values we really believed in, and if those values were lacking in our society, then we had to keep alive the chance to make those values real. For society was nothing outside us, like a distant mountain, but an organism of which we were a part; it was for us to say what we wanted that society to be, and it was for us to make sure that we could keep the right to change it in our own hands.

There was something vibrant and clean about the sense of conviction and affirmation that was rising within us as the challenge crystallized. It was something you didn't want to forget and were afraid to forget. You were afraid to lose what I believe William James once called "crisis clarity." You were determined, once the war was won, to avoid the same cynicism that followed the previous war.

Another challenge or phase of my re-education came at the end of the war, and had the impact of an explosion. When the news broke about the bombing of Hiroshima, I couldn't have been hit harder than if a report had just been flashed that an interstellar collision involving the earth was possible and likely. For it seemed to me that man overnight had come face to face with the problems of human destiny, that he had conquered nature only to discover that forces inside him were more powerful and terrifying. He had beaten back every natural challenge thrown his way: heat, cold, water, ice, sun, sand, and wind; but he had yet to comprehend that far more menacing was the environment he had created for himself. All at once, the planet became too small for his competitive urge and his quarrelsomeness. A sword was fixed with the point over his heart, and he was stumbling around in a darkened arena full of pits, holes, and knee-high obstacles.

All my life I had been a gradualist; in my thoughts on universalism and world government I had been concerned primarily with the requirements of a world community organized under law and justice, and it had seemed self-evident that it might take several generations at least before such a community could be brought into being. But with Hiroshima, it became clear that a long-range ideal had become an immediate necessity and that no amount of talk about the difficulties in the way of this universalism could dispose of the danger of trying to survive without it. The question was not whether we needed it, but only how we would have to go about getting it within the required time.

That night—the night after the day that man revealed the great design of his own destruction—I tried to sort my fears and hopes in an editorial for *The Saturday Review*. The gist of that editorial was that "modern" man had become obsolete, a self-made anachronism becoming more incongruous by the minute. He had exalted change in everything but himself. He had leaped centuries ahead in inventing a new world to live in, but he knew little about his own part in that world. Given time, he might be expected to bridge those gaps normally; but by his own hand he had destroyed even time. Communication, transportation, and war no longer waited on time. Whatever bridges had to be built and crossed would have to be built and crossed immediately.

The purpose of that editorial, I am afraid, was somewhat misunderstood. It was said that I had written a farewell to man, that I had defined a predicament from which there was neither retreat nor escape. Such was not my intention, and I have only myself to blame for not having made my purpose clear. I believed there were rational grounds for hope—tremendous hope—and I said so, but I made the mistake of bearing down so heavily on the danger that by the time I tried to discuss the possibilities of meeting that danger the dominant mood of the editorial had been established in the minds of many readers.

I am no pessimist. I doubt that any man knows enough to be a pessimist. Neither am I a reckless optimist. I do not think that things necessarily come out all right in the end if left to themselves. I do not believe that any nation or any people enjoys a natural immunity against catastrophe or a special dispensation against disaster. Survival depends on ideas and action; and before we decide what the ideas are or what the action is to be, it is essential that we become supremely aware of the danger and resolve to meet it. It was in that spirit that I wrote the editorial, which seemed to me a logical expression of everything I had learned during the process of my "re-education." Far from subtracting from an affirmative, activist philosophy built around the plastic nature of history, atomic fission added something: the powerful ingredient of urgency. I never wavered in my confidence in the *capacity* of man to eliminate war and build a just peace, or to make the changes in himself in order to meet the problems and opportunities; what I tried to do was to emphasize that capacity rested on decision, and *decision* on *recognition* of the challenge.

On the political level, one of the most compelling reasons for urgency was that time was working against us. With each passing day after the end of the war, the classic and natural causes for tension and conflict between two giant nations outside a power vacuum would assert themselves unless some way could be found of eliminating the competition for power and security. When the United States and Russia looked at each other across this vacuum, the struggle to fill it would be on in earnest unless a world organization were invested both with preponderant force and with a judicial structure which would be able to command the confidence of the world's peoples.

Two months before Hiroshima, it seemed regrettable but not unnatural that the delegates at San Francisco should fail to invest the United Nations with the power of world law. Nor did it seem strange that the United States should propose the veto, and indicate its unwillingness to submit itself to a higher sovereignty. We believed we were moving as fast as we could under the circumstances. Russia, as the other great power, was no less anxious to avoid binding commitments, and served notice at San Francisco that her foreign-policy objectives were not to be made subordinate to the Charter.

But Hiroshima made San Francisco ancient history. It was as though a man-made ice age were descending, reducing all man's political bickerings and quarrels to a preposterous thimbleful alongside the universality of the threat. For the issue was not the nation but man; and the peoples of the world were waiting for leadership which would enable them to break out of the old level on which they argued and fought, and onto a new level of awareness and responsibility equal to the danger and the opportunity.

But while peoples everywhere had been drawn together within a single potential battlefield, and while they shared a common destiny, they were without common representation and had yet to define the basis of a common hope. The nation was no longer able to protect the person, his property, his welfare—and the nation had ceased to be the ultimate outer protective ring. The nation had been the natural product of a geographic community. But what about the human community now that the geographic community was one? Something beyond the nation had to be created—adequate to meet the challenge and the opportunity; adequate to create the conditions of peace, adequate to make peace meaningful; adequate to speak for man.

I say "make peace meaningful" because I do not believe that peace is the ultimate in human achievement. Peace can be tyranny, it can be human stagnation, it can be senseless drift. If I believed that peace could be achieved only at the expense of principle, I would be against peace. If I believed that peace meant surrender to evil, I would be against peace. I say this though I have seen an atomic bomb explode eighteen miles away; though I have seen the first city in history to serve as an atomic target; though I have seen the bombed cities of Europe and Asia, their insides hollowed out by dynamite and fire; though I have seen the faces of the dead in war and the faces of the damned whose bodies, but not whose minds, survived. I say this though I know that the next war will see America's cities join the long procession that began with Rotterdam and Coventry and London and Berlin and ended with Hiroshima and Nagasaki.

I believe it is possible to avert this war, to avert it with honor, and to create a rich and purposeful peace. If I did not believe this, whatever lessons I may have learned in my re-education would have been wasted. For these lessons, in their distilled form, say that man need not lose command of his destiny, that he has deep within him the resources of courage, conscience, and the spirit to shatter his predicament, and that he can transcend the complexities and perplexities that bedevil his existence if he can but release his natural idealism, accept the concept of the human community, and build upon it.

The world today hungers for ideals—not for supposedly "practical" ways out; for the curse of the twentieth century has been a grueling, biting, unrealistic materialism seeking sanction by calling itself "practical." The nation, or rather the people, that will define the ideal of a world federation backed by the spirit of universalism as a basis both for survival and for fulfillment, will attract to itself such massed support everywhere as will dissolve what now appear to be the ineradicable components of disaster.

It may be that the leaders of one or more nations will attempt to blacken that ideal for their own peoples. No matter. The preponderance of mankind will respond at once and the rest in due course.

Such, at least, are some of the convictions that have gone into and grown out of my "re-education." This re-education is not complete—and I doubt that it ever will be; living history is a classroom in which the lessons and the room itself constantly change and enlarge. In the pages that follow I try to describe a personal odyssey to various sections of that classroom; the two broad categories of this book represent an attempt to put that odyssey in perspective. The first section is called "People and Places," the second "Ideas and Decisions." Together they raise many more questions than they dare to answer. And the biggest question of all—the one which at last brings all the others into focus—is embodied in the title of this book.

PART ONE

People and Places

"*Human knowledge and human power meet in one; for where the cause is not known the effect cannot be produced. Nature to be commanded must be obeyed; and that which in contemplation is as the cause is in operation as the rule.*"

—FRANCIS BACON

* * *

"*. . . that laws and institutions must go hand in hand with the progress of the human mind. As that becomes more developed, more enlightened, as new discoveries are made, new truths disclosed, and manners and opinions change with the change of circumstances, institutions must advance also, and keep pace with the times.*"

—THOMAS JEFFERSON

* * *

"*The age in which we live should be distinguished by some glorious enterprise. . . . Let the leaders contrive to put an end to our present troubles. The treaties of peace are insufficient for their purpose; they may retard, but cannot prevent, our misfortunes. We stand in need of some more durable plan, which will forever put an end to our hostilities and unite us by the lasting ties of mutual affection and fidelity.*"

—ISOCRATES

* * *

"*Great as the Universe is, man is yet not always satisfied with it. For there is nothing so large but the mind of the moral man can conceive of something still larger which nothing in the world can hold. There is nothing so small but the mind of the moral man can conceive of something still smaller which nothing in the world can split.*"

—CONFUCIUS

* * *

"*Every epoch has its character determined by the way its populations react to the material events which they encounter. This reaction is determined by their basic beliefs—by their hopes, their fears, their judgments of what is worth while. They may rise to the greatness of an opportunity, seizing its drama, perfecting its art, exploiting its adventure, mastering intellectually and physically the network of relations that constitutes the very being of the epoch. On the other hand, they may collapse before the perplexities confronting them. How they act depends partly on their courage, partly on their intellectual grasp. Philosophy is an attempt to clarify those fundamental beliefs which finally determine the emphasis of attention that lies at the base of character.*"

—ALFRED NORTH WHITEHEAD

* * *

"*They say that when the bombs explode over Bikini, the heat will equal the interior heat of stars. This is of the utmost interest to scientists, every one of whom owes his existence to the earth's having cooled off.*"

—E. B. WHITE

CHAPTER II

FIFTY-THREE SECONDS

Less than a year after Hiroshima, I was on my way to an atomic catastrophe. It was a deliberate catastrophe. Concentrated scientific genius was going to demonstrate what happens when it pours its highest knowledge into a gadget which acts as though it were a slice of the sun come to earth.

How did it feel to be part of Operation Crossroads, Joint Task Force One, at Bikini? It was a mixed feeling. There was, of course, the primitive, the overpowering lure of the spectacular. It couldn't be argued away on moral grounds, for the inexorable pull was on the emotions. Call it morbid curiosity, call it perverse fascination; whatever it was, you had to take into account the fact that perhaps never before in history had curiosity and fascination been under the pressure of such intense, though negative, stimulation.

But the feeling, to repeat, was mixed. There was also the feeling of a grotesque unreality, the feeling of an authorized insanity.

Thus the cosmic became the casual. One day on deck, as the U.S.S. *Appalachian* neared Bikini, we heard a lecture by a geologist who spoke in a matter-of-fact tone as he examined the possibilities of a planetary disaster as the result of the atomic-bomb tests. His calm conclusion was that there was very little chance of such an untoward development. He went on from there to consider somewhat more limited dangers, such as the claim that the bomb would set off a major earthquake in the ocean, crack open the earth's crust, and cause a tidal wave of unprecedented size and power. Here, too, he obligingly furnished calm but ample reassurances.

Even more significant than the reassurances was the historic fact—

to be reviewed, we hope, by later historians—that in the middle of the twentieth century it should have been necessary for scientists to discuss the effects of artificially induced earthquakes and various other questions bearing on the possible destruction of this planet by man. Let it also be recorded that there was nothing unusual or dramatic about these discussions; the scientists might just as easily have been discoursing upon the anthropology of the Micronesians or the comb-footed spiders of Papua.

But this was not a scientists' party. The test was set against a military backdrop, and was by and large an Army and Navy show. The stated purpose was to see what happens to fighting ships when an atomic bomb goes off. The results, supposedly, were to determine what changes, if any, are to be made not only in the way ships are designed, but in their battle formations and harboring arrangements. One bomb was to be exploded at an unspecified height above one target, another a few feet under the surface. Both bombs were to be Nagasaki models.

Yet even on military grounds the tests were vulnerable. Even assuming battleships could stand up under anything but a direct hit by an atomic bomb, could they prevent rockets with atomic warheads from blasting the cities? Why would an enemy with a limited or even unlimited supply of atomic weapons bother to use them against secondary or intermediate targets when he could more easily strike at the main objectives? If the historic purpose of the Navy was to protect the homeland, what contribution could the Navy make to the new requirements of defense? Was it possible that a Navy in the next war might come through largely untouched, all dressed up with no place to go because the home ports and home cities were already destroyed?

For almost three weeks aboard ship, the tension slowly mounted. There were daily press briefings and lectures. Two lectures were given over to a consideration of the problems of accidents and what we would be expected to do. And even though such happenings were described as remote, the mere fact that they were discussed fitted into the general atmosphere of uncertainty and even fear.

It was not a conscious fear, although the chaplain aboard ship later told me that a number of hard-boiled reporters who had never attended services before were somewhat concerned about their spiritual condition the morning of the test. The fear felt by most was deeply subjective. Rational man invokes the intellect to outlaw or at least to dominate the surface sense of fear; but the primitive or fundamental insecurity in man is not always within the reach of reason, though it is highly sensitive and responsive to external stimuli. The fact that we may not be aware of the process does not mean that it does not exist.

I suppose that any observer on the trip, if asked bluntly whether he was afraid, would honestly have replied that he knew nothing to be afraid of. And yet deep within all of us were the makings of a first-class anxiety neurosis. Each little word of speculation or uncertainty registered itself without our thinking about it, stimulating and nourishing the basic fear mechanism.

Consider, for example, so ostensibly simple a matter as the question of goggles with which to view the explosion. Very emphatically, Navy officials warned us against attempting to view the burst with the naked eye. We were told we would be blinded—not permanently, but long enough not to see the real spectacle after the flash; blinded perhaps for hours. It was announced that expensive and specially constructed goggles would be issued. And even with goggles, we were told, it might be advisable not to look at the explosion directly but slightly off to one side.

You might say there was nothing in the goggles episode that could reasonably be expected to fit into the developing subsurface tensions; yet it had its place, and was to become, as we shall see later, almost a symbol of the test itself, with all its mixed emotional content. It was interesting but not surprising to see the way some of the men twirled their goggles at the last press briefing, asking questions that had been discussed and answered many times before, questions about the effect of radioactivity on the water; about the lethal "drop-out" or "rain" of radioactive particles from cloud formations; about the maximum speed of the *Appalachian* and how fast it could get away from something if it really had to; about radioactive-detecting Geiger counters and whether we would have one on board. It developed later that a few perhaps overconscientious souls, quite disturbed by the uncertainty of it all, wrote their complete stories about the bombing the day before it took place.

All this was part of the conditioning, part of the psychological undertone, part of the general atmosphere on Able Day as the men found vantage points for themselves on the upper decks and prepared to witness the explosion. Each reporter was assigned a sailor who would act as copy boy in rushing his dispatches to the communications room below decks. A Navy officer whose headphones enabled him to hear direct reports from the bombing plane stood behind us and relayed the position of the plane as it slowly climbed to its assigned altitude of 35,000 feet.

Twenty minutes before zero second, the order came to don the goggles. The "copy boys" were ordered to turn around and to shield their eyes with their arms. I put on my goggles. It was as though someone had covered my eyes with black adhesive. The goggles seemed completely opaque. I turned around and looked squarely at the sun. It was visible, all right, but robbed of all its brilliance, robbed almost of light itself. I turned in the general direction of the target array (we were eighteen miles away) and waited. I felt as though I had just entered a room of absolute darkness and momentarily expected someone to turn on the lights.

With ten minutes to go, the bombing plane reported it had completed two practice runs over the target at the assigned altitude. The bombardier reported perfect visibility. Then the naval officer behind us announced that the plane was making its "live" run. He called out the minutes before zero as well as the distance in miles from the target.

Six minutes. Five minutes. Four minutes. Three minutes. Two minutes. The last two minutes were the hardest. Then, in a drained, parched voice, as though he had to struggle to get it out, he said simply, "Bomb away."

For fifty-three seconds the bomb fell. It seemed more like fifty-three years. When the unknown is sovereign even for a moment, you live not one but many lifetimes. It is not that your entire life passes before you in review, as in the legend about a drowning man. What happens is that everything suddenly comes to a halt. No one says anything. You don't think about anything in particular; you are just conscious of a tight feeling somewhere about your middle. You feel that even the waves have stopped moving. Though it is impossible to look at your watch, you know that even the second hand's motion would be imperceptible to the human eye. And still the bomb falls. It is too far away to see; even if it weren't, everything is black before you. In that total darkness, you merely exist—exist in a vacuum of time and space.

And then, suddenly, the flash. It is deep and round and large. You rip off your goggles and see the rapidly mobilizing column rising from a clot of black smoke on the horizon. You see it gathering into a column of heavy peach-and-cream-colored cotton, flattening out and then spreading out at the top into the classic mushroom. As soon as the classic symbol appears, you are jerked back to reality. Then you realize that the atomic bomb is no longer a novelty on the face of the earth, no longer a phenomenon. After four bombs, the mystery dissolves into a pattern. By this time, there is almost a standardization of catastrophe. The flash, the smoke, the rising column, the mushroom—all are now as familiar as bomber formations or the sound of the cannon or the heat of a gun barrel, as familiar as death itself. Even the planet has adjusted itself to atomic shocks, and is apparently capable of preserving its equilibrium in space against additional such assaults.

Five minutes after the explosion, the mushroom-capped column of smoke was becoming increasingly obscured by a slow-moving, fat cloud formation. Then it disappeared altogether. At that precise moment of frustration, news was radioed from one of the observer planes that all the capital ships were still afloat.

The reporter next to me on the top deck of the press ship U.S.S. *Appalachian* was mumbling to himself.

"Did you say something?" I asked.

"Oh, I was just thinking that the next war's not going to be so bad after all."

I couldn't decide whether he was disappointed or relieved, or both.

And in those early minutes after the explosion, when newspaper stories had to be written and cabled, when the radio announcements had to be made, most of the correspondents relayed their first impressions which became the headline news from Bikini. The general tenor was that the bomb had been "oversold"—that it was "merely" another weapon.

Honest as these first impressions may have been, they were reported to the world without any real knowledge of what had actually happened or what was happening in the lagoon. The reports from the air were spotty and unreliable because of the distance of the planes from the contaminated air area above the target array. The real news was not available until almost twenty-four hours later;

but by that time it was already too late. The first impressions were congealed in the large type.

Later and more accurate and important reports were treated as ordinary second- or third-day follow-up stories; in short, the story was "cold" after the first big splash.

It was no surprise, therefore, to return home from Bikini after the first test and learn that many Americans reacted much the same as did many of the *Appalachian* correspondents in the first few hours after the explosion. There is, however, this significant difference: The reporters changed their minds once they had a firsthand opportunity to observe the damage and become acquainted with some highly significant facts in connection with the explosion—facts not available immediately after the bombing and which they had to dig out for themselves. These facts were duly reported to the American press back home but were relegated for the most part to the inside pages, where they lacked the striking power to overcome the initial impressions. The *Nevada* was afloat and some goats lived; what else mattered?

The first fact central to any evaluation of the first test is that the bomb turned out to be less than 50 per cent of its "normal" strength. It was a Nagasaki- or plutonium-type bomb; but there is apparently no way of predetermining the power coefficient. Much depends upon the purity of the fissionable materials used. According to the Navy itself, there was a possible range of efficiency from almost negligible to 100 per cent; and there was no certain method of insuring the latter. A fairly reliable postexplosion index to the power of the bomb, however, according to one of the scientists assigned to Operation Crossroads, was the height of the mushroom formation. At Nagasaki the mushroom climbed to 60,000 feet. At Bikini, the comparable height was 24,000 feet. As for the difference between a land and sea explosion, it seems that the sea explosion, if anything, should produce a higher mushroom because of the tremendous condensation of vapor.

The second fact widely overlooked at the time is that the Nagasaki-type bomb was by no means the most powerful nuclear bomb that can be produced. At the time, we knew nothing about hydrogen bombs. Yet a Los Alamos scientist on the expedition confirmed the report that it was possible to manufacture old-fashioned atomic bombs vastly more destructive than the ones used at Bikini.

The third key fact, by now generally known, is that the bomb badly missed its assigned target, the brightly painted battleship *Nevada*, exploding over open water almost a half-mile away. Even so, despite the poor marksmanship, and the relative inferiority of the bomb, it sank six warships, smashed several others into almost unrecognizable piles of floating debris, and put some twenty other ships—including the *Nevada*—out of commission.

The fourth fact is that radioactivity is not only less predictable than had been hoped, but constitutes under some circumstances perhaps even greater danger than the bomb's heat and blast. Though the early headlines made much of the fact that many of the goats were alive, little or no prominence was given to subsequent reports of examinations indicating prevalence of what Japanese doctors at Hiroshima and Nagasaki had called "atomic-bomb disease." Radioactive burns can produce cancer or diseases related to cancer; only continuing study can determine just how many of the surviving animals can in truth be called "survivors." So far as the ships themselves were concerned, the radioactivity permeated the structures; four years after Bikini, the ships were still unsafe.

After the first day or so following the explosion, the correspondents were not unmindful of the consequences of their disillusioning, letdown-producing first stories. Nor were they unaware of the lack of prominence their later reports of the actual damage were being given—knowing as they did that any story tends to become stale after twenty-four hours. As a result, they were much better prepared for the second test. Very few of them were inclined to prejudge the damage or to disparage the power of the bomb; when the news broke immediately after the subsurface explosion, it was carefully and cautiously handled. In this way the story was kept "open" until the accounts of the actual damage were available.

* * *

As I thought about my deck companion's curious reaction—that he didn't think the next war was going to be so bad, after all— it occurred to me that he may have thought it reassuring to know that at least we could have a planetary floor for continental debris. Perhaps it was just the normal psychological release when uncertainty resolves itself. Perhaps he was reacting to the disappointment he felt when a cloud curtain moved in front of the rising column just as it began to be fully formed. Perhaps the news that no capital ships were reported by the patrol planes as having been sunk seemed to fit into the general air of negation. Perhaps he was angry at himself for having believed the Navy about the danger of blindness if he had viewed the flash without goggles. With goggles, he had been looking too far off center and had seen almost nothing; but the sailor "copy boy" next to him looked squarely at the explosion with the naked eye without any ill effects whatsoever, had seen everything, and was being anxiously questioned by reporters who wanted to know what an atomic burst looked like.

In any case, my deck companion, in common with most of the correspondents, sat down to write his story as he knew it at that time.

Late that afternoon the "Apple" sailed within four or five miles of the lagoon, and we were able to bring the target array under observation through powerful binoculars. By that time it was known that five warships had been sunk. Off on one side we could see the *Independence* in flames. Throughout the entire area we could see heavy topside damage. The reporters began to wonder whether their first impressions were correct.

But it was not until the next day that we were able to enter the lagoon itself. Fortified with Geiger counters to detect the presence of "hot" radioactive areas, we cruised into the lagoon in small motor launches, sometimes getting within a few feet of the damaged ships. Most of the ships on the outer fringe escaped damage, but those closer to the burst were progressively hurt. Now, heavy damage as a layman sees it is much different from "heavy damage" as described in official naval bulletins. To a Navy man damage isn't really damage unless it affects the hull. So long as a ship is afloat, so long as it can sail away under its own steam, what happens topside is not considered crucial.

To a landlubber, however, damage is what meets the eye. And when you see warship after warship, the superstructures mashed and tangled, their decks ripped up and the sides bashed in, you feel you have seen "heavy damage." In the case of the aircraft carrier *Independence*, you saw a floating graveyard of steel. Eighty-foot metal walls stretching up from the sea were smashed open and ripped into shredded tin. Three decks were a meaningless jumble of tangled steel and iron.

Our government could have performed no more valuable public service than by placing the *Independence* on exhibition, towing it back to the United States, and anchoring it off each of the coastal cities, East and West. Perhaps there might have been some program notes for the observers along the following lines:

"This wreckage would take almost a year to repair working under full-shift, wartime speed. It would almost be cheaper to junk it altogether and start anew.

"Do not be misled by the extreme nature of the damage into thinking that this was the only ship badly battered. On the floor of the Bikini lagoon are some eighteen other warships, many of them shattered into unrecognizable forms. Still afloat, but virtually useless, are thirty or so other naval craft of various kinds.

"Now all this damage was done by only two atomic bombs—one of them an inferior bomb that was exploded far short of the target. Bear in mind that the entire target array could have been demolished by not more than two or three atomic bombs detonated at reasonably deep positions under the surface.

"Most of all, bear in mind that what matters is not whether a battleship can stand up under an atomic bomb—which it cannot— but whether battleships or anything else can protect the homeland against atomic attack. The question is not the effect upon steel and iron, but upon human flesh. This is the supreme weapon against human life. The millions of degrees of heat generated by the protesting atom and the overwhelming blast are only two aspects of the danger. Even more menacing is the assault upon human tissue, upsetting the rate of growth, and condemning many thousands outside the area of total destruction.

"The next war, if it comes, will be fought, not with primitive atomic bombs, as at Bikini, but with bombs that can rock continents.

"When you think about the *Independence*, think also about the people of Hiroshima and Nagasaki. Remember that new wars have a way of starting up where the last left off. Remember that no people hold any special dispensation against disaster, not even Americans.

"Remember that nations, like people, can justify their continued existence only as they can control what they can create."

*   *   *

Behind the bomb, of course, was a vast new world—a world of secret cities, sprawling laboratories, mammoth power installations, and the biggest furnaces ever built. I was privileged to see one of these new atomic centers not long after my return from Bikini. It was the cyclotron at the University of California, in Berkeley—a memorial to the genius of Ernest O. Lawrence. When seen from a distance against the spectacular background of steep green hills, it seemed like a toy roundhouse. Even when we drove our car inside the guarded area, the circular building seemed unimpressively modest against its startlingly rich natural setting.

As we approached it on foot, however, I began to get some idea of the mammoth size of the structure. And the moment I stepped inside, the circular shed seemed large enough to enclose a football stadium. Facing the doorway was a massive pile of concrete blocks, suggesting an oversized but square igloo. There was the smell of raw voltage, difficult to describe to anyone who has not been inside a power plant when a giant dynamo is starting up. A deep and steady vibration was seemingly synchronized with a concentrated electrical hum.

The workhorse of the cyclotron is an electromagnet weighing 4,000 tons. Its job is to push and prod nuclear particles until they generate cosmic speeds. Deuterium ions, or deuterons, for example, are chased up to speeds greater than 80,000 miles per second. In this process the cyclotron handles 600,000,000,000,000 deuterons per second. The high-speed particles are used by physicists to investigate the properties of atomic nuclei. The basic data and approaches to the hydrogen bomb depend on such research.

The control room or atomic headquarters of the cyclotron is located along the circular wall. It is an electronic fairyland, with countless black panels speckled with hundreds of indicators, clocks, lights, buttons, and switches. Blue, green, and amber moving lines flash their messages on calipered dials. Sitting calmly on a stool in the center of all this is a mere human being, who decides what it is the electromagnet is to do, and who can shut off the whole atomic shooting match with one finger. The human being observes the dials and makes his calculations.

Here, inside this shed, and inside many other circular sheds like it throughout the world, a new environment for man is being shaped. It is an environment which, for better or worse, will replace the environment man has created for himself these past thousands of years. It has nothing in common with his natural environment; it has a character all its own, with elements previously unknown (on this planet, at least) made possible by a successful invasion of nature's innermost fortress, the atom.

It occurs to you that there is only one trouble with this new environment: it requires the perfect man. Only the perfect man— perfect in a moral, political, ideological, and spiritual sense—could avail himself of all the benefits in the atomic cornucopia. Only the perfect man, it might seem, would be capable of operating a society in which atomic energy could eliminate want, destroy disease, and provide for a rich and purposeful existence.

But to talk about the need for perfection in a man is to talk about the need for another species. The essence of man is imperfection. Imperfection and blazing contradictions—between mixed good and evil, altruism and selfishness, cooperativeness and combativeness, optimism and fatalism, affirmation and negation. It would be wonderful if suddenly everywhere in the world there would be perfection, which is to say, a regeneration of the heart of man, enabling all men to see themselves as cells in the larger body of mankind. It would be wonderful if suddenly people everywhere would see themselves in others and bring about a moral oneness to go along with the geographic oneness.

Yes, it would be wonderful, but it is not likely to happen—at least not in our time. Is there nothing, then, to be done that can head off the approaching collision?

One thing most certainly can be done: we can discover what the real nature of the challenge is and act upon it. The challenge at this point is not to make the world safe for this or that ideology, but to make it safe for its differences. The challenge is to make the world safe for man's imperfections and his contradictions. The challenge is to keep his differences, real and supposed, from catching fire. The issue is not whether one side can impose its will on the other, but how we can keep both sides from fusing inside an atomic incinerator.

It is an interesting question, of course, whether imperfect man can create a world tolerant of his imperfections. But at least imperfection is something man understands; he is not without precedent in dealing with it. What is law—whether in the community or nation—but the attempt to deal with imperfection, to deal with error and error-makers? What is government but a political contract to set well defined limits to permissible error, to make distinctions between errors of consequence and inconsequence, between legality and illegality? What is justice except protection against imperfection in the application of law itself?

Where, then, is the government of the whole? Where is the machinery that can cope with error on a world scale? Where is man's protection against imperfection, protection against himself? Where is the world leadership concerned with humanity at large, rather than with atomic battalions? Man may be somewhat lower than the angels, and he may be imperfect, but these questions are well within his ken.

CHAPTER III

MAN REMAKES HIMSELF

In the summer of 1948, I visited Germany as a member of a citizens committee invited by General Lucius D. Clay, the American Military Governor. Our job—Arthur Garfield Hays's, Roger Baldwin's, and mine—was to examine and make recommendations relating to German democratization in general and civil liberties in particular. The survey was to cover both American military administration and German civil government.

One aspect of the survey involved the centers for displaced persons. As part of my own work, I visited all the D.P. camps in the Frankfurt military-post area, there being a dozen military posts in all in the American zone. Included in my brief tour were the camp at Hanau, "home" of some 5,500 Esthonians, Latvians, and Lithuanians, who had no particular anxiety to return to their lands while the Soviet was in control; Zeilsheim, a center for almost 3,000 Jewish displaced persons; Butzbach, a departure camp for about 1,300 D.P.'s of all nationalities lucky enough to gain admission to other countries; and Bad Nauheim, a "D.P. neighborhood" for about 2,000.

I was especially anxious to see the camp at Bad Nauheim because I had heard somewhere that conditions there were worse than anywhere else in the Frankfurt military-post area. Frankly, I had wondered whether the camps I had seen at Hanau, Zeilsheim, and Butzbach might not have been somewhat in the nature of unrepresentative display-case pieces, for I had been pleasantly surprised to find them not "camps" so much as communities. They were not roped off or separated in any way inside the cities of which they were a part, but were, rather, neighborhoods in which the residents could circulate and intermingle freely in the city itself. Once a week or once a month there was a roll call, but no daily check-in. People were permitted and encouraged to work in the cities, if they were lucky enough to find jobs. The camp supervisory staff and police were either drawn or elected from among the D.P.'s themselves. In Hanau, for example, the head of the camp was elected by popular vote; his job was not nominal but actually the top administrative position. Similarly, the hospital was staffed by D.P. doctors, nurses, and attendants; the schools by D.P. teachers, and so on. All work connected with the upkeep was done by D.P.'s, who received regular salaries.

This did not mean that Hanau or Zeilsheim or Butzbach was what one might call a vacation paradise. "Freedom of movement" would never have enough meaning unless it also meant freedom of exit. Living conditions were heartbreaking. Sometimes six or eight persons had to share a room not larger than an average-sized American kitchen. This had to serve as a combined bedroom, living room, and kitchen. In one room I counted seven "beds" placed so closely together that you would have to climb into them from the ends. The "beds" at Hanau consisted of thin mattresses placed over wooden boards about two feet off the floor. Camp food was so meager and monotonous as to be shocking to an American accustomed to the luxury of leftovers.

It might be said parenthetically, however, that these deplorable living conditions were not peculiar to the camps but reflected in large measure the crisis in food and housing throughout Germany. The official calorie rate both for Germans and for D.P.'s ran to 2,000 per day, but supplements (food bought on the outside or brought in by D.P.'s themselves—with the full approval of the authorities) added up in many cases to a better all-around diet for D.P.'s than for many Germans.

In any event, what I had seen at Zeilsheim, Hanau, and Butzbach —even giving full weight to the seriousness of the food and housing problem—was a far cry from the picture I had had of a slightly modified version of a concentration camp enclosed by barbed wire and patrolled by armed guards. And when I heard that Bad Nauheim came much closer to fitting the popular conception of a D.P. camp, I lost no time in making the trip. This time I decided to visit the camp without notifying the military in advance, for I was anxious to avoid any intimation that a semi-official inspection party might arrive, as well as to eliminate any possibility of a guided tour. In fairness to the military, however, it should be said that I was given complete freedom of travel and inspection anywhere in the American zone of Germany. The car placed at my disposal was without restrictions, although I was advised against the feasibility of sight-seeing in the Soviet zone.

With an old German road map as guide, I started out one morning for Bad Nauheim, about forty miles from Frankfurt. It was the longest forty miles I had ever traveled by car in my life, requiring some three and a half hours over some of the bumpiest and narrowest roads I had seen anywhere. Many links in the road had been bombed out during the war and had yet to be repaired. Later I learned to my great chagrin that I had been using an obsolete road map, for a four-laned concrete Autobahn (highway), in perfect repair, ran directly from Frankfurt to within a half-mile of Bad Nauheim.

Seeing the city of Bad Nauheim after living in Frankfurt and Berlin was like wandering into a garden in full flower after a lifetime in a wasteland. Bad Nauheim is a postcard manufacturer's paradise; like Heidelberg, it was undamaged by the war, and derives its beauty from the combination of a gorgeous natural setting, steep cobble-stoned streets, and old German architecture. And because Bad Nauheim was unbombed, its people were better housed, healthier, and seemed to be going somewhere in particular when they walked through the streets—unlike Berlin, where people seemed aimless, walking out of memory rather than purpose.

The D.P. camp at Bad Nauheim was located directly in the heart of the city, but even after asking half a dozen persons for directions I had difficulty in finding it. The reason, it developed, was simple. The "camp" was no camp at all but a community; in fact, it could hardly be called a community, for it was not located in a single area with a single group of buildings but was spread around the center of the city with houses here and there.

I discovered this fact only after I spotted a synagogue, walked up the steps, and tried the door, which was locked. A neatly dressed man came over and asked whether I would like to go inside. I said Yes, and thanked him. He went away to get the key. While he was gone, I examined the building. It couldn't have been more than a year or two old. It had clean, unornamented lines, with just a suggestion of classical Near Eastern architecture. The doors were freshly painted and the grounds well kept.

When the gentleman returned, he brought with him not only a key but three other men. All four introduced themselves as D.P.'s who were either community or religious leaders. One of them was a physician, Dr. Lomask, who acted as my interpreter. We went inside the synagogue, and I could see at once that it would do credit to any American community; it was small but impressive, and there was no mistaking the pride with which one of the men drew back the curtain and showed me the holy scroll.

Dr. Lomask told me that the synagogue was less than three years old and that it was the gift of the American Third Army.

"Your soldiers—you call them G.I.'s, no?—they built this church for us. For many of us, the G.I.'s were our first hello to America, and we will never forget them."

In the basement of the synagogue were two meeting rooms. In one of them, prominently tacked on the wall, were large posters over the names of various governments. Dr. Lomask surprised me by saying that many nations competed with each other in inviting the D.P.'s to emigrate to their countries. There were posters from Belgium, the Netherlands, Great Britain, Australia, Canada, New Zealand, Chile, Brazil, and Argentina.

"But it is not as good as it seems," Dr. Lomask said. "Most of the countries want only young strong men without families. This is a nice poster from Belgium, but they want only men who will work in the mines. England is very good. She will take families and the old ones too. Canada and Australia will take families. But they are already taking more than their share and can't take them all. Most of the other countries are looking only for young labor."

"If the people here had freedom of choice, with assurance that the nations would accept families and the old ones," I asked, "which country would they pick?"

"Until a little while ago, most of them wanted to go to America. They had heard so much about it, and they were very much moved when the American soldiers built them the synagogue. But America would not take us. Even then we waited. But then we heard that America passed a law to take in many D.P.'s, but there is something in the law that says our people cannot go there.

"And now everyone wants to go to Palestine. Each week some

more are leaving. Last week eleven left. Next week nine will go.
My friend here, Dorach, is going next month. It is the only thing.
There is nothing else. It is not that we think we would not make
good citizens for America or other places. But can we go where
they will not take us? We can bring our families and the old ones
to Palestine, and we can work. It will not be easy because there
will be many different peoples who came there long before us, and
we will have to try to find a place for ourselves. Work. It is the
main thing. The men here talk about it all the time. They are afraid
they have forgotten their trades. But they will be all right again
when they have work to do. That is what they want, I think, more
than almost anything else.

"We know there will be great trouble in Palestine. After the
Arabs, there will be much internal disorder. Many different factions.
We shall have to cope with it as best we can."

We left the synagogue and began walking toward some of the
houses which had been taken over for D.P.'s. I asked Dr. Lomask to
tell me about himself.

He was Polish and the sole survivor of a family of five. Two of
his three children, both of them girls, had died in concentration
camps, one of tuberculosis, the other of pneumonia. His wife and
eleven-year-old son were exterminated in the gas chambers at
Majdanek.

I could see that Dr. Lomask was scrutinizing me closely.

"It is all right," he said. "You can ask it. Everyone else does.
You want to know how it is I am living and my family is dead.
All of us here in Bad Nauheim have been asked that question so
many times that we have—what do you call it?—a guilty conscience
for being alive. That is not it exactly. I mean a guilt complex; yes,
that is it, we have a guilt complex because we are alive.

"No one knows what he really is until something very terrible
happens. You know they are coming for you and your family. You
know they are coming to kill you. Then you go out of your mind
with terror. You do what you can to save your family. You love
your family. There is no question about that. But then somehow
you find yourself trying to escape. There is only room for one.
And then there is the nightmare of being an animal, of throwing
away values that should be more important than life itself. And
after it is over, after you find yourself alive and the others are dead,

you have no mind left, you have only a body struggling to stay alive when there is no reason to be alive. I know. It happened to me."

He paused, took a pipe from his pocket, didn't bother to freshen it with new tobacco, lit it, and puffed very slowly as we walked.

"I can see it in your eyes," he said. "You don't like what I tell you. You condemn it. You condemn me—us. I ask you please to believe we are not different from other people, no different from you or your friends or anyone you love, and I pray to God that nothing will ever happen to you or to anyone ever again to prove I am right.

"You think self-respect, conscience, pride ought to see one through? You are right—at first. In the first few months of the concentration camp you stand up under the beatings and kickings—the kickings with the high, hard boots. Even the foul stuff they give you for food doesn't bother you too much—at first. But day after day it continues. Day after day whittling you down like a piece of wood. And little by little they whittle off your pride and self-respect till you get to thinking that maybe they are right, maybe you are what they say you are, a stupid animal who must grovel and whine for the favor of being kept alive.

"After a year or two of this, after you see how cheap life can be—cheaper than rats, because at least rats have people to live off and we had nothing—after you see your own children die and other children die, so many of them you find it hard to know when it happened and how it happened—after all this, you're no longer a person. What is left? I find it hard to remember. I remember only that by that time you live with the primitive instinct of an animal, getting by from one day to the next, and you do what you have to do; you lie, you cheat, you steal, you bribe, you turn on your friends.

"And when you hear that they are planning to kill you and your family, and you know that this is the end of everything, one would suppose you would say, 'Thank God, now it is over,' but you don't. You scheme and whine and crawl on your belly and you try to get out of it even though you know your family can't. Sometimes I ask myself: 'Who was it that acted like that, so craven and deceitful? Was it me? Was it man as God made him, or was it man as man remade him?' "

I had been watching Dr. Lomask as he spoke. He was about fifty, of better than average height, but his stoop made him seem shorter and less thin than he actually was. His face was pale and gray, with little contrast against his rapidly graying hair. He had humility without weakness in his manner and carriage, and there was about him an air of great gentility and quiet dignity. He was soft-spoken, and I had the feeling that he spoke slowly and carefully not only because English was not his native tongue but because that was his accustomed way of speaking.

And yet, as I looked at him, I was puzzled and disturbed. I found it difficult to picture him as he had pictured himself. I couldn't reconcile this genteel, self-effacing man with the embittered image that came to mind as he spoke.

"Dr. Lomask," I said with some hesitation, "I know that I have no right to ask this, but what you tell me has moved me so deeply that I am anxious to find out whether you have been able to recover from the shock of those years. Have you been able to recapture your earlier values or ideas about life? Have you been able to un-make, to use your own words, the man that man remade?"

He smiled. "You mean there have been two Dr. Lomasks, and you want to know which one I am now. Maybe neither. Maybe there is a third Dr. Lomask. Maybe the third Dr. Lomask is part of the first and part of the second but mostly part of something new.

"What I mean is that life starts up again, and it is never the same. Even the deepest wounds in the soul have a way of healing over. Little by little the new problems and new opportunities create a new world, and before very long the ugly things are memories. But mostly it is the things you do. When you have to take care of other people, and you know these people trust you and need you, you start to build up your self-respect all over again. It is not easy to rebuild. But you add new bricks to the building each day. That is how, little by little, the man remakes himself.

"I have a wife now. We met here at Bad Nauheim two years ago. Her husband had been in a concentration camp, too, and died only two months after the end of the war. And we have a baby, a little girl. She will have her first birthday next month, and we will have a little party. My wife has already arranged for the cake and for children from the neighborhood to come over. When life grows around you, it is a lot easier to forget. It is a lot easier when you can grow with the young ones.

"So when I say there is a third Dr. Lomask, I mean new life is growing around me and in me."

I asked Dr. Lomask whether he thought the other D.P.'s at Bad Nauheim—or, for that matter, D.P.'s throughout Germany—were similarly able to create new life in and around themselves, or whether they were living out the fierce nihilism of the concentration camps.

"I am not sure," he said, "but I think maybe I have been lucky because I am a doctor. You see, a man wants to feel he is needed in the world. He wants people to come to him and say: 'Please help me, I am in trouble. I need your advice,' or, 'You can do this so well, won't you give me a hand?' And it is good medicine. Wounds of the mind need medicine like that.

"But many people here are without important work to do and without families to give them a feeling—what would we call it— perhaps a feeling of intimate responsibility. These are the people who still carry the open wounds. These are the ones who still live under the shadow of the concentration camps.

"These are the unlucky ones, the cursed ones. They have nothing to hold on to, nothing to live for, and they still haven't been able to throw off the moral emptiness of their lives in the concentration camps.

"They say that the D.P. camps are the center of the black market in Germany. It is not true. But it is true that there is much black market among D.P.'s of the type I just described. It is important we understand why it is, for until these people have something to live for, many of them will act as they were taught to act at the concentration camps, like scavengers. The American military understands. It would be easy for them to condemn all D.P.'s as black-market operators. But the American military understands that not all D.P.'s are in it and that those who are in it are the ones who still haven't been rehabilitated, and the surprise is not that there is so much black marketeering but that there is so little, considering what the situation is. I am not excusing them, only trying to tell you why it is.

"And remember that the black market is not really the black market but the open market where goods are bought and sold according to the law of supply and demand. So long as some things are scarce, like cigarettes and soap and coffee, people will try to get what they can for them."

As we walked, I observed a group of D.P.'s. Most of them were young persons. The girls were neatly and brightly dressed in their short, pre-New Look dresses; most of them wore lipstick and had their hair attractively arranged. Most of the young men wore American-looking suits, and freshly laundered, though somewhat frayed, shirts. I remember thinking that the entire group, just as it was, could be set down in a large American city, say New York or Chicago or Detroit, without anything about them that might indicate they were different in any way.

Dr. Lomask explained that it was the Sabbath, when whatever finery an individual possessed was donned with great pride.

"Some people, though, dress better than the others all during the week," he said. "They have been able, even without the black market, to buy clothes and other things they need. They have been able to recover some of their old belongings or valuables, or they have friends in other countries who are helping them. Some of my friends are able to hire German girls from the neighborhood to help with the cooking and to take care of the children. Some have been able to buy bicycles for themselves and their children.

"But, in a little while, I will take you with me to some of the houses where people live who have nothing at all—where the only clothes they wear are just about the only ones they own. They live miserable lives. I know it is hard for outsiders to understand that something of the same range of personal circumstances exists here that exists in the outside world. This doesn't mean that the range is all the way from millionaires to paupers. Anyone here who can put his hands on the equivalent of twenty-five dollars a week is considered to be very wealthy indeed."

Dr. Lomask went on to say that there were similar differences with respect to general background, cultural attainments, education, politics, and religion. Some D.P.'s were "modern" in their outlook, well educated, and actively interested in ideas, books, music, art, the ballet. Others were barely beyond basic literacy. Some were rigidly orthodox in their religions, spending much of their day in religious study and prayer, and observing religious customs and costumes going back hundreds of years in Central Europe. Others believed in a reformed church, still others were pantheists or deists, and so on.

"When you have human beings, whether they are D.P.'s or anyone else, you will have differences," he said.

There was something else I was anxious to find out. How did Dr. Lomask—how did all the others—feel about the Germans? How did they feel, living among their former tormentors, who were responsible for their long misery? Were they resentful or embittered?

"It is hard to talk for everyone, so I talk for my wife and myself. Maybe you think it strange, but things that happened at the concentration camp now seem to us very far away, and if you don't try to remember too hard it is easy to forget. And it is better that way. Why should we feel bitterness? It is an acid which burns only on the inside. It was an evil thing that attacked us, but it is an evil thing that could happen anywhere, not only in Germany. For it is not the people but the evil that can be planted in them. Sometimes I wonder who was the most guilty—those who did the evil with their hands or those who could have stopped the evil early enough but who stood by and let it happen."

I was thinking, as he spoke, about a conversation I had had a few days earlier with a German laboratory technician who told me that during the war he had worked with a blood-plasma unit. About one year before the end of the war, there was a mixup; some directives had been placed in the wrong envelopes accompanying a large supply of blood shipped to the laboratory for processing. These directives revealed that the blood had been obtained through forced bloodletting of concentration-camp victims. A report had been included with the directives, telling of the "blood-culture" experiments in which people were kept and cultivated for their blood, which would be drained off at regular intervals. But the needs for blood were stepped up tremendously as the result of heavy fighting in Russia, North Africa, and France, and toward the end desperate measures had to be taken. The directive said that there was to be an intensification of the drive against those suspected of political irregularities in Germany. These people were to be picked up and shipped immediately to certain centers, there to be bled to death, for there was a drastic shortage that had to be met. The directive said that more Poles and Balts were needed for the same purpose.

I thought of all this as Dr. Lomask spoke of his feelings toward the Germans, and I admired him tremendously, for I asked myself whether I would have been capable of the same gift of inspired forgiveness, and I was not sure of the answer. But Dr. Lomask had thought and felt it all through for himself, and there was no hesitation as he spoke.

"I have visited Frankfurt several times," he said. "I have looked at the skeletons of houses and at the rubble which covers so many thousands of bodies. It will take one hundred years to rebuild the large cities. If I had the power to punish, would I do more than has already been done? Would I do as much? I don't know. I know only that there is much hunger and homelessness, and it will get even worse. Whether that suffering is enough, I cannot say. But I think rather it is important that the things that created the evil should not be allowed to happen again—in Germany or anywhere else."

Then, looking squarely at me: "But tell me, I am worried about America. I am told that prejudice is growing in the United States very fast. Is this not so?"

I was unprepared for the question, but I tried to answer it as honestly as I could by telling him that the fight against prejudice in the United States had been going on for a long time, and that periods of depression or insecurity, or war fears—such as we are now going through—made the fight both harder and more necessary, but that there were many people you could count on to see the fight through to the end.

We turned into Frankfurter Street, where most of the large houses for D.P.'s were situated. These houses were indistinguishable from the private homes, except for the small clusters of people around them and occasional painted signs over the entrances. Dr. Lomask suggested that I inspect some of the houses. From the outside they looked every bit as substantial and impressive as some of the old medium-sized Fifth Avenue mansions. But the moment you entered the front door, you knew you were in something approaching a tenement. This impression was the inevitable result of the overcrowding. Some seventy or eighty persons were squeezed into a house originally designed for a family of perhaps eight or ten, including servants. Each of the rooms had been converted into an apartment; as at Hanau, it had to serve as a combination kitchen, bedroom, living room, and dining room.

Dr. Lomask, who stayed behind on the second floor to talk to some people, had suggested that I continue my explorations up-stairs. He had told me not to bother to knock, for the tenants on the third floor had left for a picnic outside Bad Nauheim.

As I entered one of the rooms, I was embarrassed to find a young lady of perhaps six or seven sitting by the window, braiding her long dark hair. I began an apologetic retreat, but before I was halfway through the door she had quickly and nimbly crossed the room to my side. She insisted upon my staying, and when I started to explain how sorry I was for having intruded she laughed at my awkwardness. She took me by the hand, squeezing it as she led me across the room, and sat me down facing her.

"My name is Brisca," she said. "What's yours? Are you married? What are you doing here? Can you spend the afternoon with me? Will you have dinner with us tonight? Can you come back tomorrow?"

All at once!

"Can't you speak?" she asked sternly. "I can speak four languages —English, German, Polish, Russian.

"I learned the languages in three concentration camps during the war," she went on. "Look, this tattoo mark on my arm was my number at Buchenwald. This one on my leg came from Oranienburg. I've got two other tattoo marks. We were moved to different camps."

My charming companion with the long hair and dancing brown eyes, lovely little Brisca, was one of several hundred children at the displaced persons' camp at Bad Nauheim, in the American zone of Germany. Almost all of them, like Brisca, had known nothing of the world except what they had seen at concentration camps and D.P. centers. Many had miraculously survived the ordeal of birth at Buchenwald or Dachau or other camps. And many of them had never seen their parents; the gas chambers at Majdanek had put in prior claims.

Meeting Brisca that day was one of the highlights of my trip. She was about the size and coloration of one of my own daughters, and she succeeded in giving me one of the worst cases of homesickness known to man.

She was thin and small for her age, I thought, but fairly healthy. Certainly there was nothing wrong with her grip as she took me by the hand and showed me the rest of the house. But I wondered how it was that Brisca was not off on the Sunday picnic with the others.

She explained that she had two things to do and decided that it might be easier to do them with everyone away. One was to braid her hair, for her mother had taught her how to do it regularly when she was two years old; that was five years ago, at Buchenwald, one year before her mother died. Another thing Brisca had to do that day, she said, was to write a letter to a little Polish boy at Zeilsheim.

"Joseph is eight years old," Brisca said. "I met him a long, long time ago. Poor, poor Joseph. He doesn't know who his mother was or who his father was. No one knows. He was here one year ago, and Mr. Libsten said he found Joseph at Belsen. Another boy sixteen years old was taking care of Joseph, but that boy didn't know who Joseph was, and no one could tell because the Nazis forgot to tattoo the number on his arm.

"Mr. Libsten made believe he was Joseph's grandfather and took him here after the war. But Mr. Libsten was a very old man, and he had friends in Zeilsheim, and they said they would take very good care of Joseph, and that is where he is now. So I write to Joseph in Polish. And I tell him how much I want to see him again and how much I like him and what all the boys and girls here are doing and how is he feeling and I tell him I will be going soon to see him in Zeilsheim."

Brisca's most treasured possession, I later learned from Dr. Lomask, was her memory of her parents. She was all of three when she lost them, but she remembered things her mother taught her, and she remembered that her father would play on the floor with her. And now she felt a sense of personal responsibility toward Joseph because not only did he have no memory of his parents; he knew nothing about them and had no way of finding out who he himself was. At least, as Brisca said, she has tattoo marks to prove who she is. Thus, by a hideous irony, the indelible label of a concentration camp became the badge of belonging to the human race, while unmarred flesh was not regarded as the sign of a free man but as a mark of the disinherited and the anonymous.

When Brisca and I went downstairs to meet Dr. Lomask, we saw that he was still engaged, and we decided to go off by ourselves. We first visited the public dining room, where one meal a day was served. (The other meals are prepared by the D.P.'s in their own rooms with food distributed on a ration plan.) Brisca said she had bread and cereal for breakfast and sometimes warm milk; soup and bread for lunch, and soup again for supper—sometimes with a spoonful of meat in it—and potatoes and sometimes another vegetable. A woman who happened to be in the dining room at the time said that the food had been much better until only a few months ago but had fallen off so badly that it was now the chief source of complaint among the D.P.'s in Bad Nauheim. I asked her how the food compared with what was available to the Germans, and she said that the general feeling was that it had perhaps been superior until recently but that it was now a good deal worse.

We went outside. I told Brisca that I had brought a brief-case full of American chocolate candy bars and chewing gum to give to her friends. (Brisca knew how to translate chewing gum into all four languages.) We walked down Frankfurter Street, and it was no time at all before my bag was empty. I was warmed by the delight of the children but embarrassed by their excessive gratitude as they danced around to get their candy. They seemed healthy, though not robust or sparkling. I was surprised to learn that many of them were actually two to four years older than their size made them appear.

On the way back to say goodbye to Dr. Lomask, Brisca asked about America. She asked me about my children and their friends and what they did and what their school was like and what they wore and about their toys and whether they had circuses and carnivals like the ones that sometimes came to or near Bad Nauheim. Then:

"What is America like? Is it a large place?"

I told her it was a very large place, so large that many countries could fit inside it—Poland and Germany and France and Austria and Czechoslovakia, and Great Britain. I told her that there were farms in America almost as large as the entire city of Bad Nauheim and that you could travel for hours and hours and see nothing but rich wheat growing in the fields. I told her about the large cities and the small villages.

"I think I would like to go to America," she announced. "Will you take me? Will you take my aunt and my uncle and their little children?"

What could I say? How should I have answered Brisca? Should I have told her that it was a large country but not large enough to take her and her aunt and uncle and two cousins, not large enough for her friends or the other people whom she had known during and after the war? Should I have told her that the people who didn't think it was large enough were the people who made the laws? But then, how would I have explained to her that the men who made the laws decided to allow some displaced persons to come to this country but that there was something in the law that ruled her out and her family and her friends because they came from certain sections of Europe and because they had a certain religious background? Could I have explained to her what technicalities were or meant and why they were more important than friendship, more important than understanding, more important than the right things that had to be done?

"Don't you want to talk to me any more?" she asked. "You haven't answered me."

I answered her as best I could. I told her that the war made things very difficult and very complicated all over the world and that it might take some time before enough people could get over their fears and hates and understand how much they needed one another.

I told her that I didn't know how long it would be before it would be different but that there were many Americans who were trying very hard to help them. I told her I would ask my government if I could bring her and her uncle and aunt and cousins to live with me.

I think she understood.

*   *   *

On the way back to Frankfurt that afternoon, I knew a sadness heavier than I had felt for many years. I suppose it was because little Brisca looked so much like one of my own little girls and because I knew that the war that had happened before to cause this misery could happen again, and that there was not yet in being in the world the mobilization of sanity to prevent it.

"Theft, incest, infanticide, parricide, have all had a place among virtuous actions. Can anything be more ridiculous than that a man should have the right to kill me because he lives on the other side of the water, and because his ruler has a quarrel with mine, though I have none with him?"

—BLAISE PASCAL

* * *

"Think continually how many physicians are dead after often contracting their eyebrows over the sick; and how many astrologers after predicting with great pretensions the deaths of others; and how many philosophers after endless discourses on death or immortality; how many heroes after killing thousands; and how many tyrants who have used their power over men's lives with terrible insolence as if they were immortal; and how many cities are entirely dead, so to speak, Helice and Pompeii and Herculaneum, and others innumerable. Add to the reckoning all whom thou hast known, one after another. One man after burying another has been laid out dead, and another buries him; and all this in a short time. To conclude, always observe how ephemeral and worthless human things are, and what was yesterday a little mucus tomorrow will be a mummy or ashes. Pass them through this little space of time conformably to nature, and end thy journey in content, just as an olive falls off when it is ripe, blessing nature who produced it, and thanking the tree on which it grew."

—MARCUS AURELIUS

* * *

"Care for distress at home and care for distress elsewhere do but help each other if, working together, they wake men in sufficient numbers from their thoughtlessness, and call into life a new spirit of humanity."

—ALBERT SCHWEITZER

* * *

"If we find men with whom our hearts are in accord we become intimate friends though thousands of miles may separate us, while next-door neighbors remain total strangers if their hearts do not agree. In the world we have many acquaintances, yet those with whom we know our hearts agree are very rare. Even brothers do not know each other's hearts. Do not resent the fact when the world fails to know you. . . ."

—KAIBARA EKKEN

CHAPTER IV

DINNER IN A HUNGRY CITY

The visitor to Berlin during the early years after World War II realized that there was more to the city than the four sectors under the separate military rule of America, Russia, Britain, and France.

First of all, there was the Berlin that met the eye. It was a strangely calm and composed Berlin, a city of trudging old people with improvised pushcarts that served as moving vans. It was a city of permanent transients who were shifting from one section to another—wherever they could find food and coal. It was a quiet city but a tired city, where cars and people moved slowly and even the low clouds seemed clotted and motionless. It was a city of small vegetable patches carved out of the empty spaces between the ruins or out of the gray dirt of vacant lots, and the people lived in these patches in crude wooden huts and sealed themselves in behind wooden barricades.

This Berlin—the remote, unhurried Berlin—was the core center of world crisis. On the surface, at least, it seemed curiously apart from its own place in the world, as though it were trying to disprove any connection with the world of motion and force—of which it was a mainspring.

There was very little surface evidence of the high-voltage tensions or fierce uneasiness that animated the outside world.

There was no thunder of daily newspaper headlines, no newsstand competition in bludgeoning black headlines, and when you read about Berlin in the European edition of the *New York Herald*

Tribune it was almost as though you were looking at yourself in the mirror through the wrong end of a telescope.

Then there was the subsurface Berlin. It was a Berlin of plot and counterplot, a place where giant opposing swords were stretching toward each other and were beginning to feel each other. It was a place of endless depths and sublevels, where new German forces were being shaped and old forces regrouped, a subterranean spawning ground for revolution and intrigue.

This was the Berlin where the cold war was gathering heat and momentum. Every once in a while, there would be brief eruptions breaking through the apparent surface calm—clashes or demonstrations or riots, which were actually only the wisps of smoke above an impending volcano. All sought to control the volcano, or at least to direct it. That it could set off a civil war was self-evident. For, day by day, the sides were gaining in definition and shape among the Germans themselves.

Despite the surface appearance of a dull, detached city, the people were dividing themselves: the line separating East from West for the most part was an open one, and the political and geographic entities of a civil war were well advanced. If an explosion came—and almost any incident could touch it off—it could represent the focal point of world eruption rather than that of Germany alone.

A tremendous momentum had been building up, and was more important, more menacing, than the deliberate moves of Russia or America. It was a momentum so great that it could trigger a war quite outside the precise calculations or timing of the nations involved.

Finally, there was the symbolic Berlin—the Berlin that told us more about twentieth century civilization than we might care to know. It was not a city but the charred skeleton of a city, hollowed out and jagged, yet with a massive and permanent aspect to its debris, for there was too much left to clear away, and too little left on which to rebuild.

A bombed city, when first you see it, smashes across the eye and mind with poleax impact. It is not only the scale of destruction, but the supreme abruptness of destruction that hits at you. A hundred earthquakes spilled from the sky out of the hands of men and a thousand years of the works of men, put together piece by piece, are ripped open, and their creators with them. It is the minute asserting its sovereignty over the age itself, a single swift scoop with the spoon that empties the seas.

But that was not all. The symbol of Berlin in the modern world was that of a grotesque normalcy. For actually there was nothing abnormal or unique about Berlin. Most of the great cities of Europe and Asia were now part of an enveloping pattern of destruction— London and Coventry and Manchester and Birmingham and Southampton and Cherbourg and Calais and Madrid and Barcelona and Rotterdam and Warsaw and Kiev and Milan and Turin and Stalingrad and Leningrad and Frankfort and Aachen and Cologne and Essen and Darmstadt and Mannheim and Munich and Stuttgart and Hamburg and Shanghai and Nanking and Canton and Peiping and Chungking and Hangchow and Tokyo and Yokohama and Hiroshima and Nagasaki.

No, there was nothing unique about Berlin. The only uniqueness in the world was in the Western Hemisphere; and I wondered whether the American people knew just how unique they were— that their cities were standing only because of the accident of history or the twist of fate that saw the V-2 developed at the end of the war instead of at the beginning.

I wondered whether this uniqueness held any special meaning for Americans, whether they were able to see the world whole and understand what had happened to the larger city of man in our time, or whether they accepted their good fortune as having no particular significance or consequence.

For the thing that hit hardest as you walked through the streets of Berlin, the thing that continued to grip the mind long after you left, was the fact that not long ago the city was alive and intact and its people walked through its streets or lived in its apartments or worked in its offices. If they had known then what they know now, you asked yourself, what would they have done that they failed to do? If history could somehow be turned back, but with a certain knowledge of things to come, what different decisions would they have made? It was important to ask these questions because they applied equally to the people of the cities that are still standing. What do these people think about as they perform their daily routines? Are they able to accept the reality of Berlin as applying to themselves? If so, what should they be doing that is different?

Would this comprehension of reality lead to dedication and action
or to futility and escape?

*   *   *

One evening shortly after I arrived in Berlin during the airlift
in 1948, I played host to twenty-six university students at dinner.
It had started out as a small buffet for just a few young people, but
in a matter of a few hours I discovered I had let myself in for one
of the largest private dinners since the Occupation began. And
three hours before the dinner, all I had been able to scrape together
was six bunches of carrots and four packages of peanut-butter
crackers.

But before telling how I eventually managed to get the food,
perhaps I ought to explain how it was that I found myself in such
a scrape.

In the course of our survey on German civil liberties, it became
necessary to talk to a number of anti-Nazis who were now leaders
in the struggle to democratize Germany.

One of them was a trades-union leader—let us call him Mr. Soeller
—a Social Democrat who had lived in the United States for some
years and who was now working with the American Military Government in helping to combat Communism and to infuse German
unions with democratic ideas and objectives.

Toward the end of our discussion he suggested that I speak to
some of the university students in Berlin who were active in the
pro-democratic movement in Germany. At least once in a week, he
said, his wife prepared hot soup for rotating groups of them—perhaps the only hot dish they would have all week.

If I could come to the next dinner—and he smiled ironically when
he said "dinner"—I could talk to the students and find out at
first hand just what the youth of Germany was thinking and
doing.

Mrs. Soeller said that a group of six was coming the following
evening. Would I care to join the party?

I promptly climbed out on the end of a long limb and announced
rashly that I would like to be host for the dinner, and told the

Soellers to bring as many students as they wished to the Harnack House as my guests.

"I think you will find that Germans aren't exactly welcome at hotels and restaurants set aside for Americans," Mr. Soeller said.

As he spoke, I recalled the "For Americans Only" signs I had occasionally seen in Germany—signs barring Germans from wash-rooms at the air terminal and at Military Government headquarters, signs barring them from certain cafés and roadhouses.

I recalled, too, an experience I had had at Bad Nauheim when, on my way to a D.P. camp, I had stopped for a sandwich at an outdoor terrace restaurant. No sooner had my German driver picked up a tray than he had been ordered to put it back. When I had remonstrated with the headwaiter, I had been told that the restaurant was operated for Americans only. "Not my fault," he had said laconically. "Orders."

My thoughts were interrupted by Mrs. Soeller, who urged that the "dinner" take place at her house. I agreed, but insisted—and carried the point—that they allow me to act as host and be responsi-ble for the food. I said I was certain my hotel would make up a large food package to take out—sort of a picnic-dinner affair.

The next morning Mrs. Soeller phoned and asked in embarrassed tones whether it would be all right if the dinner party were to be enlarged somewhat. Apparently the word had spread, and she didn't have the heart not to extend the invitation to eight others, making it fourteen, exclusive of the Soellers and myself. But she assured me that even if I could not obtain the additional food, the students would gladly share what little there was.

I winced. I had not yet figured out a plan of battle for acquiring the necessary vittles for six, let alone fourteen.

"Of course it will be all right," I said, swallowing hard. "I'll try to get the groceries to you early in the afternoon."

The first thing I did was to call the manager of my hotel and ask whether it might be possible for him to prepare a dinner food basket to take out that evening.

When the manager asked, "Food for how many?" I dug deep down inside of me for a casual note. "Twelve to fourteen," I said matter-of-factly.

"Fourteen!" he exploded. "Why, fourteen in one party I could not serve even in the dining room. It is against regulations to serve parties of more than five!"

There was only one thing to do. I decided to throw the entire problem into the lap of the American Military Government. After all, I had gotten into this mess in the course of carrying out my assignment. At least, that was what I kept telling myself.

I found General Clay's office most sympathetic. Yes, a civilian assistant said, it was a wonderful idea to have the students for dinner. No, I would not be thrown into the hoosegow for violating regulations—considering the purpose of the dinner, and, besides, a hot meal wouldn't do the youngsters any harm.

And what about food . . . ?

Well, that was another question. The commissary happened to be closed today. There was no way, short, perhaps, of an order from the general himself, of getting it reopened. Would I want to refer the matter to the general? I weighed the needs of the air lift against a hot dinner for fourteen, and told the general's assistant not to bother; I would try something else.

At 12:30 P.M., I sneaked out of a luncheon meeting and phoned my hotel. There were two messages—both from Mrs. Soeller. The first was that the size of the party was no longer fourteen but nineteen. The second was that if I ran into any serious complications in getting the groceries for a full meal, not to worry, because she could always make soup do, though it would be helpful if I could supply the soup vegetables.

At three, when I phoned the hotel again, the guest list had grown to twenty-six. At three-thirty, I pried myself loose from my last meeting and started to make the rounds of the Army Post Exchange stores. On my way I saw a vegetable store, went inside, and bought it out—which is to say, six bunches of carrots.

At about three-forty-five I walked into the Post Exchange, plunked all my ration coupons down on the counter—coupons for food, candy, cigarettes, and toilet articles which were supposed to last for two weeks—and told the young German girl waiting on me that I wanted everything I could get that was edible.

She started to sort off coupons, then told me that she could accept only those falling due that week. Besides, each coupon was tied to specific goods. I could get, if I wished, twelve packages of cigarettes, twenty packages of chewing gum, twenty bars of chocolate-coconut candy, two tubes of toothpaste, four bars of hand soap, two large bars of laundry soap, three boxes of Rinso, six boxes of razor blades, two large tubes of shaving cream, writing paper, ink . . .

I explained my problem to the German girl, who said that perhaps I ought to see the manager. The manager, an American from Detroit, was most sympathetic.

"Let's see," he said, "I think we just got in a big new supply of anchovies." He disappeared into the back room for two minutes, then emerged triumphantly with five tins of anchovies, three enormous bags of beer pretzels, a pound can of salted peanuts, and wonder of wonders, a two-pound box of Domino granulated sugar!

Things were looking up. I couldn't help wondering, though, how anchovies and pretzels went with soup.

Then the manager called me aside and said with a grin that he had telephoned a friend who supervised one of the largest places assigned to American personnel and that he might be able to help me out.

I expressed my very deep thanks, then rushed over to the address given me, where the supervisor, an understanding and generous soul if ever there was one (a native of Philadelphia, to be consistent about it), bade me follow him to the larder in the cellar, a wonderful fairyland where every type of food imaginable was stored.

He moved around the larder with a big basket in one hand.

"Suppose we start at the beginning," he said very professionally. "We'll probably want some appetizer. How about this canned crabmeat? That means you'll also need some tomato-and-chili sauce. Then for soup, we'll probably want some canned beef and noodles. Five cans ought to do it. Then for the main course, I'm afraid I can't give you a steak, but we do have some tinned Richardson & Robbins chicken. And three of these bologna stockings and a pound of tongue ought to lend a little more color to the main course. I'm afraid we haven't much in the way of fresh vegetables, but if the woman who's preparing the meal for you can get any potatoes she ought to be able to make some potato salad with these jars of mayonnaise and a bottle of vinegar. That brings us to the dessert. Let's see, now; we're a little low on fancy desserts. How about some canned plums? Two of these five-pound tins ought to do it."

I almost reeled at the magnificence of the bounty. But that wasn't all. Out of the icebox came margarine and cheese, and off a shelf four wondrously large loaves of white bread.

"Aren't you likely to get into trouble on my account?" I asked anxiously as I observed the supervisor jotting down all the items he had taken from the shelves.

"I don't think so," he said. "That call from the P.X. wasn't the only one that came in asking me to open the pantry for you. Someone over in OMGUS * headquarters phoned, too, and asked me to put it on him in case any questions were asked. I think it'll probably work out all right. Now let's get this stuff out to the car."

Just before I drove off, the supervisor asked me to wait a moment. When he reappeared he was carrying five bottles of sparkling burgundy, which he presented with his own compliments.

Thanks come hard when you're under the open end of a cornucopia, but I did the best I could to tell him how grateful I was.

When I arrived at the Soellers' shortly after five, I felt like a combination of Belshazzar's delivery man and a walking display case for the Marshall Plan.

*   *   *

I wish I could say the dinner was an unqualified success. I wish I could say I came away from it deeply inspired by the vision of new, vital democracy being forged by the youth of Germany. I wish I could say the dinner convinced me that the disease of hypernationalism is dead in Germany.

Artistically and gastronomically, of course, the dinner was everything I had hoped it would be. Mrs. Soeller was able to work wonders with the culinary Noah's Ark I had brought. In less than a halfhour, or so it seemed, most of the food was ready, and the group sat down to eat in relays. The tables were attractively set. Mrs. Soeller had borrowed additional silver and dishes from neighbors, several of whom had come over to help with the serving.

I don't think I'll ever forget the unrestrained looks of wonder and incredulity on the faces of the students when they took their

* Office of the Military Government of the United States.

places at the table and saw the wineglasses and the individual packs of cigarettes for each person and the bowls of nuts in the center of the table and the butter plates and the fresh napkins. And when the main course was served—chicken and beef tongue and potato salad— they lost all reticence and broke out into open cheers. I need not report their reaction to the sparkling burgundy.

There were fifteen young men in the group, and eleven girls. Most of them were graduate students, the average age being perhaps twenty-five or twenty-six. Medicine and law and architecture accounted for most of their fields of study. I was surprised to learn that there wasn't a single prospective physicist or chemist or biologist or engineer in the lot. Almost as surprising was the fact that only two or three were interested in writing or music. Surely, I thought, this group could not be a representative cross section, but later I learned that this wasn't too far from being the case.

The initial problem at the dinner was to put the students at ease and to convince them, without making any specific statement to that effect, that I had no ulterior purposes in arranging the meal and that nothing was expected in return. Little by little, they loosened up; by the time the main course was cleared away the conversation really began to flow.

They were pleasant, affable, engaging, although a few of them were embarrassingly deferential. Most of them looked underweight, one or two severely so. But for the most part they seemed sturdy and healthy, with good tone to their skin and with clear eyes.

They were neatly but poorly dressed, with not a single unfrayed shirt or jacket in the crowd. The girls were all pre-New Look and perhaps even prewar with their knee-length skirts and dresses— evoking in an American visitor a perhaps pardonable nostalgia. They had a clean, scrubbed look about them, though you could tell from their use of cosmetics and from the way they arranged their hair that they were loyal subjects of the world's greatest sit-and-see kingdom—the American movies.

At first we spoke about the war. Without a single exception, the men were veterans. And it developed that with but a single exception they said they had all fought on the Russian front and had not faced Americans or British in action. In response to my direct question, one by one they identified themselves and spoke briefly of their war service—on the Stalingrad front, on the Leningrad front, on the broad front directed toward Moscow.

Was it a coincidence that out of fifteen German veterans gathered together only one should have been in action against the West? The exception, a dark, slight young man of perhaps twenty-two, had fought Americans and British in North Africa, where he had been wounded.

They all seemed so sincere and straightforward that I wondered whether I was doing them an injustice when there came to mind something an American sergeant in Frankfurt had told me.

"Brother," he had said, "no one in Germany knows anything about the war against the United States or Britain. No one fought against Americans. They all fought the Bolshies. Go up and ask them. Go up and down the streets and ask them. Ring all the door-bells and ask them.

"Yup, they're veterans, all right, but they were all taking their whacks at the Russians—you know, common enemy and all that stuff. Who was it, I keep asking myself, who took my brother pris-oner and let him starve so that when we found him he weighed ninety pounds and was blind and didn't even recognize me when I saw him just before he died? Who was it operated the concentra-tion camps? Brother, try and find out—if you can."

I remembered, but I remembered, too, that the big job was to see whether there was anything we had to work with in laying down a new track in Germany away from power ideologies and Father-land missions of destiny that twice came close to ruling and then wrecking the world. And the most important part of that job was finding or creating and then developing a real movement which could take over the responsibility for running a non-militaristic and democratic Germany.

No one knew whether this was really possible, but the attempt had to be made; and surely there could be no more promising place to look for the form and substance of such a new movement than in the active democratic and anti-totalitarian groups among the young people. Perhaps, I thought, the uniformity of their replies on the war-service question was a poor test of their sincerity.

In any event, I decided to stop nibbling around the edges and to ask direct questions, the replies to which might furnish the crisp, easy-to-take-hold-of information I was looking for.

As we finished the meal, I asked whether any of them believed—and by this time I think we were on sufficiently informal ground so that they need not have feared they would incriminate themselves by their answers—whether any of them believed that Germany was justified in starting the war.

One of them, a short, blond, somewhat stocky young student who was studying architecture, spoke up.

"We don't believe it is true that Germany started the war," he stated with great earnestness. "Germany fought because she was attacked and had no choice."

"Attacked by whom?" I asked.

"By Poland."

"Surely," I said, "you can't believe that Poland, with an army of hundreds of thousands against Germany's millions, and with toys for planes and tanks against Germany's highly developed war machine, attacked Germany."

"But Poland was instigated by Britain and Russia," he said.

I asked whether this was logical in view of the fact that Russia and Germany had signed a non-aggression pact which actually set the war in motion and under which Russia became a partner in the partition of Poland. As for Britain, didn't the German people know that after Czechoslovakia had been given to Germany at Munich, Britain had informed Germany that the limit of Nazi expansion had been reached and that any move against Poland would mean war?

"That's just it," another student said heatedly, "the German people weren't told any of that. We had no way of knowing what was happening."

Without sarcasm, I asked him whether the German people had known about Austria, about Czechoslovakia, about Danzig—whether Germany had occupied those countries in self-defense—about the building up of the greatest military machine the world had known until then, about the concentration camps for enemies of Nazism, about the gas chambers.

Was it logical to expect me or anyone to believe that the German people knew about none of this?

Four or five of them began to reply at once. The last wall of restraint had been broken through; they were animated, even eager to do battle.

Each of the four took his turn. The burden of what they said was that Nazism was the inevitable reaction against the injustices of Versailles and that the German people turned to Hitler almost in self-defense. Yes, after Hitler came to power there were many outrages, but that was all over now and finished and the German people were now opposed to Nazism and they, the students, were today very active in the anti-Nazi movement in the universities. But the outrages under Nazism were things the students and most of the German people didn't know about at the time. It was only now that they were finding out about the cruelty toward the Jews and about the concentration camps and the gas chambers. But how could they be blamed at the time if they didn't know—or knew so little that they might just as well have known nothing at all?

I said that this interested me deeply, for I had not known that any of these things had been kept secret. I said I had thought, for example, that when young boys and girls had been trained virtually from infancy for a place in the Nazi military machine, and that when almost every male was in uniform and almost every worker was working in a war industry, the German people might know that all this might have something to do with war. I said I thought that when smaller nations had been gobbled up and when they were garrisoned by German troops, the folks back home might have some intimation of the fact.

I asked whether everyone had been looking the other way when Catholic churches and Jewish synagogues had been desecrated, and when Jewish shop windows had been smashed and the stores confiscated and turned over to Nazis, and when Jews were forced to scrub the streets and were kicked and clubbed, and when political opponents of all parties disappeared, and when Hitler and Goebbels and the others had made speeches boasting about these facts and using them as a warning to dissenters.

"That's just it," a girl student said. "That's just it. Even those who knew dared not oppose. I was in high school when the plebiscite on Austria was taken. My chemistry teacher had been opposed to the Nazis from the start, and every once in a while he would say little things in class that were not flattering to the Nazis. When the plebiscite was taken, he voted *nein*, and then he was no longer our teacher. No one knows what happened to him.

"It is all right for those who have a free country where you have free elections to talk about what others less free should have done;

but when you know that something terrible will happen to you if you oppose the government it is different. You think: 'Why should I risk my neck? Why should I, only one person, try to fight the entire government which after all knows best?' "

I told her that she was right about one thing: That it was highly improper of me to have the impertinence to tell others what they should have done. But I also reminded her that when we spoke of what happened in Germany, we were speaking of something that was far from being a local matter. When the war's dead totaled sixty millions, and when the homeless and starving were numbered in the hundreds of millions, perhaps a non-German might be justified in being somewhat inquisitive about this recurring disease.

As for the chemistry teacher who voted *nein* and then disappeared, I asked what they thought would have happened if forty million Germans had voted *nein*. Would all forty million have disappeared? Where would the government have sent them? What would have been left? Suppose forty millions of Germans decided that each was willing to risk his neck because of the question of right and wrong involved—isn't it possible that no necks would have been lost? Was it possible for any government to stay in power indefinitely without the consent of the people? Yes, the government might possess all the power, but there inevitably comes a point where the government has to call upon its people in an undertaking that would not be possible without the *cooperation* or the *sanction* of the people themselves. When that point came in Germany, what were the people thinking about? Their own individual necks?

This opened up the entire question of individual responsibility for acts done by the people acting as a nation. Was it fair to ask, I put it to them, whether any of them had any sense of personal responsibility, any sense of personal guilt, for Nazism or the war or any of the evil by-products of Nazism, such as concentration camps?

There was silence for a moment, then one of the older graduate students, whom I judged to be about thirty, spoke up.

"We are all anti-Nazis," he said, "so you must not think we are trying to excuse what happened. But we could not help ourselves. You ask if we have any feeling of guilt. I have thought about this a great deal before. But how am I supposed to feel any guilt if I couldn't do anything other than what I did? I had orders. I followed them. I had no right to question. It would have been immoral to disobey orders. If I did what I was told to do by my country, why should I feel guilt?"

There it was—*orders*. Morality began with discipline. "Would you say that orders are always moral, even when the acts are so immoral, so evil, that an individual must be totally lacking in all sense of right and wrong if he were to obey them?" I asked. "Take the case of the soldier who is ordered to beat political prisoners, or the soldier who is ordered to drain off the blood of innocent persons before killing them so as to fill up the blood bank. Or the soldier who leads innocent victims into the gas chamber. Or the soldier who commits any crime in the name of his government. Or the officer who orders the soldier. Or the higher officer who orders the lower officer. Would you say it would have been immoral for any of them not to carry out their orders?"

"Don't you see, though," the student countered, "that those men had no choice in the matter? They were not responsible for the decisions which made them do what they did; they had nothing to say about it."

I tried to demonstrate that they *did* have a choice: They had the choice of killing or being killed themselves. What kind of "morality" was it that justified any debasement or any crime against human beings, so long as the orders were properly signed and transmitted?

As I asked these questions, I realized that we were at the core center of the entire issue. The discussion had cut through to the innermost recesses of Nazi psychology. When everything else was stripped away, there were exposed the deep sources of authoritarian behavior: the respect for established authority, devotion to a "moral" code built upon the hard rock of obedience, a completely relativistic approach to questions of right and wrong. What I wouldn't have given at that moment for a copy of Thoreau's "On Civil Disobedience," or Emerson's essay "Man the Reformer," to read to them then and there.

I said I had a confession to make. I wanted to confess, for my own part, to a sense of personal guilt for what had happened in Germany. Before the war I had been doing a lot of fancy talking and writing against Nazism, but that was easy enough to do from the safety of America, where there were no penalties for what I said and where there were plenty of supporters for that point of view.

But if my convictions were worth anything, I should have been over in Germany, taking my chances with the others on the firing line against Nazism. When Hitler's car was passing through Berlin and the people were tossing bouquets, I should have been there tossing a hand grenade. I felt guilty because so much of my anti-Nazism had been just talk.

Up to this point the young veteran who had fought the Americans and the British in North Africa—the only one of the entire group whose war experience was not confined to Russia—had sat silently listening to the others. Now he began to speak.

"I think I have felt a personal guilt," he said slowly. "It is worse than that. There are times when I have felt a guilt not only for being a German but for being a human being—especially when I look around the world today and see how cruel and senseless men and nations—not only Germans—can be.

"But that is not what I want to talk about. I want to talk about everything that was said tonight.

"I don't think we have been honest. I think we have been talking excuses but not facts. I think we are making excuses to ourselves.

"Why should we fool ourselves? We know what happened. We know that even before there was Hitler, there was the beginning of Nazism in our homes.

"We know that even before we were old enough to read, our parents were showing us pictures from the family album—pictures of war heroes all the way back. You almost had to wear a uniform before you could get into that album.

"And our parents would tell us about the glorious deeds of Germany and about the wonderful things that happened to a young man when he went away for his military training.

"And they were right. Think now. In military training we did the things our fathers did and their fathers before that. We wore glorious uniforms and played games and drilled and sang songs. We got a mysterious sense of fulfillment; we became saturated with a sense of destiny. We learned the beauty and the righteousness of discipline.

"Were we victims of Nazism? Nonsense; we made Nazism possible. We didn't have to go in for persecution or the other unpleasant things ourselves. We could leave the dirty work to the others. But Nazism was the total expression and outlet for achieving the purposes which we believed all our lives to be sacred.

"Another thing we haven't been honest about tonight was in not saying truthfully what Nazism was actually like. Why don't we all admit what is the truth—that for maybe 90 per cent or more of the German people, Nazism was wonderful. The people had jobs and they had music and they had festivals. Salaries were good, health benefits were good, and there were more parks and games and concerts than ever before. There was no inflation. Men who worked could come home to their families and know there would be food. If a child was sick, there would be a doctor.

"As for the bad things that were done—the fires and the tortures and the cruelty and the disappearing people—well, so long as our own bellies were nice and round, so long as the Gestapo didn't come rapping on our own doors in the middle of the night, we would pretend it never existed. And we went on having a wonderful time.

"We were all cowards. Even now we are cowards. We say we are anti-Nazis. We are afraid to say the truth, that we were not anti-Nazis when everything was coming our way, when we were riding high only because we were sitting on someone else's neck. You are cowards because secretly in your hearts you are all hoping for another Hitler who can bring back the good old days.

"Admit it; you secretly hope and even believe that Hitler is alive somewhere and that in the end he will not fail us, that he will come back and redeem the Fatherland.

"And if it is not Hitler but a powerful communism that sweeps across Germany, and if communism gives us a chance to be on the winning team, we'll become a red dictatorship instead of black.

"That is why I want to get out of here. That is why for ten years I have been trying to get out somewhere—I don't know where. Not America. I am afraid America, like Germany, is becoming too much concerned with security through force.

"I think now I want to go where people haven't yet beaten back nature, where they still have to worry about fighting the jungle or the weather and haven't got any time or energy left to fight each other.

"When I was in North Africa I thought many times I would desert and go south into the heart of Africa. I had to smile to myself when I thought of Leftenant Kunz reading my departing note: 'Dear Leftenant,' I would say, 'I have decided I want to capture lions instead of General Montgomery. Not British lions— just plain lions like we see at the circus. I don't think I like this war very much. I don't think I like you very much. I don't think I like Hitler very much. Dear Leftenant, you know what you can do? You can just take the war and Hitler and all your orders and—."

He broke off and sat down. He said what I was waiting to hear; and while he spoke I had been observing the faces of the others. You could tell he had been drilling on an exposed nerve. They were increasingly uncomfortable, then taut.

Finally, the short blond veteran, who had said earlier in the evening that Germany had gone into the war to defend herself against Poland, got to his feet.

"You must not listen to Brecker," he said. "Brecker has always been like this. He is a romanticist, a dissident, and yes, Brecker, I'll say it in front of the American as I've said it to you—you're a troublemaker. Always you're making trouble. Before the war you made trouble and during the war you made trouble.

"Mr. Cousins ought to know that Brecker was brought up for court-martial in North Africa and got off only because we desperately need radio technicians. But it was terrible. They had to bring Brecker back from the front because they caught him firing over the heads of the enemy. As a soldier he was a disgrace to Germany.

"Mr. Cousins," he said, "we all hope you will overlook Brecker's outburst and bad manners. As for what he said, I am sure you must know he speaks only for himself. None of us—indeed, very few Germans—would agree with what he has said."

I assured him that I had no doubts on that score.

*　　*　　*

Later that night, walking through the darkened city of Berlin and looking up at the ragged, jagged walls of brick that seemed to lean against the sky for support, I tried to sort out my impressions. I was disheartened, but what, after all, should I have expected?

That I would run into a flock of Jeffersons in the heart of Germany? That I would find students spouting John Stuart Mill and Milton and Paine? Just because they were identified with the pro-democratic movement in Germany was no reason to suppose that they could throw off at once the accumulated weight of at least fifteen years of saturating indoctrination in the dogma and mythos of the leadership principle and the tradition of hypernationalist glory.

It would take a long time—longer perhaps than most of us had realized—before all this could be replaced by a non-authoritarian, democratic ideology with real roots that would send up shoots which wouldn't topple over at the first sign of a strong wind.

But democracy in Germany required much more than the willingness or readiness of the Germans to have it. And in basing all our hopes for a better Germany upon a program of re-education or de-Nazification, we were missing the main point.

The future of Germany, whether we liked it or not, was not being shaped by a settled American policy as to what we should like Germany to become, or by the will of the German people. The future of Germany was being shaped by the cleavage between the world's two greatest power systems. All the things we vowed we would never let happen again in Germany—the rebuilding of the German war potential, the political centralization of Germany, the resurgence of nationalist groups—were in the making again because Germany had become the first major power vacuum in the cold war.

Decisions being made on both sides about the day-by-day problems of Germany were being filtered through the screen of military necessity. Both America and Russia were in the strange position, virtually, of vying with each other for the favor of the defeated common enemy. So far as Russia was concerned, her major objective was to shape her eastern zone into the pointed edge of a wedge into Europe. So far as America was concerned, the dominant issue seemed to be whether we could rebuild Germany in time as a retaining wall against the East.

All this seemed insane, but no more so than the directly related fact that the fabric of world peace was fast unraveling; no more insane than the fact that the world organization charged with keeping the peace had become, in Mr. Churchill's phrase, a "mere cockpit in which the representatives of mighty nations hurl reproaches, taunts, and recriminations against one another"; no more insane than the grotesque unwillingness of the American Government to lead the way in yielding essential power to the United Nations, an example being our continuing support of what we officially described as "the protection of the veto"; no more insane than Russian obstructionism and intransigence; no more insane than the tensions which day by day were spiraling upward toward the last of the Wars of the Sovereignties.

The reality of all this was raised to a new dimension as you walked through a shattered, smashed city, its insides hollowed out by dynamite and fire. You felt depressed—inevitably so, but you also knew that there was still time—late as it was—to build a flooring for peace. And you knew that the leadership would have to come from the American people; only America had the combination of moral and physical resources that could provide dynamic initiative for a crusade to give the United Nations the powers of government.

I had come all the way to Berlin, but I learned, as I should have known all along, that the future of Germany and the blockade and the air lift were not nearly so critical to the peace of the world —important though they might be—as the decisions that the American people had to hammer out by, and for, themselves.

"There is no profanity in refusing to believe in the gods of the people: the profanity is in believing of the gods what the people believe of them."

—FRANCIS BACON

*　　*　　*

"I would rather die having spoken after my manner, than speak in your manner and live. . . . The difficulty, my friends, is not to avoid death, but to avoid unrighteousness; for that runs faster than death. I am old and move slowly, and the slower runner has overtaken me, and my accusers are keen and quick, and the faster runner, who is unrighteous, has overtaken them."

—SOCRATES

*　　*　　*

"Mind alone is the cause of the bondage and liberty of men; if attached to the world, it becomes bound; if free from the world, that is liberty."

—MAITRAYANA,
BRAHMANA UPANISHAD

*　　*　　*

"All that we are is the result of what we have thought: it is founded on our thoughts, it is made up of our thoughts. If a man speaks or acts with an evil thought, pain follows him, as the wheel follows the foot of the ox that draws the carriage."

—THE TEACHINGS OF BUDDHA

*　　*　　*

"Reason commands us far more imperiously than a master; for in disobeying the one we are unfortunate, and in disobeying the other we are fools."

—BLAISE PASCAL

CHAPTER V

"THE MAN BEHIND HITLER"

In September, 1948—several weeks before a de-Nazification court absolved Fritz Thyssen of the charge of being a "major" Nazi—I sat with the former industrial king of Germany in a parked American military staff car outside the court at Königstein, near Frankfurt, and discussed his relationship with Adolf Hitler.

Herr Thyssen, on the basis of a preliminary investigation by American officials in Germany, had been passed up for trial as a war criminal because of insufficient evidence. But, like other prominent Nazis or former Nazis not indicted as war criminals, he was now being tried before one of the many de-Nazification courts. These courts were strictly the affair of German civil government. While the occupying powers frequently sent observers, the trial was independent of the military governments.

I had been in Frankfurt two days when I learned that only a few miles away, in Königstein, the trial of Fritz Thyssen was taking place.

The next morning, I joined a group consisting of Janet Flanner of *The New Yorker*, Fred M. Hechinger, the American education writer, and Dr. William M. Hitzig, New York City Police Department surgeon, for the drive up to Königstein through beautifully patterned hills that reminded one of the Berkshires. Königstein itself is a small unbombed town attractively situated on a hillside. On the main street, as you near the center of the town, is a white inn, not very large or impressive from the outside. The dining room of the inn had been converted into a makeshift courtroom. It was low-ceilinged, with a long row of window-doors on one side.

About one hundred and fifty persons were crowded into the room, in the front of which was a long improvised bench for the judge and representatives of the various German political parties. Flanking the bench were two parallel tables—one for the prosecution, the other for the defense.

Herr Thyssen sat in the enclosure formed by the tables, his back to the spectators. He sat deep in his wooden chair, his hands cupped in front of him. He was trim and well dressed; his illness and advanced years were noticeable in the tremor of his hands and in his general manner.

The testimony at this particular session centered in correspondence between Thyssen and Hitler and Göring, published by *Life* in the issue of April 29, 1940. Thyssen readily acknowledged its authenticity and said it had been published with his cooperation in an attempt to give the outside world a clearer picture of Nazi tactics and duplicity. The letters, covering a period of more than a year, traced the events and disagreements leading to an open rupture between Thyssen and the Nazi leaders. Thyssen, according to the letters, was opposed to the war, demanding that Hitler and Göring respect their promises to him. After the correspondence had reached a certain point, Thyssen left Germany. This was followed by confiscation of his property by the Nazis, although Göring made clumsy attempts to lure Thyssen back to Germany in letters promising the industrial magnate complete security of property and person.

When the court adjourned for the day, I went up to speak to Herr Thyssen. People were milling around, and it was difficult to talk. The only spot I could think of that afforded any privacy was an American staff car outside. Herr Thyssen readily accepted the invitation to meet with our small group. The next hour or so was as memorable as any I can recall. Thyssen, picking his words very carefully in English, answered questions fully.

We began by asking him flatly whether he felt any responsibility at all for Nazism, mindful of the picture of him as the man most responsible for Hitler.

"Yes," he said. "I make no attempt to hide the fact that I supported Hitler back in the early 1920's when Ludendorff spoke to me about Hitler and suggested I help the Nazi party. I gave Ludendorff money then for Hitler. Then, over the years, I became more and more convinced that Hitler could save Germany, especially when France and the Allies persisted in their ruinous policy of reparations and when France tried to seize the Rhineland."

"Precisely what form did your support of Hitler take from the time he came to power up through 1939, when you left Germany?" Miss Flanner asked. "How much money did you give and to whom?"

"I gave no money during those years. In 1933, when Hitler came to power, I gave him my moral and political support. I believed him. I believed in his sincerity and honesty. I believed he could save Germany from revolution. Later, much later, I learned he was a liar and a dangerous man."

"And when was that?"

"About 1937. I was becoming increasingly disturbed about the rearmament program. I didn't like the direction his foreign policy was taking."

"Did you have any feeling about Nazi dictatorship itself—about the fact that Germany had become a police state, about the political murders, the destruction of civil liberties, the persecution of Jews?"

"Yes," he said. "That was bad. Very bad. But there was no way of knowing before that this was what Hitler would do."

I had the feeling that the entire anti-Jewish episode seemed somewhat unreal to him, and perhaps not too significant. I reminded Herr Thyssen that Hitler's plans for a police state and his position on the Jews had been made perfectly clear in *Mein Kampf* long in advance.

"Sure, but who read *Mein Kampf*? Almost no one. Everyone owned a copy; no one bothered to read it."

"Did you read it?"

"Parts of it."

"Didn't you see the long sections in which Hitler told exactly how he felt—about his contempt for democracy, Germany's need for a dictatorship based on the master-race idea, and about his prejudices on race and religion?"

"Yes, but that was just propaganda. Hitler needed a *blitzableiter*— a lightning rod—to divert the lightning that threatened to strike all around him, and he picked on the Jews. But I never believed he would carry it to the lengths he did. It got completely out of hand. I don't think Hitler himself believed everything he said about the Jews. Hitler once told me, when he learned that Furtwängler was using some Jewish musicians in his symphony orchestra, that he summoned Furtwängler and said to him: 'I don't want to criticize you for using these men, and I am sure they are good musicians, and some of them are probably good friends of yours. But we have got to be careful about what we do in public.'

"Hitler also said that he himself might be fond of a pretty, young Jewish lady, but that he couldn't afford to be seen with her in public. He said he told Furtwängler not to break his friendship with these men, but that it might be embarrassing to have them in the orchestra. Furtwängler dismissed the musicians."

I asked Herr Thyssen whether what he had read in *Mein Kampf* hadn't convinced him long before 1939 that the Nazi program would lead to war.

"But I must remind you again that no one took *Mein Kampf* seriously. I began to differ with Hitler in 1937. I thought he was betraying his promises to me that he made before he came to power. If everything had gone as planned, Hitler would have retired long before 1937."

"What do you mean by 'retired'?" I asked. "What had been planned?"

Thyssen leaned forward and rested his arms on the back of the driver's seat.

"It was never intended that Hitler would remain in power," he said. "Hitler was supposed to be temporary. The plan was to have him strengthen Germany and then step down in favor of a restoration of the Hohenzollern dynasty."

This was startling news indeed. I asked Herr Thyssen whether Hitler had agreed to this plan.

"Agreed? He didn't have to agree. It was his own idea. He himself proposed it. That was why we supported him. There were four promises Hitler made to me, none of which he kept:

"1. That after Germany's position, internally and externally, had been fortified, he would bring back the monarchy, turning the government over to the Hohenzollerns.

"2. That he would undertake and conclude with the Vatican a special Concordat guaranteeing Catholics full religious rights inside Germany.

"3. That he would undertake and conclude a comprehensive peace treaty with England, so that whatever might happen England would be on our side.

"4. That he would undertake and conclude a special peace treaty with Poland, as protection against Russia.

"If Hitler had been true to these promises, there would have been no war."

I asked Herr Thyssen how it was that he had permitted himself to be taken in by these promises.

He smiled wanly. "Hitler was the most persuasive man I ever met in my life. He had a way of looking at you when he spoke and a way of talking directly at you so that you wanted to do anything he asked you to. Everyone who met him believed him.

"Many times I asked myself just what you have asked me: 'How is it I could have believed him?' And I have thought a long time about it. I think Hitler was a master psychologist, perhaps even hypnotist. When you were with him and under his power, he could make you do almost anything. Once I asked him about it.

" 'Mein Führer,' I said, 'what is the secret of this strange hold you have over people?' This is what Hitler replied:

" 'I think I know what it is. Before I get up to speak before an audience, I study it. I search the faces carefully and try to sense a mood. Then when I get up to speak, for the first ten minutes I exploit this mood. I work hardest during those first ten minutes. Those first ten minutes are the important ones. I try to create a single personality out of all those faces. I create a single mind and a single will, so that when the people think, they think as one person; when they respond, they respond as one person. Then I identify myself with that one mind. I get inside that mind and possess it, so that there is not the many minds of the audience but one mind—my mind. After that, I can say anything I wish and they will believe me. I can speak absolute nonsense for two hours, and they will believe every word of it.' "

Thyssen reached into his pocket, took out an American cigarette, lit it with quivering hands, and went on with his story.

"I keep thinking about that power of Hitler's. Just the other day I picked up a copy of a book by Gustave Le Bon, *The Crowd: A Study of the Popular Mind*. Very interesting. He talks about hypnosis applied to groups. I think that is what Hitler did."

I asked Herr Thyssen whether he thought another hypnotist could come along and do the same thing to Germany again.

"I think so, yes," he said. "Germany is not like America, where you have traditions of democracy and where it is not easy for a charlatan or dictator like Hitler to come along and fool the people. In America you have a big country and you can make mistakes, but they are not too serious. But here in Germany, when the people make a mistake, they can't get out of it.

"I don't think democracy can work in Germany. The people have lived under militarism too long. They want to be told what to do. In a democracy, Germany breaks into many parts and a dictator has to put them together again.

"Germany needs a constitutional monarchy. It has to be held together by a family around which the nation can rally. Otherwise, it will go Nazi again, or Bolshevist. A democracy would only create the confusion in which the extremes could come to power."

I asked Herr Thyssen whether Hitler's promise about the restoration of the Hohenzollern monarchy may have been nothing more than an attempt to say the very thing that Thyssen most wanted to hear. Since Thyssen was a devout Catholic, wouldn't the promise about the Concordat with the Vatican fit in the same category? What I was trying to find out, without asking it in so many words, was whether Thyssen realized that he himself had furnished a remarkable demonstration of the very gullibility he had just described in the German people.

"I was fooled," he replied. "And when I discovered how badly I was fooled, I tried to fight it as hard as I could. But it was then too late. There was nothing I could do to stop Hitler's all-powerful onrush, and I fled."

In April, 1940, Thyssen was in Paris. When the Nazi military machine began to roll across France, the French Government took Thyssen into protective custody.

"There was a good deal of pressure brought upon the French Government to turn me over, and finally they gave in. And I was probably worth a lot to the Germans, because a bargain was made and I was traded for two French generals who had been captured by the Germans."

Thyssen smiled wryly as he told of the exchange. Then his face changed. It became tightened and tense again as he told of his experiences of the war years. He said that the Nazis first sent him to a lunatic asylum, and he spent "a long, long time" in solitary confinement. Then he was sent to Oranienburg, where he was kept for about two years. At Buchenwald, toward the end of the war, he was in a cell next to Léon Blum, for whom he developed considerable fondness.

"Very fine man, Mr. Blum. Very honest. Very intelligent. Very sympathetic. We became good friends. I was anxious to see him again."

And then, when the American armies broke through and liberated one concentration camp after another, the Nazis kept moving him back to camps far in the interior of Germany. Finally, "they decided to shoot me, but the Americans came one day too soon."

I watched Thyssen closely as he spoke. His usual spryness of manner and ready smile were gone now. Instead, there was only a sick old man through whose mind there ran ugly and bewildering memories. Not very long ago in his life he had been regarded as one of the most influential, powerful, and respected figures in Germany —and perhaps also in a large part of the outside world. Then he enlisted his passions in the crusade to recover the Rhineland, recognizing in Hitler a subordinate ally. Then came the fast-moving events—Hitler's rise to power, rearmament, the fast-spiraling tensions, voluntary exile, war imprisonment, liberation, imprisonment again. . . . And now?

"I am an old man. I am being tried by the Germans. They say I was the man behind Hitler. It is not so. The Americans who investigated me know it is not so. The Americans examined very carefully all the records and spoke to many witnesses.

"I am not complaining because I am being tried now. I admit I once supported the Nazis. I admit my part. And if they want to punish me for that part, that is all right. But I was never a major Nazi."

We got out of the car. I wanted to ask one more question. Had Herr Thyssen seen the new issue of a German magazine featuring a picture of Hitler on its cover? The story speculated on the possibility that Hitler was now alive, planning to reappear at a propitious moment.

No; Herr Thyssen hadn't seen the magazine. He hadn't been doing too much reading lately. He said he had no way of evaluating the article, though it was true that some Germans secretly hoped that Hitler would some day return triumphantly and make good his promises to the German people. They still believed in ultimate victory for Germany and in Hitler's personal invincibility.

"Maybe the old hypnotism still holds. But what difference would it make if Hitler were actually alive? Maybe things are working out as he would have wished them to. I must go now. Please to remember that I was not Hitler's chief, as they charged at the trial. Remember that I never gave him the million marks that got him started, as they charged. He was always against the things I stood for, but I didn't realize it until it was too late."

Thyssen walked slowly toward the improvised courtroom, an old man with a cluttered and troublesome past. It was a past filled with repudiations, and now there was no group which was ready to receive him. His early deals with the Nazis hadn't worked out, and when he withdrew, the anti-Nazis, whether of recent or prewar vintage, didn't believe him or trust him. He was a man without a living country. The country of his allegiance had actually died with the Hohenzollerns.

As his bent figure mounted the steps to the porch, I tried to visualize the man at the height of his power—a key figure in Germany's industrial output, someone to whom the nation's top political figures once came with hat in hand. And then came the fall, sudden and calamitous. What was the mighty crowbar that dislodged him from his power and his pre-eminence? It was something so simple that he himself now found it difficult to recognize.

What had dislodged him was that he believed what he wanted to believe. He wanted the restoration of the Hohenzollern dynasty; Hitler said he would bring it about, and Thyssen believed him. Meanwhile, everyone else was doing the same thing for a different reason. Hitler was telling different things to different people, and it didn't matter that the things were contradictory. Each man blocked out from his hearing everything except that which suited his purpose. Once the commitment was made, there was nothing to do except to go through with it, for the people were all bound to one another in a community of terror and guilt. It was an object lesson in the march of totalitarianism, but I was afraid that the value of the lesson was being lost by the outside world. People were too caught up in new involvements to pay much attention to yesterday's lessons.

Was this what Thyssen had in mind when he said that it didn't make much difference whether Hitler were alive or not—"things were working out as he would have wished them to"? Of one thing we could be certain: almost everything that had happened since the end of the war was in line with Hitler's most ominous wishes for his victors. So much so, in fact, that it almost seemed that the script for the cold war had been written in Hitler's cellar during the big fire of Berlin.

In *Mein Kampf* Hitler had told the German people there was no such thing as peace; there was only a single struggle toward ultimate victory in which intervening defeats were to be regarded as setbacks, capitulation as strategic military maneuver. In the lexicon of *Mein Kampf*, military defeat would merely mean that the battle had moved to a different level, but the object would remain the same. *Mein Kampf* virtually instructed Germany to sign any papers it was asked to sign, so long as it advanced that central objective. According to this strategy, Germany would attempt to play off the big nations against each other. And in the situation growing out of World War II, it was in an ideal position to do so. Separated into zones, Germany could transform itself into a whetstone for sharpening the conflict between the large powers.

At first the differences between Russia and the West in Germany would be administrative. Then, as the suspicions and general tensions inevitably grew, the differences would take place within a military context. Each side would find it necessary to bargain for Germany's favor. Out of it all would come either the rearmament of Germany or German unification—and possibly both. The West, faced with the need to make Europe secure against the Red Army, would try to refashion Germany into the first line of defense. But it couldn't do so without rearming Germany. And it couldn't rearm Germany without rebuilding Germany's heavy industries. Russia would attempt to counter by professing to lead the movement for the restoration of German geographic and national unity. In either case, Germany was bound to come out on top. And Germany, the vanquished nation, would become the principal means in Europe for priming the pump of war between the West and Russia, both of them her enemies.

And Germany was now in a position to do so because of the failure of the nations to think through the problems of the peace. While the war was on, all talk about the requirements of the coming peace was brushed aside as secondary to the need of winning the war. But once the war was won, the urgency and sense of dedication quickly vanished. There was a settling back.

The basic problems bequeathed by the war were deferred. The lack of a durable and workable framework for the world itself meant that there was nothing into which the various parts could be fitted. The problems of Germany and Austria, for example, were to be met, at least for the time being, on the basis of the military holdings of the victors at the end of the war. It was hardly to be expected that the military factor would remain static indefinitely. Moreover, instability under these circumstances was an important Russian asset.

Little wonder that within a few years after the end of the war it would be possible for an old and bent figure, Fritz Thyssen, on trial charged with having been the man behind Adolf Hitler, to say that "things were working out" as Hitler might have wished them.

CHAPTER VI

NOTES ON AN ANNIVERSARY

In July, 1949, I was flying over the Pacific again, over many of the same islands we had visited on the trip to Bikini. This time I was on my way to Japan to attend ceremonies in Hiroshima marking the dedication of a world peace center on the occasion of the fourth anniversary of the atomic bombing of the city. The event virtually coincided with the fourth anniversary of the end of the war.

The long Pacific flight furnished ample time for anniversary reflections. In August, 1945, if you had asked an American or an Englishman or a Frenchman or a Russian—or even a German or an Italian, for that matter—what the beginning of the peace meant to him, you would have had pretty much the same answer. The coming of the peace, you would have been told, meant that the organized killing was over and that people could dare to hope again.

But by August, 1949, the world's people were in the grip again of the same explosive tensions that held them in the late thirties. If in August, 1949, you asked people what the peace meant, your answers would have contrasted sharply with the ones you received in 1945. If you asked your question in America, you would have found the general belief, in and out of Government, that the peace was but an elusive armistice. Paradoxically, you would have found that while on one hand the atomic bomb's destructive power was being exalted, on the other hand the American people were being prepared psychologically to stand up under atomic attack themselves, with assurances that atomic warfare would not be as fiendish as some had supposed and that people could actually survive if they weren't too close to the burst.

If you looked in Russia for an answer to your question, you would find a Government-sponsored uneasiness. You would find that the actual naming of the enemy was only part of a powerful and official effort to generate a deep hatred of the West. You would find that the social democracies of Europe were regarded as even more vile and wicked than the out-and-out "capitalist" or "bourgeois" states. You would find that the pump of national pride was being primed with a heavy hand and that great swells were being created behind the idea of Russian world leadership in many of the principal inventions of the past century, and in science and the arts in general. You would find that the most significant thing about the Iron Curtain was not so much what failed to get out, but what failed to get in. You would find that whatever the distortions of the West may have been concerning what went on inside Russia, these were as nothing alongside the distortions in Russia concerning what went on outside. You would find general confidence that the world was either ripe or about to be for the picking, and that the inexorable sweep of history was towards communism.

If you looked to Germans for your answer, you might find a hard and knowing smile, for Germany was already collecting bids from West and East as they lined up against each other. You might find many Germans who were saying, as did the students at the memorable dinner in Berlin, that the final phase of the war was about to begin in line with Der Führer's prediction that the West and the East would tear themselves to pieces with Germany emerging as the center of a new balance of power.

If you asked the question in China, then convulsed in civil war, the answer would be drowned out by the groans of the dying. If you asked it in India, or Southeast Asia, by the groans of the living.

All these things you would have found if you had asked about the meaning of the fourth anniversary of the peace as you went around the world. But those answers, disturbing though they might have been, would not be nearly so disturbing as the answers you might get if you had asked your question, not of Americans as Americans or of Russians as Russians or Chinese as Chinese, but of people as representatives of humanity-at-large—their primary concern being the condition of man rather than the dilemmas or ambitions of the national and social groups within which man has divided, subdivided, and incarcerated himself.

Asking your question about the peace on this higher and more consequential level might have produced an answer that would have been in startling contrast to the answers that were given against a compartmentalized background. The answer in this case might be that the glory and destiny of the human being was never under greater challenge; that the very faculties that have differentiated man from the other orders of animals now defined his predicament at its largest. He was endowed with awareness and intelligence which enabled him, alone among the millions of species on this planet, actually to advance over previous generations, to examine the record of experience, and to apply its lessons to his own time. Only he had the capacity to define goals and to attempt to meet them. Only he possessed the quality to inspire and be inspired. Only he held the magic of hope. Only he knew the meaning and the power of conscience. Only he could contemplate his own nature and the nature of the universe and conceive of a higher nature than either.

It might be asked what man was doing to justify such gifts and endowments as he stood midway in the twentieth century. The answer might be that with all his faculties he has been unable as a species to cope with himself, that in the midst of the potential splendor of orderly existence he was a pauper chained to chaos.

These were among the answers you might find if you stood on a platform high enough to see man in the total sense. But though those answers are oppressive, it is only on that higher platform that the problem can be fully seen. And only by getting enough peoples to stand in their oneness on such a platform can real hope be defined and realized.

*   *   *

The flight to Japan, by way of the Hawaiian Islands, Johnson Island, Kwajalein, and Guam, was uneventful. When the air is smooth, a plane trip is the most exhilarating form of transportation devised by man. The sky is the dining room of the imagination. It spreads a table of such self-perpetuating wonder and variety that the eye and mind become willing gluttons, the craving increasing, expanding with each dish. No sunset or sunrise seen from a mountaintop ever gave the optic nerves a finer time than when they have the clouds for a floor instead of a ceiling. The spectacle is a total one in the sense that it is circular; everything gets into the act and the picture, held together by a vast frame of continuing color. As for the clouds themselves, Guy Murchie has a passage in *The Practical Cogitator* well worth quoting:

If winds are the spirit of the sky's ocean, the clouds are its texture. Theirs is easily the most uninhibited dominion of the earth. Nothing in physical shape is too fantastic for them. Some are thunderous anvils formed by violent updrafts from the warm earth. Some are the ragged coattails of storms that have passed. Some are stagnant blankets of warm air resting on cold. Some are mare's tails floating in the chill upper sky. In the afternoon I've beheld a quadruple rainbow moving against a stratocumulus layer below. Not an ordinary rainbow that forms an arch, but the special rainbow called the glory, known only to those who fly: a set of complete circles, each inside the next concentrically. These formed a sort of color target that sped along the clouds on the opposite side from the sun with the shadow of the airplane in the center.

You get a sense of stretch up here, you have the feeling that this is the natural habitat for men who think they'd like to work together. You find it easy to understand why the Acheson-Lilienthal Report on Atomic Energy was largely hatched up here in the blue. After long hours of earthbound indecision, the committee members would adjourn to a conference room ten thousand feet up and discover ways of getting the hang of what the other fellow was talking about and arriving at basic agreements that previously had seemed elusive or impossible. There was little intervention by the individual ego and a good deal of a disposition to consider rather than to confront.

Dealing as they were with what comes pretty close to the ultimate, the members of the committee had only to look out of their window for establishing the true nature of the problem, which was not the atom but man. And their window was a complete frame of reference. For when you get up above a mile, you see only the evidence of man but nothing of man himself. You see his roads and his fields and his cities, but never man. Going by the evidence, you might conceive of him in terms of units of electrical energy rather than of matter. And if, assuming you were able to scrutinize him through powerful microscopes and could establish the fact that he was matter and energy both, you would be able to discern virtually no differentiation between one man and another—no matter how many specimens you examined from different areas. And yet you could tell from the evidence that these differentiations seemed to man to be more important than life iself.

You would wonder, considering how small is the fraction of the earth's surface he occupies, how he could find his way from one distant area to the other to get at the throat of someone just like himself. You would wonder at the faculty which enables him to identify such a person as totally different and to proceed to attempt to kill him and his kind for a reason which, from the perspective of your sky platform, would seem as incomprehensible as a war between the forests. Up here, at least, you have some idea of what the real challenge is. You see that the dominant portion of the earth is not land but sea. You can see that very little of the land is congenial to man's existence and development. You can see vast areas where there is too little rain and other areas where there is too much. If you fly over Europe and Asia, you can see that the typical city is the destroyed city, and that the pattern of destruction is not static but enveloping, suggesting unity of a sort if man rejects the unity which sanity might produce. I wondered whether even Hiroshima, which I was soon to see, could be more instructive on the predicament of modern man than my celestial classroom.

If the proper study of mankind is man, up here in the blue was the place for it. Such, at least, was the frame of mind in which I approached the city in which this Atomic Age was christened.

"Only at quite rare moments have I felt really good to be alive. I could not but feel with a sympathy full of regret all the pain that I saw around me, not only that of men but that of the whole creation. From this community of suffering I have never tried to withdraw myself. It seemed to me a matter of course that we should all take our share of the burden of pain which lies upon the world."

—ALBERT SCHWEITZER

* * *

"It can hardly be a matter for surprise that our race has not succeeded in solving any large part of its most difficult problems in the first millionth part of its existence. Perhaps life would be a duller affair if it had, for to many it is not knowledge but the quest for knowledge that gives the greatest interest to thought—to travel hopefully is better than to arrive."

—SIR JAMES JEANS

* * *

"The dogmas of the quiet past are inadequate to the stormy present. The occasion is piled high with difficulty, and we must rise with the occasion. As our case is new, so we must think anew and act anew. We must disenthrall ourselves."

—ABRAHAM LINCOLN

* * *

"Mankind is now in one of its rare moods of shifting its outlook. The mere compulsion of tradition has lost its force. It is our business—philosophers, students, and practical men—to re-create and reenact a vision of the world, including those elements of reverence and order without which society lapses into riot, and penetrated through and through with unflinching rationality. Such a vision is the knowledge which Plato identified with virtue. Epochs for which, within the limits of their development, this vision has been widespread are the epochs unfading in the memory of mankind."

—ALFRED NORTH WHITEHEAD

CHAPTER VII

THE FIRST CITIZENS OF
THE ATOMIC AGE

Hiroshima wasn't what I expected.

I expected resignation; I found rehabilitation. I expected desolation; I found rejuvenation.

In Hiroshima I found people who, having survived atomic catastrophe, restored their lives, and, even more important, restored their faith in the human race and their faith in themselves. The citizens planned to make their city one of the most beautiful in the world.

From the back yard of the small inn where I stayed, I had a fairly good vantage point for viewing the city, with its many rivers and levees. In front of me, across the river, I could see perhaps six square miles of the city, stretching along the banks of the river and sprawling out beyond. The city itself is fairly flat, built at sea level. Hiroshima is a seaport, though from this vantage point it seemed completely surrounded by a ring of mountains.

The hurry-up, improvised quality of the wooden buildings on the other side of the river gave the city something of the appearance of an American mining town in the West a century ago. The resemblance was even stronger because of the mountains in the background.

From where I stood, I could see the general area hit hardest by the atomic bomb; I could see what is now the most famous landmark of the atomic explosion—the dome, or what used to be a dome, of the old Industrial Exhibition Hall. Just enough of the curved steelwork was left so that you could tell it was a dome. Another four- or five-story structure, off to the left a few hundred yards away, showed evidence of considerable damage.

Apart from these two buildings, Hiroshima was completely rebuilt—rebuilt, that is, on a sort of overnight basis. The homes, the stores, the industrial buildings were thrown up very hastily. But the greatest difficulty hasn't been putting up the new buildings and shacks. The greatest difficulty has been clearing away the rubble.

The river in front of me was at low tide; you could walk across its full width of about five hundred feet without getting your ankles wet. I looked out across the river and could see the streets clearly marked—electric and telephone poles, very little open area, and no rubble or evidence of the bomb whatsoever, except for the old dome skeleton.

Of course, when I actually walked through the streets I could see many wounds still open. There were the gutted foundations of the concrete buildings, even though four years of weeds and grass do a great deal to smooth over and conceal the old ruins.

Right next to the small inn where I stayed was the wreckage of what was once a fairly large two-story stone home. All that was left was part of a wall, the large concrete gateposts, and the iron gate itself—most of it twisted out of shape. I went poking around behind the wall and came across a family of five living under a piece of canvas propped up by boards, with the stone wall as the principal inside wall surface. Directly in front of their home, if you want to call it that, which measures about seven feet by seven feet, the family had cleared away the rubble and planted a vegetable garden.

*   *   *

On the fourth anniversary of the atomic bombing, I stood at the spot which is believed to mark the center of the atomic explosion. Directly in front of me were two fairly thick and round stucco columns or gateposts on a very small plot raised about one foot off the ground level as a marker and memorial.

These columns were all that was left of Dr. Shima's hospital, which was directly under the atomic burst. A new hospital had been built right in back of the old gateposts. It was a two-story affair, painted white. Patients waved from the windows.

As you stand at the spot marking the center of the atomic explosion, it's difficult to describe the things you feel. Here, four years ago, there was a flash of heat which at the split second of fission was many times the surface temperature of the sun. And suddenly, even before a stop watch could register it, the heart of a city was laid open with a hot knife. I talked to dozens of people who were in it—dozens who were crippled and burned and suffering from diseases of radioactivity—and their stories were very much the same.

The sudden flash of light brighter than the morning sun—much shorter, much more intense than lightning, much more intense than any light ever seen before on this earth. If you lived through that second, you found that your clothes were on fire, and your arms and legs and face were on fire, and you rushed out into the street and ran, for everyone else was running—no one knew where. And everything was now blazing, and you were inside the fire, trying to run somewhere. Then someone yelled, "Run for the river!" and you threw yourself into the river, and thousands of others did the same thing, and you wondered what happened to your family, to your children or your parents. No one knew where anyone was, but there were people all around you, and other people were jumping from the bridges into the river, and the dead bodies were all around you in the river; but you could hardly hear the people crying because the blaze was like rolling thunder sweeping over you. And all day and night the fire ate your city and burned your dead, and all night you stayed in the river to cool your burns; but the tide ran out and you buried yourself as deeply in the mud as you could and prayed for the tide to come back in again with the water from the sea to cool your fevered body, even though it was salt water and it cut into your burns, but at least it was cool. The hours passed slowly, and you searched the sky for the light of morning, but the city was a torch and it was difficult to see the sky. But then morning came, and you joined the thousands of others running through the black smoke, stumbling over the wreckage of the buildings, the sounds of the dying all around you. You were too much in a hurry to notice you had no clothes; it was hard to see that others had no clothes either, for their bodies were like charcoal.

This, then, was Hiroshima in the first hours of the Atomic Age. It was something new in the solar system—getting at the heart of matter and ripping it apart, and causing the smallest units of nature to smash each other and set off a flash as though a piece of the sun itself had broken away, and sending out strange rays that went through the bones and did things to the composition of human blood that had not been done before or dreamed of before. This was the triumph of mind over matter in the ultimate and most frightening sense.

As you stood in front of the large stone columns from the old hospital gateposts, and you reached over and felt the rough, raised surface of the stone, its composition altered because the surface had been melted by the explosion, you wondered why people would ever come back to the city again—not merely Hiroshima but any city—any city that man ever built, for by this bomb he had placed a curse on every city everywhere. You wondered what the lure could be that could bring people out from the hills and back to this place of compressed agony. You wondered, but you didn't have very far to look for the answer, for the answer was all around you. You could see it in the faces of the people who passed on the street. You could see it in the brisk life-loving walk of the young people. You could hear it in the full laughter of children. You could see it in the eagerness of young boys and young men playing ball with each other wherever there was a place to play ball. The answer you found was that there are deeper resources of courage and regeneration in human beings than any of the philosophers had dared to dream. The answer you found was that the greatest force on this earth—greater than any device yet conjured up in the laboratories— is the will to live and the will to hope.

As you looked around you in Hiroshima, you saw a young woman of about twenty-four or -five with a baby strapped to her back. She was wearing Western dress, though she had on Japanese wooden shoes. There was nothing defeatist about the girl. She was starting out to raise a family; she was going to do it in Hiroshima, and nowhere else; she believed in life, and nothing could change it. And as she passed you, and you looked at the back of her neck and down her left arm, you saw the seared and discolored flesh that is the badge of citizenship in Hiroshima today. The girl stepped to one side to allow a modern bus to pass—it was a bus filled with Japanese baseball players in uniform, for baseball has become the national pastime in Japan to an extent not approached even in America.

The baseball players were singing, some of them, and you thought you saw, but couldn't be quite sure—you thought you saw the familiar atomic burns on one or two arms and faces.

Another thing you wondered about was what the people themselves thought about the bomb and America. You spoke to them about it, and it was hard to believe that what they said was the way people can or should feel after having lived through an atomic explosion.

There was no bitterness, except in one or two cases. They said, most of them, that if it hadn't been Hiroshima it would have been another city and that they had no right to ask exemption at the expense of their fellows.

They said, most of them, that they had taken part in something that would save the lives of millions, for they believed, most of them, that Hiroshima, in the words of the mayor, Shinzo Hamai, was an exhibit for peace, a laboratory that had demonstrated the nature of the new warfare so dramatically that it would destroy war itself.

They believed that two years of blinding, grinding warfare were squeezed into a single bomb and that the smashing of Hiroshima made it possible for many millions of Japanese to stay alive, for they then knew by this bomb that the war was forever lost to them.

Some of them, of course, said things they thought you wanted to hear, but their voices and their eyes would frequently give them away.

And then, as counter-balance perhaps, you would find a woman— a woman barber who took over the shop after her husband died in the explosion—who would turn her head and say that she never wanted to look at any American, for she was afraid he would see the hate she had in her heart for the people who could stain their honor as Americans did by dropping such a bomb. She lost her husband and two children, and when it pained her heart to think about it she would think of America and know that such evil could come only from evil people.

Then there were some who blamed it on the Japanese Government, who said that when Japan first bombed China they were certain that God would visit the crime on the Japanese a thousandfold. Some blamed it on the Japanese Government because it had converted Hiroshima into a military base and shipping point, and they were certain that America would find this out and destroy the city.

This was the first I had heard about Hiroshima as a city of military importance. As I spoke to people and questioned them, the picture began to take shape. When a girl of nineteen told me about her experience in the bombing, she spoke of all the soldiers running past her house on the way from the barracks near the old castle. When the photographer who took films for me told about his experience in the bombing, he spoke of his sensation while riding a train two miles away from Hiroshima on his way to work. He said that when he heard the explosion he thought the large ammunition supply center near the old Parade Grounds had been blown up, for the explosion was too loud for even the largest bomb. Others on the outskirts of the city spoke of the same feeling. I spoke to one man who operated a bus to the ammunition dump; he gave me some idea of its size and said that many thousands worked there during the war.

It was freely admitted, once you referred to it, that Japan was divided into two military zones: the headquarters for the North in Tokyo, and the headquarters for the South in Hiroshima.

Later that evening I discussed with Mayor Hamai the military importance of Hiroshima during the war. He spoke freely and fully. Hiroshima had been Japan's chief port for sending soldiers overseas. It had housed large ammunition supply depots.

I asked the mayor whether it was true, as I had heard in some of my conversations, that as many as 60,000 soldiers had been stationed in Hiroshima at the time of the bombing. He was familiar with the reports but believed that the number may have been closer to 40,-000. Then I learned for the first time something I had seen in no report about Hiroshima since the end of the war. I learned that 30,000 soldiers had died in the atomic bombing of Hiroshima and that this figure had been suppressed by the Japanese police, then under orders from the Japanese Government to conceal the military death toll and the military importance of Hiroshima as well as to minimize the general damage and civilian death toll. Japan had been taken completely by surprise, and didn't want the United States to know how effective the weapon had been, so that what little bargaining power she had at the peace table might not have been further reduced; and that, once having announced false figures, Japan was reluctant to embarrass herself by giving out the true ones.

I learned that the only figures since used by the American Government about Hiroshima have been supplied by Japanese sources and that the original figures supplied by the Japanese police had never been corrected. I further learned from Mayor Hamai, who was in charge of rationing in Hiroshima during the war and who was given the responsibility for issuing new certificates after the bombing, that the population of Hiroshima had decreased 110,000 when a check was made three months after the bombing—and that this figure did not include 30,000 military personnel or the many thousands of volunteers from outside the city brought in to construct fire-retention barriers, or the thousands who have died since. The city's own estimate today, said Mayor Hamai, is 210,000 to 240,000, which includes all those who have died since. The highest previous figure made public was 100,000.

The following day Mayor Hamai took me on a tour of Hiroshima's hospitals. It was an experience difficult to put out of your mind, and you tried hard to put it out of your mind because you saw things that whatever sanity you might have had cried out against. You saw beds held together with slabs of wood; nowhere did you see sheets or pillows; you saw dirty bandages and littered floors and rooms not much larger than closets with four or five patients huddled together. You thought back to what you saw in the D.P. camps in Germany, and you knew that nothing you had seen in Germany or anywhere else put human pride to such a strain.

You looked in on an operating room that seemed little better than a crude abattoir. You saw rooms where whole families had moved in with the patient. You saw all this with unbelieving eyes, and then you had some idea of what Mayor Hamai meant when he said that Hiroshima needed America's help to take care of the sick. For all the hospitals in Hiroshima were destroyed or gutted or severely damaged by the bomb, and hospital facilities in Japan are not easy to come by. People can throw up shacks to live in inside a week or two, but a hospital is nothing to be thrown together. Everything is needed that makes a hospital a hospital, Mayor Hamai said: surgical equipment and rubber gloves for operations and sterilizers and X-ray equipment and beds and pots and pans.

As he spoke, I thought of the millions of dollars being spent by the United States in Hiroshima in the work of the Atomic Bomb Casualty Commission—excellent work and important work, for it can tell what happens to people in atomic warfare. Nothing of those millions goes to treat the victims of the atomic bomb. The Casualty Commission only examines patients; it doesn't treat them. And you had the strange spectacle of a man suffering from radioactive sickness getting thousands of dollars' worth of analysis but not one cent of treatment from the Commission.

On the second floor of the Memorial Hospital in Hiroshima, near crowded rooms of children who are serious tuberculosis cases, a woman rushed out to me and fell at my feet, sobbing as I have heard few people sob. Dr. Akio Asano, the tall scholarly, youthful head of the hospital, told me that she had heard an American had come to Hiroshima and that she had just been praying to Kami for the American to come to the hospital so that he might be able to see how sick her little girl was and how badly she needed certain medicine they didn't have in Hiroshima. She had been praying when I walked in. The little girl was seven years old. Her father had been killed in the atomic explosion. Her name was Nobuko Takeuchi. She had been ill of tuberculosis for several months, complicated by a series of mastoid infections, for which there had been several operations. But now she had what Dr. Asano described as the worst case of tuberculosis he had ever seen in a child of her age, and she might not live for more than a few weeks unless she was able to get large doses of streptomycin. But nowhere in Hiroshima could you get streptomycin.

That night I became a black marketeer. We established contact with what are called sources in Japan, and a few grams of streptomycin were rushed over to the hospital. But little Nobuko needed forty to fifty grams, and we sent wires to Tokyo and even to the United States to get the medicine in time. The Church World Service in the United States heard about the appeal and rushed a fairly substantial package of streptomycin by air-mail. (The medicines kept Nobuko alive for almost a year; then her frail body succumbed to an attack of meningitis.)

After we left the hospital, Mayor Hamai told me of his dream for a modern hospital in Hiroshima that would become part of the Hiroshima Peace Center, for which the Reverend Kiyoshi Tanimoto, of the Nakaregawa Church of Christ in Hiroshima, had gone to the United States in search of support. I had been working with Mr. Tanimoto in the United States, getting groups together to advance the idea of a Hiroshima Peace Center, but not until now did I realize how important were the units that were to go into it. The Peace Center would have, in addition to the hospital, an orphanage, a home for the aged, a civic recreation center, a peace institute study center, and a medical research center.

The next tour was of the orphanages for children whose parents were killed in the atomic explosion. I should like to report on one of them in particular—the Yamashita Orphanage, located about eight miles outside the city on a hillside. It is operated by Mr. and Mrs. Yamashita as a public service with whatever help and support they can get from the city and its people, and from the outside world. It is the largest of the four orphanages for Hiroshima children, providing care for almost one hundred youngsters ranging in age from four years to seventeen years. The youngest was born just a few hours before the bombing.

Mr. and Mrs. Yamashita were able to survive the bombing despite severe burns. Mrs. Yamashita, who had been close to the center of the explosion, said that suddenly there was a bright light and her body was on fire. She was carrying her two-year-old baby at the time, and the first thing she did was to smother the flames that enveloped the child. Then she picked up the baby and ran until she reached the fields outside the city, where she lived for three days on the ground before word came that people were returning to the city.

On her return with the child she found Mr. Yamashita, already under treatment. Recovery was slow for both of them, but after six months they were able to resume their lives, and they decided to dedicate themselves to the care of orphans. They got land and homes outside Hiroshima and built their little colony.

Mr. and Mrs. Yamashita were now completely recovered, except that the old wounds burn and itch in extremely warm or cold weather. Mrs. Yamashita said that she had been unable to have a successful pregnancy since the bombing, having experienced four miscarriages. She spoke of other women in Hiroshima in like circumstances.

The Yamashita Orphanage was, I think, the high spot of my visit to Hiroshima. Living conditions were better and brighter than I had seen almost anywhere else in the city. The children there were more alert, more responsive, and seemed quicker and happier than

I had seen almost anywhere in Japan. The food was adequate and well prepared; there was ample play space; and, what was more important, the children were not starved for want of affection. Dozens of the younger ones hung on to Mrs. Yamashita like kids hanging on to an American mother's skirts in a department store. The quality of the teaching in the orphanage was as high as you would find anywhere in Japan. There was only one thing wrong with the Yamashita Orphanage. There was not enough of it. It ought to be five times as large, and would be, if outside help were forthcoming.

Before coming to Japan, several people had told me that they would like to adopt Japanese children orphaned by the bombing. Under the Oriental Exclusion Act, however, these adoptions were not possible. It occurred to me that the next best thing might be *moral* adoptions. By moral adoptions I was thinking of Hiroshima children who would be adopted by American families and who would carry the names of the people adopting them. The children would continue to live in Japan—perhaps in some place such as Mrs. Yamashita's—but the American families would be responsible for their care and upbringing. Then, later, if Congress passed a law permitting Japanese children to come to America, these morally adopted children could become legally adopted as well.

The next morning Mayor Hamai took me to the site of the old castle that had been destroyed by the bomb. Here, on an artificial hillside, you could overlook the city with its seven rivers and its many bridges. You could see the many homes and stores going up. The sound of the city, with its old trolleys, and the sounds of the pile drivers and the hammers and saws blended into a drone, as it sometimes does high up in a skyscraper.

There on the hillside that morning, a small group of citizens broke ground for the Hiroshima Peace Center, and rededicated their city to the cause of peace by renaming it the Peace City. Mayor Hamai, in introducing me, spoke of his hope that within a few years there might rise on this site an institute for the study of world peace, as part of the Peace Center project.

I said I came to Hiroshima expecting to see the end of the world. Instead, I found the beginning of a better one. I expected to find that Hiroshima, like many of the cities I saw in Germany the previous year, would be flattened out, its only heights those of rubble.

True, there were few stone or concrete buildings in Hiroshima by contrast with such cities as Cologne, Aachen, or Berlin, but the wounds here went as deep as, or deeper than, any city in any war had ever suffered. Yet what was most important about Hiroshima, I said, was not that the debris and the remains of the old city have been cleared away and that a new city is in the process of being rebuilt. What was most important was what has happened inside people. I was not referring to the lack of bitterness, for even if it were bitterness it is doubtful that history would completely withhold sanction. I referred to the proof of personal regeneration, the rediscovery and reinforcement of personal purpose, the capacity for personal rededication.

I tried to make the point that hope cannot exist, either in the individual or society, without the prospect of regeneration. And yet the power of regeneration is undervalued by modern man. The idea of regeneration in too many cases has been tied to the idea of immortality, identifying it as the principal means of achieving ends beyond life, rather than as an end in life itself, essential and attainable.

The sense of personal regeneration in Hiroshima was discernible and unmistakable. There was not only proof of the power of life over death, but of the individual discovery of fathomless physical, emotional, and spiritual resources. This regeneration soared far beyond personal rehabilitation to a restoration of vital faith in human destiny. There was in the making there, I said, a larger definition of the purposes of man than it seemed within our ken to imagine only a few years ago. In the days following the bombing many people in Hiroshima must have believed that they were witnesses to the death both of a city and of an age—and in a sense they were right. But that feeling had changed color and composition with the passing of the months. Today there was a new vision in Hiroshima. The city had a mission to explain itself to the world, to offer itself as a laboratory specimen in the making of world peace.

Such a vision was important and good, for personal recovery must be part of a larger pattern. However impressed we may be with man's capacity for regeneration, we must ask ourselves: regeneration for what? So that man may be afforded an even larger test of his capacity to survive atomic catastrophe? Hiroshima was an ideal classroom for history, but little will have been learned if the only lesson is that survival and regeneration are possible. Regeneration was possible in Hiroshima because it had the rest of the world to draw on. But what will the rest of the world draw upon?

Not survival but the condition of man is the problem. Not whether he can endure atomic fire but whether he can avert it. And in dedicating itself to this purpose the city of Hiroshima defined a mission as urgent as it was noble.

Even as we broke ground for a new Peace Center, we were aware that peace in the world was less a fact than it was a word and that while the will to peace was deep inside peoples everywhere there was as yet no adequate means by which this will could be translated into effective reality. There existed nowhere on a world level an agency responsible to mankind as a whole, an agency which could listen and act to the end that human life may be protected and developed. To say that such an agency is more easily imagined than achieved, and is therefore to be avoided, is to condemn the history of progress.

Certainly true peace will be difficult to achieve. Life itself is difficult. But an honest effort is required before we can be sure that what is difficult may not also be possible. And such an effort—a supreme, common effort in the name of the world's peoples—has yet to be called for, let alone attempted. The problem confronting us is neither interplanetary nor supernatural. It is a man-made problem, one well within our reach to examine and solve.

*   *   *

When I returned to the United States, I had in my pocket a message that Mayor Hamai asked me to convey to Americans. It was written in his own hand. It was appended to four large bound volumes containing the signatures of 106,000 citizens of Hiroshima sending their greetings to the American people. This was the Mayor's message:

"There is much I would like to say to America. First of all, I would like to thank those Americans who have helped us to bring a dead city back to life.

"It is not my place or purpose to try to tell Americans what ought to be done. But what I can do is to tell them about what will happen to the world's cities if something is not done to stop war. The people of Hiroshima ask nothing of the world except that we be allowed to offer ourselves as an exhibit for peace. We ask only that enough peoples know what happened here and how it happened and why it happened, and that they work hard to see that it never happens anywhere again.

"We the people of Hiroshima are sick at heart as we look out at the world and see that nations are already fighting the initial skirmishes that can grow into a full war. We know that stopping war is not a simple thing and that there are grave questions that have to be solved before the world can have true peace. We know, too, that peace is not to be had just for the asking; all nations must agree to it.

"But we also know that some nation must take leadership in building the type of peace that will last. And we are looking to America for that leadership. America can call for world law, and all the world will listen. Leaders of a few nations may not want to listen, but their people will hear. Let the call go out from America for a federation of the nations strong enough to prevent war, and a thrill will be known in the hearts of millions of people everywhere. This is the best hope for averting a war which would see thousands of Hiroshimas. And this is the message the people of Hiroshima ask that you take back to America."

"*If there is any ethical thinking at all among us, how can we refuse to let these new discoveries benefit those who, in distant lands, are subject to even greater physical distress than we are? In addition to the medical men who are sent out by the governments, and who are never more than enough to accomplish a fraction of what needs doing, others must go out too, commissioned by human society as such. Whoever among us has through personal experience learned what pain and anxiety really are must help to ensure that those who out there are in bodily need obtain the help which came to him. He belongs no more to himself alone; he has become the brother of all who suffer.*"

—ALBERT SCHWEITZER

* * *

"*. . . the triumph of my art is in examining whether the thought which the mind of the young man is bringing to the birth is a false idol or a noble and true creation.*"

—SOCRATES

* * *

"*The fellowship of those who bear the Mark of Pain. Who are the members of this Fellowship? Those who have learned by experience what physical pain and bodily anguish mean, belong together all the world over; they are united by a secret bond.*"

—ALBERT SCHWEITZER

* * *

"*The mind must be restrained in the heart till it comes to an end that is knowledge, that is liberty; all the rest are extensions of the ties which bind us to this life.*"

—MAITRAYANA,
BRAHMANA UPANISHAD

* * *

"*Despots themselves do not deny that freedom is excellent; only they desire it for themselves alone, and they maintain that everyone else is altogether unworthy of it. Thus it is not about the value of freedom that we differ, but about the value greater or smaller that we set on mankind.*"

—ALEXIS DE TOCQUEVILLE

CHAPTER VIII

THE ANATOMY OF FRIENDSHIP

One summer evening in Hiroshima, during the 1949 trip, some of the young folks proudly called my attention to what at the time was the city's only neon sign. It served as the blinking crown for a new night club. When lit it looked like an incandescent infection against the dimly lit background of a still crippled city.

"It is wonderful, is it not?" said a girl of about nineteen. "It is just like the pictures we see in the American magazines. In the room downstairs, they serve drinks and cocktails. Upstairs, we have a dance hall. We play only American music and we do only American dancing—the same as you do, ballroom dancing, jitter-bugging, and jive.

"The young people are disturbed," she continued, "because some of the old-fashioned people are talking of getting rid of the night club or making it close earlier each night. They are very much tradition-minded, the older people. They are deeply shocked to see boys and girls dancing together and drinking together and staying out very late. But the older folks will never do anything more than talk about it. They know they are powerless. Now it is a new day for Japan with new ideas and new customs like you have in your great and powerful democracy. We like it this way. We like your freedoms."

Not far from the dance hall was a sign advertising two new motion pictures—one American, the other Japanese. Both ads looked as though they had come off the same assembly line. The sign on the top showed a golden-haired American beauty struggling to keep a clawing maniac from divesting her of the few remaining square

inches of cloth which clung insecurely to her body. The companion
sign at the bottom showed a Japanese gangster, a smoking revolver
in his hands, making a fast getaway.

The older folks, I was told, keep their heads down when they
pass these movie placards. They are bewildered by some of the
aspects of the new order and have come to regard democracy not so
much as a necessary revolution in thought and social and political
conduct as a revolution in manners and morals, generally for the
worse. If this was the phoenix of democracy rising from the atomic
ashes of Hiroshima, and if it was not to be opposed, then at least
the old folks could keep their heads down in their futility.

In more prosperous Tokyo, comparatively speaking, the young
girls wore tight sweaters, short skirts, and American style shoes.
They chewed gum, went dancing, liked hot music, preferred American movies and Japanese vaudeville to the traditional Kabuki
theatre. The old folks blinked at this, too, but rarely tried to assert
the old authority. Since America was the model, somehow that made
it all right.

But to be loved or praised for the wrong reasons is a precarious
business. It is too easy for that type of acceptance or admiration
to be turned into contempt. Gum, jive, jazz, tight sweaters, yo-yoes,
comic books, neon lights, movie thrillers, dance halls, and chromium
trim all are part of the American story but they are the smallest
part. Certainly they are not the reinforced concrete foundations
on which the meaning of America rests, or the solid base on which
to build our relationships with other people.

At that distance, in Japan, it seemed to me that the whole
story of America—a story worth the telling and worth the understanding—began with an idea. This idea is actually the political
expression of a basic law of nature—that there is strength in
diversity. According to this idea, America is a place where people
can be themselves. It is a human experience rather than a purely
national or cultural experience. It is built upon fabulous differences—religion, race, culture, customs, political thinking. These
differences, or pluralism, as the sociologists call it, are actually the
mortar that holds the nation together.

According to this idea, too, there is a constant and wonderful
process of shuffling, so beautifully described in Edward Bellamy's
Looking Backward. People are climbing up and down social and

economic ladders, reaching for the stars most of the time and actually getting close some of the time. An immigrant shoemaker dies happy because his son is a world-famous surgeon. A wealthy industrialist dies unhappy because his son has dissipated the family fortune and disgraced the family name. A man whose grandparents fled from Europe to America becomes a Presidential candidate.

Sometimes things, like people, get all mixed up and the nation has a collective headache, as during an election year. But this disorder somehow works, certainly much better than the orderly and immaculate elections in which all the X's are fitted into one row of neatly arranged squares and where there are no arguments over the counting of the ballots. Sometimes persons in advantageous positions stick their hands into the nation's pockets and keep them there too long. But at least the rascals can be hunted down in public. The government cannot insulate itself from the consequences of its own errors. Shocking as the corruption is, it is not nearly so shocking as having the corruption carried on by a government without watchdogs, without an opposition party hungry to return to power—hungry, too, to seize upon anything to embarrass the incumbents.

As another barrier to continuity in corruption are the reformers, who, it develops, have far more tenacity than the crooks. Indeed, American democracy sprouts reformers the way Italy sprouts opera singers. In many respects, as Theodore Roosevelt once observed, the reformer is perhaps the most interesting and unique product of all.

But for all this diversity, complexity, unconformity, and informality, I was certain there was a single pulse beat to America. It was something that didn't make the headlines, was seldom talked about, very rarely even defined. It was the individual's determination to keep the American combination alive. He knew that, basically, democratic government was his show, and he wanted to keep it that way—even though he might spend most of his time complaining that he was politically helpless.

But how do we make this America known?

If our history lays any special charge upon us it is this: that we try to project an idea of America as a human center in which government and ideologies are subordinate to a free man's nobility or meanness, or the sum total of both. And it is for this that we should take pride in being known. It is always nice to be loved, but especially nice to be loved for the right reasons.

* * *

Frequently, in Japan, I found myself wondering about the democratization program under the American Occupation. I wondered how much of it would stick; I wondered how much of it the Japanese were really digesting and making part of their working political philosophy, how much of it was being worn like an outer garment.

An incident that occurred in Yokohama furnished some of the answers.

For it was in Yokohama that I ran into the story of Tami Taguchi and Orville ("Pinkie") Pohlman. They were both World War II veterans. They had fought on opposite sides. Tami was from Yokohama, but no one seemed to know where Pinkie lived in the United States; in fact, that was the point of the story.

The story grew out of an evening I spent with a group of students at the home of one of their professors in Yokohama. There were about fifty young people in the group, many of them war veterans and all of them active in the Japanese pro-democratic movement. They believed that the only permanent cure for Japanese nationalism and militarism was world citizenship.

After dinner, we discussed some of the problems of world federation. Some of the keenest and most knowledgeable questions came from a young man who spoke English extremely well, though with an accent at once unusual and charming—Japanese mixed with Australian cockney. I later learned that the Australian part of the accent came from his father, who had worked there in his youth.

The young man's name was Tami Taguchi. As the evening wore on, most of the conversation was steered through him. The students asked about the world-government groups in America. They were well informed about the activities of the United Nations, had studied the Charter carefully, and were interested in the possibility of a U.N. revision conference, and in plans advanced in England for a People's World Constitutional Convention.

Before I left, the group demonstrated its world-mindedness by singing American, English, and French songs. I was 10,000 miles from home, but when they sang "Auld Lang Syne" at the end of the evening I couldn't have felt more nostalgic than if I had come across a peanut-and-popcorn stand in the middle of the Sahara.

This was something I wanted Americans to hear for themselves, and so I managed to have the entire group come up to Tokyo for a recording that I could use in a radio report back home. Led by Tami Taguchi, the students turned up well ahead of time in the studios of Radio Tokyo, which is to Japan pretty much what a combination of CBS, NBC, ABC and Mutual are to the United States. While the recording of their songs was in progress, Tami Taguchi handed me a note on which he had hastily scrawled the following:

Please, sir, if it would be possible for me to sing "Show Me the Way to Go Home," it would be very much appreciated by me. Maybe Private Pohlman will hear me, or maybe some people in America they will hear me and they will know where he is, Pinkie, my friend.

I scribbled a line at the bottom of the note telling Tami to please sing his song but to be sure to explain who Private Pohlman was and why he wanted to hear from him. I sent another note into the control room to alert the engineers.

I had heard "Show Me the Way to Go Home" sung many times and under a wide variety of circumstances, but never more eloquently or with more originality than by young Tami Taguchi. His voice was somewhat high-pitched and it wavered, and sometimes you couldn't tell the words for the accent; but there was no mistaking the fact that he sang it as though it were the only song in the world. While still in front of the microphone, Tami went on to tell the story of his meeting with Pinkie. Here, as well as I can remember it, is that story in his own words:

"This song I have just sung, 'Show Me the Way to Go Home,' was taught to me by a very wonderful and great friend, Private Orville Pohlman. Everyone called him 'Pinkie' because his face was so red.

"When I met 'Pinkie' it was Christmas Eve 1945. I think it was maybe two or three o'clock in the morning. It was snowing outside. I was sleeping. Suddenly, there was a great noise. I jumped up from my bed. Someone was pounding on the door. Quickly I realized what was happening. The Americans were coming to kill me—just like my officers in the war said they would if Japan lost the war. At first I wanted to hide but I knew they would find me anyway and they would think I was a coward. I went downstairs to open the door. I was so frightened I forgot to put any clothes on over my underwear. All this time the pounding on the door kept getting louder.

"When I opened the door I knew that what I was afraid of was true. There was an American soldier standing there. It was the first time I had ever seen an American that close. He was a giant, just like they had said all Americans were. I knew he could crush me with his bare hands. I looked at him and didn't say anything. I was trembling with fear. He looked at me and didn't say anything either. Then he smiled and I thought he was laughing to himself because I looked so funny standing there in my underwear. Then I guess he thought I was trembling from the cold, because he took off his big overcoat and put it around me. It was so heavy and I was so surprised that I could hardly stand up inside it. But I knew right then that this American giant had not come to kill me, for he smiled again and said:

" 'Anybody here speak English?'

"I said, 'Oh yes, I speak English. My father lived in Australia and he taught me to speak and read.'

"Then he said, 'Thank God. I'm lost. My jeep went dead about a mile from here and I'm trying to find my way back to my barracks. It's somewhere around here, but I'll be darned if I can find it without any lights.'

"I knew where the barracks were but it was about two miles away and I knew that even I could not find it in the dark. So I said to the American giant that maybe he should wait until morning and to please come inside and spend the night. At first he was afraid he should not do it because he didn't want to disturb my family, but I told him no one would be disturbed.

"When he came inside I went to get him some sake to warm him, and he drank the sake. He said it was good and asked for more. I gave him the bottle and I think he liked it very much. He began to talk and to tell me about himself. He said his name was Orville Pohlman, private first class, but that all his friends called him

'Pinkie,' and he grinned and pointed to his face. It was redder than any face I had ever seen in my life. And as he drank sake to warm up, it seemed to me it kept getting redder and more wonderful all the time.

"We talked for hours before we went to sleep. I was the first Japanese he had met who spoke English, and he asked me many questions about the Japanese people and about the Army. I was seventeen at the time and had not yet been in active service, but I had completed my training, and I could tell him about the strange way Japanese boys were trained for war—how the officers tried to make us hard and brutal by beating us and then ordering one of us to stand still while they made his best friend hit him with the broad side of a sword. It was a very bad thing to do, but it was supposed to make you forget your kindness and think only about how to kill.

"Mr. Pohlman—that is what I kept calling him for a long time even though he told me to call him Pinkie—Mr. Pohlman said that the best soldiers were those who understand why they were fighting and who knew that killing was bad but that there were things more important than killing and dying. He told me about Pearl Harbor and about Nazi Germany and about what happened when people were made to kill the kindness inside them and to hurt their friends, as my officers had made me do during my training.

"Then we began talking about other things—about baseball and sports and music. I always have liked baseball more than other sports and after a little more sake, because it was cold in the house, we were showing each other how to slide under the throw, and then we began to teach each other songs. One song he taught me that night he said he had been singing to himself after he had lost his way when his jeep broke down. It was 'Show Me the Way to Go Home.' He said it was one of the most wonderful American songs to sing with your friends, especially when you warmed yourself up with a drink like sake. I think it was while he was singing 'Show Me the Way to Go Home' that I finally fell asleep.

"Mr. Pohlman—I mean Pinkie—and I became very good friends. He was eight years older than I was and he helped me in many things. He brought me clothes and had them shortened so that they would fit. He gave me food at a time when Japanese had very little to eat. He gave me American books to read, history books and books about the American people. He came to see me three or four times a week and I felt that he had adopted me like I was his son.

"What I remember more than anything else about Pinkie was what he used to tell me about America and the American people. I would read the books he gave me and we would talk about them. I remember so well the stories he told about Abraham Lincoln and what he said about democracy—to the people, of the people, for the people, from the people, and by the people.

"Three months after the Christmas Eve I first met Pinkie he came to see me and he said he had something sad to tell me. He had been told that his long period of service in the Army was over and that he could now go home to see his family again. He had to leave in a hurry, right away, right then. I was very glad that he could go home but inside I felt like the time I learned that my mother was very sick and I might never see her again.

"Two days after Pinkie left I realized that I had been so sad and mixed up that I had forgotten to write down for him my address, and he had forgotten to give me his address. An address in Japan is very complicated; there are many things to put down, and mail is not easy to receive if the address is not right, and when the mail is lost, sometimes it is never returned to the man who sent it.

"It is now four years since I last saw Pinkie. I have had no letter from him. I am worried about him. I know he is worried about me. I have sent letters to him in care of the United States Army in Washington but I have heard nothing. I hope he is all right and his family is all right. That is all I want to know.

"Pinkie—maybe you are listening to this broadcast. That's why I sang 'Show Me the Way to Go Home.' Maybe someone you know may be listening. Please write down my address now. I've been able to get a simple address. The American Army has been good and has given me an American Army address like the one you used to have. This is the new address, Pinkie: It's 8th Motor Pool, APO 503, Yokohama.

"That's all, Pinkie. I want to come to America some day to see all the things you used to tell me about. But most of all, right now, I want to hear from you. It's been four years."

Tami finished and sat down.

*   *   *

Unfortunately, the short-wave radio broadcast on which Tami made his appeal suffered from poor atmospheric conditions and a large part of Tami's message was lost. Consequently, when I returned to the United States, Pinkie's whereabouts were still a mystery.

The Reader's Digest carried the story. For two months nothing happened, then one day while I was in Minneapolis I was summoned to the telephone. It was my office in New York. "We think Pinkie's been found!" my secretary said excitedly.

At last! "Was it California, or another state ending in 'ia' as Tami had guessed?" I asked.

"Nothing of the sort," said my secretary. "Hold on to your hat. It's Wisconsin. Appleton, Wisconsin—only a couple of hours from Janesville, where you're going to be tonight."

I gasped, for on the very day that my itinerary called for me to be in Wisconsin I would find myself only a hundred miles from the young man about whom I had heard so much in far-off Yokohama.

"There's just one thing that puzzles us," my secretary said. "It seems to be Pinkie, all right, though he seemed pretty vague when the reporters got to him, and some of them think either that he's not the real Pinkie or that his friendship with Tami was a lot more casual than Tami made it out to be in his story."

Well, if it weren't the real Pinkie it would be easy enough for me to find out. And if he were, but was turning his back on Tami, it might be interesting to have his side of the story.

When I arrived in Janesville I sent a telegram to Orville Pohlman, Appleton, Wisconsin, asking him to phone me that evening in Janesville.

At 10:35 P.M. the phone rang. The voice on the other end of the phone seemed somewhat muffled.

"Is this *Pinkie* Pohlman?" I asked. "Tami Taguchi's friend?"

"Yes," he said in a drawl. "Yes, sir." His voice was pleasant and friendly.

"Pinkie," I said, "it would mean a great deal to me if I could see you and visit with you. But first, tell me something about yourself. What do you do?"

"I work on a railroad, the Soo Line Railroad. I'm a yard hand. How long will you be in Janesville?"

"Not very long. I'm supposed to take a train out of here in about an hour. But there's a plane leaving Milwaukee early tomorrow morning for Chicago, where I can make connections for Akron. Pinkie, I know this is damned nervy of me, but is there any chance of getting you to fly down with me tomorrow—as my guest, of course. You can be back in Appleton tomorrow night."

"Why sure, Mr. Cousins," he said. "Everybody in Appleton's been asking me when I'm going East to meet you. I can get the yard to give me the day off."

We arranged to meet at the counter of Wisconsin Central Airlines at the Milwaukee Airport the next morning at 10:45.

I arrived early. Exactly at 10:45 I was paged at the counter for a telephone call. It was Pinkie.

"This is terrible, sir," he said slowly. "I'm afraid I won't be able to make the plane."

I groaned. "Where are you, Pinkie?"

"Outside Milwaukee. My car broke down. I've been trying to get a cab or something but I've had no luck. I guess you better go without me."

"Pinkie," I said, "the plane may be late in leaving. Grab a cab, and I'll see what I can work out on this end."

The plane wasn't late. Indeed, it was already on the ground. The problem was put up to the pilot, Captain R. B. Parkinson.

"For *The Reader's Digest* Pinkie? You bet your sweet life we'll hold up the plane. We're due out at 11:15. Maybe we can hold it up six or eight minutes, ten at the most. We've got close connections at Chicago and they'll have my neck if I miss out."

At 11:25 A.M. Captain Parkinson shook his head. "Ten minutes overdue. We'll give him three minutes more."

Two minutes later word was flashed along the sentry line. It was Pinkie. He had come by cab and was almost blitzkrieged as he stepped out. When I grabbed his hand, he was the most thoroughly bewildered young man I had ever seen in my life.

Inside the plane Pinkie grinned as he strapped himself to his seat. I sat opposite, and for the first time since we met I had a chance to look at him closely. He was a towhead, with strong even features and light eyes. He had an open, honest, friendly face, was hard and lean, weighing somewhere in the vicinity of 180 pounds, and seemed extraordinarily shy, reminding me of Gary Cooper in one of his big-hearted-but-embarrassed roles.

I asked Pinkie directly whether my story about him and Tami had been embarrassing to him, telling him that some of the reporters were not too sure that he valued Tami's friendship as much as Tami valued his.

"Oh, no, sir," he said. "Tami's a wonderful little fellow and a real good person, and we were pals, just like he said in your magazine story. When I got home from Japan I tried to send a note to him, but it came back, wrong address.

"One day last week everything happened, so all of a sudden. A lady came to the house and began to ask me questions. Then people began to swarm down on the house, everyone asking more questions."

The "lady" who discovered Pinkie almost a month after he had become the object of a national search was Mrs. Herber H. Pelkey, of Appleton. Mrs. Pelkey read the article in *The Reader's Digest*, then turned to her telephone book, as many *Digest* readers throughout the United States had done, in the hope of finding a listing for Orville Pohlman. There were a half dozen Pohlmans.

"Mrs. Pelkey began calling all the Pohlmans in Appleton," said Pinkie. "Each time she asks, 'Do you have a Pinkie in your home?' Fourth time, someone answers, 'Not here, but my brother-in-law's name is Pinkie.' Then Mrs. Pelkey asks if I served in Japan, and first thing you know she was over at my house, with reporters and photographers and everything."

"What did you tell them?" I asked.

"When I found out what it was all about, I couldn't say much. They tried to make me out to be a national hero or something and I didn't know what they were all fussing about. Plenty of G.I.'s did the same thing. Plenty of them in Japan got to know decent Japanese people and made friends with them and helped to take care of them. I had buddies in other countries who did the same thing.

"Of course, Tami, he sure appreciated every little thing. He learns quick. Sing a song for him, fifteen minutes later he sings it back to you, words 'n' everything. He had a tough time getting enough food or clothes, and we did what we could for him."

The plane began the descent for the Chicago Airport. There we had two hours between plane connections, and over soup, sandwich, and a glass of milk Pinkie told me the story of his life. He was born in Black Creek, Wisconsin, twenty-nine years ago. He was one of seven children. His father was a road-repair man, and his mother was ill most of the time and unable to take care of the children. Work for Mr. Pohlman was irregular—but even when he was on the job his pay was insufficient, and the state stepped in to help.

"The county sent us to live in different places, but every once in a while Dad might have a streak of luck and was able to put enough money together to take care of us, and some of us would live with him.

"Things got rough during the Depression. I was about ten years old when they moved me to a dairy farm and I lived there a few years and got close to the people there, and they wanted me to live with them, like I was their son. I left the farm and quit school just after I got out of the grades. I was about fourteen, and I got a job on another dairy farm making about $10 a month.

"I stayed on at that dairy farm a long time—maybe four or five years. They were paying me $25 a month, and I could send some money home. They were nice folks. One of the kids, a girl about my age, was why people got to calling me Pinkie. We all ate together, the farmer and his family and the dairy hands, and this one night there were some visitors—I don't remember exactly—but the table was more crowded than usual. And the daughter—she was a bright girl and very pretty—she squeezes her chair in next to mine, so close I could hardly move my arm, and the other fellows, all they did was look at me and wink at each other. My neck felt like it was burning right off the top of my spine, it felt so hot, and next day the fellows started to call me Pinkie. When they wanted to have some fun with me they spoke about that time at the table, and my neck lights up like a neon sign."

"What happened to the girl?"

"Oh, soon after that I left for another job, and I never knew what happened to her. My next job was working in the railroad yards. It was tougher work and longer hours, but it paid almost twice as much, and they had a ball team nearby.

"When the war came they asked me to go back on the farm—they were short of help—and I worked there a couple of years before I went into the Army. By the time they shipped me out of the country the war was about over. I guess I was with the first troops going into south Japan.

"Like most G.I.'s, I was sore at what the Japs had done to my buddies. Feeling was running pretty high and the first week after we landed the people stayed under cover, and we thought the place was deserted. But after a while they began to hang around the camp and watch us and give us souvenirs.

"The first Japanese I got to know real well was Tami. I called him Tommy. It was on Christmas Eve or New Year's Eve, 1945. I don't remember exactly how I got to knock on his door. I think I was asked by some Japanese to come to his home to celebrate, but I went to the wrong house or something. I remember making a big racket knocking on some door and how a young kid came down to open it and his standing there shivering in his long gray underwear, and how I couldn't keep from laughing.

"I suppose I took such a liking to him because his life had been so much like mine as a young kid. He had to start working for himself and he had a tough time, too. I said to myself, here's a kid 8,000 miles from Appleton and many times he must have felt like I felt when I grew up, almost never seeing my mother because she was so sick, and not seeing my father too much either.

"Tami says I told him a lot about America. Well, he told me a lot about the whole Far East and about the ways of people there. Anyway, we swapped all we knew. He says in the *Digest* story that I gave him a lot of things. I don't remember giving him very much but, like I said before, he is very appreciative and makes you think you've given him a meal ticket for the rest of his life when all you've given him is a can of soup.

"But I saw a lot of Tami in the three or four months before I returned to the States. I would go over there in my free time and we would play baseball together or we would talk or sing. How he loved American songs! 'Show Me the Way to Go Home,' that he told about in the story, was only one of his favorites."

"What happened when you had to leave Japan?" I asked.

"Nothing especially. I had to say goodbye to Tami quick-like but I was darned glad to be getting back to the States. Then things began happening to me at home. I got my job as a hand at the Soo Line railroad yards in Appleton and met the girl I married. She's got a fine education and it's the best thing that ever happened to me that I met her and married.

"We've got two kids. Phyllis is almost two years old, Ronald seven months."

I asked Pinkie what his plans were for his youngsters.

"Plans, sir? I don't suppose we've really got plans. But I suppose the thing every parent wants to do is to give his kids a lot of the things he didn't have. We've got a real healthy family, my wife is a wonderful mother to the kids, and we're moving along.

"Anyway, one thing I know is, Ronnie won't have to cut out from school at fourteen to play nurse to a barnful of cows. My wife is a marvel at saving money, and we already own our own home. Six rooms. Not very large, but real nice."

I asked Pinkie how much he earned.

"Every two weeks, about $125. It may not seem like a lot of money, sir, but it's a lot of stuff just for pushing trains around a yard, and it comes to four figures each year—something that didn't use to happen. And we're putting something away. Did I say 'we?' I meant my wife. Not that she saves on the important things. You know, we order nine quarts of milk a day. That's one thing I always had plenty of as a kid and it really pulled me through."

"Are you going to write to Tami?" I asked.

"Write to Tami? I've already written to Tami. Wrote him air mail the first night after Mrs. Pelkey came over. I'm not good at writing, and I'd rather milk a couple hundred Jerseys with soggy tails than set myself down to a postcard. But I wrote a long letter to Tami, telling him how glad I was to know his address and telling him he'd become famous."

Two days later, back in New York, I learned that Pinkie's letter had dead-ended in Japan. Tami Taguchi had disappeared! The Army postal authorities reported that a considerable number of letters addressed to Tami from America were being held until Tami could be found. Then the letter almost every G.I. in Japan was waiting for—from Pinkie to Tami—arrived and was promptly spotted.

The Army moved into high gear. The Pacific edition of Stars and Stripes featured the story and intensified the search for Tami, who left no forwarding address after he wound up his work for the Army driving a truck—just as Pinkie used to do.

Major Charles Emard, in charge of the Army postal service, personally supervised the effort to find Tami. Within three days after Pinkie's letter arrived Tami was found. He was pedaling a rickshaw bicycle, or pedicab, in Yokohama. According to Stars and Stripes, Tami could hardly believe his good fortune. After he had read and reread Pinkie's letter with moist eyes, he took up the letters from other well-wishers in the USA.

A little later, according to the news stories, a happy but be-wildered Tami was sitting behind a table writing a letter to Pinkie, while flash bulbs of Army and press-association photographers lit up the room.

*   *   *

The story of Tami Taguchi and Pinkie Pohlman has had a strong symbolic significance in Japan. Pinkie had proved that goodwill wasn't only the result of large-scale information and service pro-grams but of the genuine regard and warmth one man may have for another.

The relationship between the two men had answered many of the questions I had asked myself about the impact of America on Japan. A great deal had been said about the carelessness of American soldiers stationed in foreign lands. But what the critics frequently overlooked was the remarkable talent for making warm and lasting friendships of the average G.I. Of one thing we can be certain: America has an almost limitless need abroad for Orville Pohlmans—in Japan and elsewhere—who know that the best foundation for real understanding among peoples is on the level of a working friendship.

*   *   *

Within little more than a year after my return from the 1949 trip to Japan this problem of goodwill among peoples was to send me back to the Far East.

"*Truth and understanding are not such wares as to be monopolized and traded in by tickets and statutes, and standards. We must not think to make a staple commodity of all the knowledge in the land, to mark and license it like our broadcloth, and our wool packs.*"

—JOHN MILTON

* * *

"*When will the West understand, or try to understand, the East? We Asiatics are often appalled by the curious web of facts and fancies which has been woven concerning us. We are pictured as living on the perfume of the lotus, if not on mice and cockroaches. It is either impotent fanaticism or else abject voluptuousness. Indian spirituality has been derided as ignorance, Chinese sobriety as stupidity, Japanese patriotism as the result of fatalism. It has been said that we are less sensible to pain and wounds on account of the callousness of our nervous organization!*"

—OKAKURA-KAKUZO

* * *

"*Should a traveler, returning from a far country, bring us an account of men, wholly different from any with whom we were ever acquainted; men, who were entirely divested of avarice, ambition, or revenge; who knew no pleasure but friendship, generosity, and public spirit; we should immediately, from these circumstances, detect the falsehood and prove him a liar, with the same certainty as if he had stuffed his narration with stories of centaurs and dragons, miracles and prodigies.*"

—DAVID HUME

* * *

"*Sovereignty lies in knowing men, and giving repose to the people.*"

—CONFUCIUS

* * *

"*It is a flattering and consolatory reflection, that our rising Republics have the good wishes of all the Philosophers, Patriots, and virtuous men in all nations; and that they look upon them as a kind of Asylum for mankind. God grant that we may not disappoint their honest expectations, by our folly or perverseness.*"

—GEORGE WASHINGTON

CHAPTER IX

ASSIGNMENT IN ASIA

It's a tough assignment, and you mustn't hesitate to turn it down."

The speaker was George C. McGhee, Assistant Secretary of State whose area of the world included India, Pakistan, and the Near East. He was giving me a preliminary briefing on the assignment that was to send me to the Asian subcontinent on what one of the men in the State Department jokingly called "Operation Yak-Yak."

Mr. McGhee explained that his office had received many requests from State's representatives in the field for Americans who would talk about the United States and answer questions about the American people under conditions that could hardly be described as ideal. There were resounding misconceptions about the United States in Asia—not all of them the result of sheer accident or misunderstanding. Communist propaganda against us in many Asian countries, he said, was intensive and apparently effective.

"Congress has recognized the problem," Mr. McGhee said, "and has passed the Smith-Mundt Act for the express purpose of advancing better understanding among Americans and other peoples. If you accept you will not be required to turn out blurbs or commercials nor to say anything you don't believe. In fact, the worst thing we could do would be to send out someone who would sound like an apologist or a hired propagandist.

"Public opinion in India and Pakistan, to a large extent, is the result of what happens in the literate and artistic groups. Newspapermen, writers, students, teachers, government people—these are the opinion leaders on the subcontinent. And if you accept this assignment, you will find that most of your talks will be in these circles.

You can expect heckling—plenty of it—especially in the universities. There is a good chance that in one or two places you may even be publicly attacked as a paid propagandist. But we believe that the overwhelming majority of your audiences will accept you in the spirit in which we send you: an independent American who has had a chance to see and know a great deal of his own country and who will try to answer fully and fairly the many questions put to him."

I accepted the assignment, which came little more than a year after my return from Hiroshima. I wouldn't have missed it for the world. It was an awesome challenge, and I fully recognized my limitations in attempting to meet it. But there was nothing I would rather do. As I wrote in the opening chapter, there was much that impelled me in the direction of the subcontinent.

* * *

Not many weeks after I received the details of my assignment from Mr. McGhee, I was in a plane heading out across the North Pacific for Japan. On a trip like this, which began on December 31, 1950, close to the shortest day of the year, a sense of almost continuous night dominated all my impressions. It was as though we were fleeing from the sun, trying to outrace it hour after hour. Seemingly, we were suspended in a smudge for almost twenty hours. There was no sense of motion, for there was nothing to see against which to fix a position. It was a moonless night from the moment we jumped off into the black at Anchorage, Alaska, where the sun rose not long before noon and set at 2:30 P.M.

This annihilation of light and motion was matched by the annihilation of the clock. The most futile thing in the world anyone could have done up there was to ask the time. There were about a dozen time changes between New York and Tokyo—if you feel punctilious about those things. What time did you decide to eat or sleep by? The time you followed yesterday? That time was as meaningless up there as sunglasses. The time you looked at just a short while ago? That, too, told you nothing. Meanwhile you flew over the International Date Line and a full day vanished, although it would not have been day even if it didn't vanish. There were four changes of crew after we left Minneapolis, to correspond with the major portions of the flight, each of which averaged from nine to ten hours. Except for the Edmonton-Anchorage hop, each portion of the flight was handled by the crew as a regular night flight—which is to say that pillows and blankets were distributed and your chair adjusted for sleeping. But you became fatigued from being put to bed four times in the same night, all the more so when the night lasted a full day.

Over Canada and Alaska it had been entirely different. In the four or five hours of daylight that we enjoyed out of Edmonton, we passed through an endless white paradise, the like of which I had seen nowhere in the world. This was the land of glaciers and white miracles of mountains, dwarfing the Rockies or the Alps in height and splendor. The term "white supremacy" belonged to this and to nothing else. The sun was high enough to give a glitter both to valleys and to peaks, low enough to provide the contrast of a strong and smooth blue sky; low enough, too, to enable the peaks to throw off colored patterns and shadows.

About three flying hours out of Shemya, the bleak jumping-off airstrip in the Aleutians for the long hop across the Pacific, we flew over the loneliest boat in the world. It has a crew of about thirty whose job it is to keep the ship fixed in position and to worry about bad weather—of which there is plenty.

The ship is a flighthouse, which sends out radio beams instead of light beams. But it is hardly ever seen by the planes overhead, for it is anchored in a section of the Pacific invariably closed in by fogbank or cloudbank.

"That's my idea of the most forlorn spot in the world," the pilot of my plane said after we passed over the approximate position of the flighthouse. "I have a friend who once met one of the crew on leave. He said it's cold and dark. The darkness bothers the men even more than the cold. This time of year it's dark for all but a short stretch each day—and the light they get wouldn't wake an owl.

"Every once in a while there is a break in the weather, and the men actually see the plane overhead they're trying to guide with their radio—and they all rush to the deck to see it, watching the lights flicker, watching until the lights finally twinkle out.

"You can't blame them for being excited when they see us. Brother, you'd stand up and cheer your head off if you actually saw something going somewhere after you'd been swallowed up in this black stuff day after day and night after night with only the clock to tell you where daytime is somewhere else. You get awful hungry to get a good square view of something going where there's some daylight. Up here there's just an awful lot of night and practically nothing else."

The contrast between the white paradise of Alaska and the endless night of the North Pacific seemed almost symbolic of the trip itself. For behind us was an America prosperous, as yet untouched by war in its homeland; ahead of us were Korea and China and India and a battered world in hunger and revolution. It was difficult to bring the two worlds into single focus, but the long night of this trip furnished an effective if gloomy transition.

* * *

On the morning of the second day across the Pacific, with a weak orange sun rising behind us, we could discern Japan on the horizon. Fujiyama, with its white cap, seemed to preside over the black stretch of land rimming that part of the horizon. Then, as we approached, we could see the jagged shore line. Underneath were the giant fishing nets, laid out in tremendous, evenly drawn squares. As we came in for a landing, we could see the blinking early-morning lights in the streets of the small towns and villages surrounding Tokyo.

Within a day after I arrived in Tokyo, I had to rub my eyes. The change in a year and a half was startling—a change in both place and people. When I had seen Japan in the summer of 1949, the people were making progress but they were run down at the heels. Their clothing was skimpy and tattered. Their faces seemed drawn and tense. The food shops had little volume and variety. Housing was still a critical problem. But it was different today. The Ginza, Tokyo's main thoroughfare, was lit up by neon lights. The shops were crowded. About the only thing you couldn't buy was a television set. There were refrigerators, washing machines, electric bed warmers, fancy luggage, delicate lace lingerie—even pogo sticks. Food was plentiful. The people were comparatively well dressed and had far more bounce than when I had observed them eighteen months ago. "Better than before the war," a university professor told me. "Japanese people are grateful for American help in rebuilding ourselves."

What I saw in Tokyo was reinforced in Hiroshima. In contrast to my visit a year earlier, it was now difficult to tell that this entire area was devastated only five years earlier by the first atomic bomb in history to be dropped upon a city. True, there were still some ugly scars—the skeletoned dome of the Exhibition Hall Building and the discolored façade of the City Hall. But Hiroshima in 1951 looked like a different city. Wide new thoroughfares were in process of construction. Modern office buildings were going up. Old trolleys were being replaced. Mayor Shinzo Hamai was busy at work carrying out his plan to make Hiroshima one of the most beautiful cities in the East. One of the principal features of the new plan was the large Hiroshima Peace Center project, to include a hospital, orphanage, community center, exhibition hall, and the institute for the study of world peace.

"Many, many changes since you were here last time," Mayor Hamai told me. "The psychological recovery is even greater than physical recovery. More people are working. More people have homes. The city has helped to put up new housing projects, like the one you see over there." He pointed to an impressive two-story building development which covered most of a short block.

I was especially impressed by the improvement in the hospital facilities. Revisiting Dr. Akio Asano's hospital, I was pleased to see that people were no longer forced to sleep on floor mats. There were beds and good mattresses for all. Dr. Asano proudly showed me his new operating room and equipment and his modern sterilizers. The miracle drugs—penicillin, streptomycin, aureomycin, chloromycetin, and others—were still not available in large quantities, but at least it was possible to obtain sufficient quantities for the serious cases. I recalled the critical scarcity just a year earlier when we tried to get from the United States enough streptomycin for little Nobuko.

It wasn't only Hiroshima or Tokyo. Other cities I saw in Japan reflected this spirit of recovery and well-being. The industrial centers were working at top speed. The shipbuilding business had had one of the most prosperous years in its history. In rolled steel the year's goal had been surpassed; a new goal of 4,000,000 tons had been set for 1951. Pig-iron production was expected to exceed 2,500,000 tons that year. In an earlier month more than 90,000 bicycles—basic transportation in Japan—were produced. A postwar production record had been established in the automotive industry with an output of 2,250 cars in November alone.

What impressed a visitor from America most of all, however, was the general atmosphere of detachment from the Korean war crisis. You had to keep reminding yourself that only a few hours away a war was going on. You seldom heard the war discussed. There were no big black headlines in the papers about Korea. I had the strange experience of being asked by an American friend, an officer in the occupation, to explain why everyone in the United States seemed to be on edge.

Among the Japanese there was little surface evidence of any preoccupation with the war news. The visits of American officials had attracted a great deal of general interest, but that was because the Japanese Government and people regarded a peace treaty with the United States as the number-one national aim. In general, however, the comparative boom served to focus the individual's attention on himself and his share in the improved national standard of living.

Culture and entertainment were thriving. The Japanese traditional folk theater was having a considerable resurgence, especially among the young people, although it had not yet replaced the American movie as the nation's favorite pastime. Strolling along a street leading to the Imperial Palace, I noticed a crowd of Japanese gathered in a large circle. A model-plane tournament was in progress, and youngsters were sending their planes aloft in a contest of speed and endurance. The planes were as sleek and as professional as any model planes I have seen anywhere. Most of them were powered by fuel engines, and they set up a small roar as they buzzed along.

Suddenly there were screeching sirens as motorcycle military police cleared the way on an adjoining thoroughfare for a caravan of U.S. Army ambulances carrying American boys wounded in Korea to our hospitals in Tokyo. A few persons watching the model planes turned around to see what was happening. It would have been interesting to know what thoughts crossed their minds as they watched the seemingly endless procession of trucks with their Red

Cross insignia. Were any of them pondering the irony that only a few years ago Japanese were fighting and dying in China? Then America crushed Japan and moved into Japan, doing more for the Japanese people in a few years than the hypernationalists had been able to do in half a century. Indeed, America was doing more for the vanquished foe than it was doing for many of its own allies. And then, by a strange twist of history, Chinese and Americans were killing each other while Japan became a prosperous spectator. And here were American Army ambulances speeding past a group of Japanese watching their youngsters pursue fairly expensive hobbies.

If these were the thoughts that passed through the minds of the few Japanese who even bothered to look up, I wonder what they made of it all. Perhaps they didn't even try. It's a tough one for even the historians to figure out when they get around to it.

I discussed this with a young Japanese instructor, F. Kuwano, whose father had lived in the United States before World War I.

"Strange things happen since 1945," he said. "When we lost the war, you made us realize how evil war was. You told us a nation that builds a mighty war machine will use it. You warned us about the great danger of militarism and nationalism. What you said was true. Many Japanese people agreed with you. Especially encouraged were those Japanese who always were worried about the military ideas and imperialism of the war party.

"That was why we were so anxious to prove to the world after the war that military Japan was not the only Japan. When you took our military supplies and dumped them in the ocean, we were very thankful. We wanted to redeem ourselves in the eyes of decent people. We wrote a new Constitution. In it we outlawed war and use of armaments as a way of dealing with other nations. We were not merely writing words on paper. We believed it. We wanted to prove ourselves worthy of all the fine things America was doing for us under the Occupation. Your land-reform program, very good. Before the war, whenever Japanese liberals spoke about the need for breaking up holdings of large landlords and giving land to people who worked land, they were called terrible names like Bolshevists or revolutionaries. But now General MacArthur has done much more than even liberals asked. It is good and we are grateful.

"Another wonderful thing General MacArthur has done is to improve health of Japanese people. Before the war, Japanese death rate was one of highest in the world. Rat disease, cholera epidemic, tuberculosis, pneumonia, malnutrition—all these sicknesses crippled the Japanese people. Then came Americans. One American, General Sams,* is a great human being and doctor. He made Japanese people understand how bad and dangerous are rats. He started a national campaign of education and rodent control. Then General Sams began a war on tuberculosis. Tuberculosis is the worst killer of Japanese people—reason why so many Japanese die before age thirty. Again General Sams starts with education so we can know how tuberculosis comes and how we can fight against it. Then he gives us special new medicines and treatments. Soon we see wonderful new results. Tuberculosis death rate within few years is cut in half.

"Then General Sams works to teach Japanese people about proper diet and how to grow balanced food. Japanese children are now bigger and stronger.

"All these things have made startling change in few years. Today, death rate per thousand is very low in comparison with other Asian countries. Maybe almost 40 per cent less than five years ago. General Sams, a great man.

"Another wonderful thing you did for us was help Japan conserve our natural resources. You have carried out big plans for saving our forests and for replanting millions of acres. Much less waste now of wood and coal. Fishing industry, much more efficient.

"You have helped us build schools and hospitals and roads. You have given us many new ideas for teaching our children.

"Japan today is the most prosperous nation in East. Of course, our prosperity is nothing like yours, and millions of Japanese people are still without enough food. Housing problem is still bad. But compared to other Asian countries, Japan is far ahead."

I was impressed by all this but I was somewhat uncertain about his main point. He had started out by talking about all the "strange things" that had happened since 1945. He had referred to the new Constitution and its provisions outlawing war, and then had gone on to describe the achievements of the Occupation. Was this what he meant by the "strange things"? I put the question to him.

"What I meant to say was that Japanese have a connection in their minds between the new Constitution and other democratic measures. You told us, and we believed you, that democracy and peace-

* General Crawford F. Sams.

fulness mean the same thing. And so with your help we tried to create a different national society built around peace.

"And now we are puzzled because many things are happening again you warned us against. Only yesterday you dumped our armaments out to sea; today you are asking us to make armaments again. The schools no longer teach that war, militarism, and nationalism are bad. Many of the old slogans are returning, and what is most tragic of all is that our teachers, the Americans, are the ones who are no longer interested in finishing the wonderful job they started here only a few years ago. Many of the fine democratic measures you introduced are being put aside because they would take away too much energy and money from the defense program.

"I wonder whether the Americans realize that in the new atmosphere, the old militarists and religious nationalists find very favorable conditions for restoring their prestige and perhaps, before long, their power. That is why I say many strange things have happened since 1945. What is most strange is that some of us wonder why you went to trouble of trying to remake Japan at the end of war. If your main wish for us now is that we become a war power, would it not have been better to keep Japan the way it was?"

*   *   *

Kuwano, like many other thoughtful Japanese, was profoundly disturbed by the queer and violent turns that contemporary history had taken. America and what America stood for had represented itself to him as the answer to the old militarism, but now America herself seemed to be sponsoring a repudiation of many of the things that had opened the eyes of the Japanese to the danger and immorality of their imperialist past.

I tried to tell Kuwano that perhaps we were all victims of history—not only Japanese and Americans, but all peoples everywhere. What we had done in the early years of the Occupation was no accident, nor was it a strange and insincere interlude. It was no mere quirk that no victor in history had been less vindictive than we were when we went into Japan in 1945; it was a deep reflection of the national will. The billions of dollars put into Japan, the various health, economic and education programs—these were a genuine manifestation of our desire to do the right thing.

What went wrong, of course, is that we hadn't sufficiently recognized that it would be impossible to create a design for a new and peaceful democracy without creating a design for the world itself. Japan was as dependent for its own peace and democratic progress upon a peaceful world as was every other nation and every other people. I thought back to my experience the previous year in Germany when it was clear that we would have to abandon many of the vows that we had taken about demilitarization and de-Nazification. Germany, like Japan, had become a pawn in the cold war, and many Germans were using the new bargaining power for all it was worth; and apparently it was worth a good deal.

I told Kuwano that I believed we were all paying a price for world anarchy. What was happening only a few hours away in Korea, where men were on the march again, was but part of the price. And if we were really interested in halting Communist violence and aggression, then we must realize that the aggressor could have no greater opportunity than was presented by the conditions of disorganization.

The question was exactly what it had been in San Francisco in 1945. Were we mature and wise and strong enough to have a pooling of sovereignty in the common cause?

*   *   *

Such, at least, was the mood in which I left Tokyo for a brief visit to nearby Korea—only a few hours away by air, but ages removed from the two worlds from which I had come: the world of a fast-recuperating but puzzled Japan, and the world of a strong but remote America. The Sea of Japan, however modest a body of water, seemed like outer space itself as I flew over in a hospital plane returning to Korea to pick up a fresh load of casualties.

CHAPTER X

"CONNECTING UP" IN KOREA

It didn't seem like Sunday. The sun was strong and the sky was blue and open, but nothing else made it seem like Sunday. No parks to stroll in; no people on porches working their way through the big Sunday newspapers; no baseball or football games to go to or read about; no brightly dressed children holding hands on their way home from church.

It was Sunday in Taegu, Korea, military headquarters of the United Nations.

What you did on this Sunday afternoon in Taegu depended on who you were. If you were a soldier, you fought or you waited. If you were an aviator, you flew your sorties or you waited. If you were a Korean, you trudged or you waited. War is mostly a business of waiting. While the action lasts it seems like forever, but the action comes mostly in hot, shattering spurts.

Because of the sheer accident of a birthdate, I was not a soldier in Korea.

Because of the sheer accident of a birthplace, I was not a Korean. I did not have to walk along the hard rutted roads, a bundle of family belongings strapped to my back—moving slowly in a vast procession of hollow-faced and bewildered people who were homeless in their own homeland.

These accidents enabled me to stand on the sidelines as a spectator—close enough to the tragedy to touch it with my hands, yet free to move as far away from it as I might wish. In all essential respects my credentials in the human family were no different from those of the Koreans, yet a little slip of paper in my coat pocket endowed me with the magic of exemption and option. This paper enabled me to obtain such food as I might require; it made it possible for me to find lodging; it even authorized me to fly out of this hell. For the Koreans the hell was sealed in, universal, absolute.

Hell in this case had its headquarters in the public square in front of the Taegu railroad station. Thousands of the homeless had been converging on this square. Some of them had just come from the open boxcars of the freight train that had carried them into Taegu. They had been shoveled into the boxcars like gravel, spilling over the ends and the sides, and then shoveled out again at Taegu. They were funneled through one side of the open terminal where other Koreans who were accredited for the purpose would work them over with spray guns filled with DDT. Not much was left of the human dignity we talked so much about at home; but it was probably better to submit to the temporary indignity of a delousing spray gun than to the continuing indignity of its cause.

* * *

Standing there in front of the railroad station, I had the feeling that Taegu could tell us more about our age than a convention of historians. For this was where the predicament of the individual in our time was defined at its sharpest.

The teachers were the refugees—750,000 of them—all of them supremely qualified experts. They knew all there was to know about war, political terror, hunger, homelessness, and heartbreak. Three times they had to carry their packs and their little worlds on their backs. Three times they tried to outrun violence, and failed. They streamed into Taegu because they expected that the Americans would help them find food and refuge.

On that Sunday afternoon I watched them—countless thousands of them—as they pressed into Taegu. They came in the snow and the rain. They came by truck and bicycle and oxcart. They came in open freight cars, as I say, piled high atop one another until they spilled over the sides and ends, clinging to the rungs, riding between the cars, hugging the iron underbelly. But mostly they came on foot, lugging their cumbersome bundles and carrying their babies on their backs. One woman I saw was pregnant and seemed to be approaching full term; she had a year-old infant strapped to her back and a three-year-old in her arms. On her head she balanced a large blanket-tied bundle. Her husband was not with her. Another young woman of perhaps twenty-five, one shoe missing, was frantically cutting in and out of the crowd, looking for a missing child. There were many lost children from whom to choose. You seldom saw complete families.

A Korean of about seventy, wearing the traditional clothes and the stovepipe hat of the Korean patriarchs, was coughing blood and seemed ready to give up. Other elderly men and women, heavy bags on their heads or backs, struggled to keep up with the procession. Their faces were taut, their eyes deep-set and blank. A young girl of fifteen or sixteen became hysterical and started to hit out at the military vehicles trying to squeeze through. She slapped at the cars with rage and laughed and screamed with mad delight as they veered to avoid hitting her. Another girl of about the same age, her head swathed in a bulky, dirty bandage, wandered around just looking.

They kept coming and coming, clogging the heart of the city, and they put down their bundles and waited. Near the large open area of the railroad station they jammed the main thoroughfares, making it difficult for the rolling machines of war—the lorries and supply trucks and darting jeeps—to get through. Every once in a while screeching brakes would announce a near accident, and not infrequently someone would be hit. Then the Korean military police would rush into action, yelling and screaming at the people and using their menacing submachine guns as prods. Every once in a while, too, the police would have to clear a path through the crowd for the marching Korean soldiers in American uniforms on their way to the front. They sang as they marched, the Korean soldiers, their loud but uneven voices clashing with the sounds of the crowd and the banging, banging, banging of the heavy trucks bouncing along the rutted roads.

The problem of getting military transportation through the city on the main north-south road became increasingly acute. About five o'clock in the afternoon two-way traffic became impossible, and the United Nations military police worked furiously to reroute traffic from the north in order to give right of way on the main road to supply trucks moving up to the fighting front.

During the night the South Korean authorities apparently made a heartbreaking decision. I learned about it when I returned to the vicinity of the railroad station in the morning. The entire area had been blocked off. I was startled to see that the streets were virtually empty. I went up to an American M.P. directing the fast-moving two-way traffic and asked him about it.

"They were sent back north last night," he said simply.

I was certain I had misunderstood him, and asked him to repeat.

"Just like I said, mister. North, north, north. South Korean police made the decision."

I could hardly believe it. "We didn't send them back into that hell?" I asked. "You're not serious?"

"Look, mister," he said with some irritation. "I only told you what I know. Traffic was all fouled up. Orders came to clear them out. They put road blocks on the roads going south to keep the refugees from jamming these roads any more than they are now. The only place left to send them was north, on the other side of the river where they can fan out so's not to stop traffic. Most of them are trying to get back into the city again, but they tell me the road up there is pretty well sealed off."

The M.P. remained silent a moment. He had a faraway look as though he had seen something he was trying hard to forget.

"You oughta be able to figure it out for yourself," he said. "It was plenty rough. It turned my stomach. First the Korean police tried to get them up off their bags and on their feet so's to start moving. But soon as the people realized what was up, they sat down hard and closed their ears. Then the police waded into them like they were so much cattle, working them over with the butt ends of their guns and clubs, screaming and yelling at them, and shoving them forward. Once they started moving, the toughest part was over. They were pushed in that direction"—he pointed north— "and the police kept riding herd until the street was cleared and they were out of the city." He looked at me, then turned away.

"Okay, mister, you needn't look at me like I did it. No one could do nothing about it. You couldn't do nothing if you tried. That's just it in this damned war—people getting the hell kicked out of them no matter what they do or where they turn, and no one can do nothing. I kept wanting to yell out at the Korean police as these people were being pushed back toward the Commies. I wanted to say: 'Stop shoving, you stupid bastards. These are the people we're supposed to be liberating, remember? Put down those rifle butts and leave these people alone, leave 'em rest.'

"Sure, it was easy to want to say it," the M.P. continued. "But who would listen? What good would it do? So I just watched, hard, like you're watching me now."

*   *   *

The Korean refugee symbolized the individual of our time—in retreat and without refuge. He symbolized the Age of the Great Trap—a trap which not only awaited but pursued the individual. It seemed out there in Korea that one by one the escape hatches were being closed down. Man's sanctuaries were becoming increasingly rare, increasingly remote. Instead there were clubs and rifle ends to beat him back. He was being ground down into impersonal animation.

Had there ever been a time when so many people in so many places were so desperately seeking escape from political terror or from war? Had there ever been a time when there were so many locked doors? Once not so long ago the refugee captured the conscience of more fortunate peoples. A single individual fleeing from injustice or misery would find other individuals and even nations springing to his defense. An earthquake would erupt and several hundreds would be made homeless; instantly, mercy would be mobilized and put into action.

But you had the feeling that in our time the problem had gotten out of hand. The challenge was so great that a bad case of heart-hardening had set in. Those on the outside, in failing to provide a refuge for the unfortunate and the damned, had synthesized a refuge of their own. If the tragedy engulfed enough people, it apparently lost its raw edge of reality, converting benefactors into spectators.

And the greatest tragedy of all, perhaps, is the fatal lack of connection between man caught in the Great Trap and man who wants to help but cannot. Consider the case of the American M.P. completely hemmed in by legalisms and uniforms and regulations and conditions beyond his control. "I couldn't do nothing about it," he said, and he was right. His helplessness was formalized, certified, underwritten by society itself. For he too was caught in a giant trap too large to argue with or comprehend.

In January, 1951, no one knew what the military outcome of the campaign in Korea would be. We were facing great odds, and it seemed that we might not be able to hold on. But we did know that we were fighting not only for land but for people and ideas. This planet was much smaller than it used to be and it was shrinking fast, but it was not so small that there was no room on it for people who believed us when we proclaimed ourselves their friends and benefactors.

Was there any reason why we should not have brought this issue before the United Nations, pressing hard and mightily for an adequate rescue program in behalf of the Koreans? It would have required an armada of ships that would have dwarfed Dunkirk, and many nations would have had to come forward to offer a haven until such time at least as the world became sane again. It would have been the largest operation in the name of mercy and simple justice in our age. But it would have saved lives and been a monumental symbol of hope to people everywhere.

*   *   *

On that Sunday afternoon in Korea I walked toward the bridge leading to the outskirts of the city. Bullock carts moved far to one side to make way for the lorries. On the banks of the thin, muddy river, people squatted as they worked on their soapless laundry, beating the dirt out of clothing with thick sticks or swinging the wet clothes against large, smooth rocks. A new industry had come to Taegu with the United Nations Army—one-day laundry services for the soldiers. Up and down the main streets of the city I had seen freshly painted signs proclaiming the conversion of many of the city's businesses. "Good Washes Please" or "Clothes Quick Wash Back" or "Washe U Waite Nowe" were some of the new shingles.

Not far from the bridge, on a gently rising slope, was a large area marked off by a white picket fence. In the center the fence parted for a small gateway on the top of which, in freshly painted blue and white letters, a sign read "United Nations Military Cemetery." Beyond that were white crosses—perhaps two thousand; it was hard to tell. Dozens of Korean laborers were at work over the graves, disinterring the recently buried coffinless bodies in their disintegrating shrouds. The level of each grave was being raised from six to two feet. The reason for it, I learned, was that we were preparing against the possibility that we might have to evacuate Taegu, and we wanted to take our war dead with us.

A military truck drove up. The driver, a sergeant, got out slowly, then spoke to the officer in charge of the cemetery. The officer walked over to the back of the truck, peered in, lowered his eyes, and called over some of the Koreans. The truck contained the naked bodies of ten American soldiers who had been ambushed only a few miles north of the cemetery. The sergeant had spotted them and picked them up. The Koreans helped the officer in charge and the sergeant as they lifted the bodies from the truck and placed them on a large canvas inside the gateway. The bodies had been stripped. Even the wrist identification tags had been removed. Some of the bodies had been badly riddled with bullets, torn open and fragmented. One or two were without visible marks, seeming strangely serene and detached from the raw, red cutting edges of war. And now the bodies were to be scientifically processed for identification.

Another large jeep drove up. A tall redheaded driver called out and asked the officer-in-charge where he could find the cemetery list. He was told that the list was on file at Eighth United States Army Headquarters in Taegu. I was going back that way and asked for a lift. We rode together in silence for a moment or so as the big jeep bounced and banged in and out of the deep dirt ruts.

"Third cemetery I've checked on this week," he said. "Kid brother got killed somewhere around here six weeks ago. Folks wrote to me, asking did I know where the grave was and would I stand in front of it for them and put some flowers on it for the family. All I can do is stop when I see a cemetery and look at the list. So far, nothing. Maybe I'll find something this time."

I stared hard at the half dozen bullet holes in the windshield.

"Most of those are about a week old," he said. "I wasn't driving it then. Fellow driving got it that night. Two drivers before him got it too. Nowhere near the front lines. It's like those kids stretched out there on that canvas. You never know where it's coming from. Drive on a road at night—any road, even this one, then suddenly the hot lead starts pouring in. We drive up from Pusan to Taegu on roads that are supposed to be cleared out, then there's a short burst of gunfire, two trucks go haywire, and by the time we fan out to find out where it came from the place is empty."

Overhead, six Thunderjets in formation were eating up the sky. When the heavy sound subsided, the driver looked over at me and asked whether I had just come from the States. I nodded.

"I been reading an awful lot of rhubarb about us in the news-papers and magazines," he said. "Seems the folks back home are worried about our morale. Some of them are saying that all this arguing about bombing China or not bombing China, and this busi-ness between the President and the Old Man, all this is supposed to hurt our morale.

"Nuts. That ain't what's bothering us," he continued. "Bomb China, don't bomb China—that's for the brass to worry about—and we're not trying to second guess anybody. Don't worry about our morale. Ain't nothing that's hurting it except what we read about what's going on back home."

"Such as?"

"Brother, you kidding? You don't mean to tell me you don't know what I'm talking about. Listen, what's getting us down is, do the people back home know there's a war on? We can read. We see the magazines. We get the newspapers. You can't kid us about what's happening. We're the fellows that are being shot up, and we want to know whether we're just the fall guys or whether anyone at home is giving, too. And, brother, if you just came from there you know everyone's not giving. Can't even get enough goddam blood to fill the tubes. But there's plenty of money around at home and plenty of hot times and the lid's off, and who gives a damn if a few guys are grabbed off and shipped out to this mucked-up place?

"This is supposed to be a police action, it says here. Just a cosy little police action. Well, they've got some live ammunition out here and these kids are catching it, and we don't want to have this party all by ourselves.

"You really want to know what morale is—real morale? Real morale is the feeling you get when you know you're connected up—you know you're connected up with the people at home and they're connected up with you. When you're all connected up, then everyone's in, we're all in the same show, and it's just a matter of time before we get the damned thing over with. It's a wonderful feeling, being connected up, but mister, we just ain't got that feeling. You tell me, goddam it, that I should feel all connected up with everyone and they're connected up with me and I'll laugh in your face. Would the Army have to advertise for blood like they was trying to sell laundry soap if everyone was connected up with Korea?"

I said nothing. There was nothing to say. I didn't believe that the people at home were "connected up" with the war in Korea. Yes, we were concerned, but it didn't burn into us and become real. It wasn't more important than the things we wanted to do or buy or the size of our salaries or income or the things that absorbed our interest. Sure, somewhere deep down inside there was an unhappy and uncomfortable feeling about it, but it didn't get too far beyond that.

Perhaps this was just the way people acted when the trouble was at a distance. Perhaps not until each person could be taken by the hand and brought to Korea and set down alongside a truckload of empty bodies ripped open by dynamite and lead would we be able to "connect up."

We weren't "connecting up" in ways other than the failure to give our soldiers the spiritual satisfaction that comes from knowing they have a team in depth behind them. I thought of the Taegu railroad square and my talk with the American M.P. directing traffic. What about the Korean people? Were we connecting up with them? Was there a dramatic outpouring of conscience for the millions of refugees?

"Connecting up" was a vast and vital enterprise. There were the connections to be made between experience and anticipation, between accumulating evidence and comprehension, between yesterday and tomorrow. In the bare historical sense, we had yet to act on the lesson of Korea. There was general recognition that if a United Nations army of substantial numbers had been in existence before June, 1950, there might have been no Korea. But what about the threat beyond Korea? Were we ready for that? Had we thought through the implications of the unfinished job of San Francisco? We were faced in 1945 with the need and opportunity to connect up with the lessons of World War II, but we weren't willing to do it if it meant losing sovereignty. And so the free nations kept their sovereignty at San Francisco and were losing lives in Korea. And even as the Korean casualties mounted above 125,000, we held back from the big steps that might have given deep meaning to this sacrifice. "Connecting up" in this case would have meant coming before the United Nations to propose the creation of a mighty force recruited, not on a voluntary basis, but on a compulsory basis—as part of the transformation of the United Nations into an organization with binding obligations under a rule of law.

It would not do to say that the Russians would never connect up with such a proposal. That is no doubt true. But we were already in Korea under United Nations sanction to crush Communist aggression. Was there any reason why that sanction could not be broadened to whatever extent was necessary to make it adequate? If the lawbreaker demurs, were the others to embrace lawlessness? Wasn't it possible that our best chance of connecting up with the present crisis was to convince the lawbreaker that such preponderance as the free world then enjoyed would not be frittered away? That this preponderance would be consolidated under law directed at the creation and preservation of true peace under justice? That such an organization was open to all those who accepted its obligations, and was constructive and affirmative in character, and would invoke force only to forestall or combat the use of force? That it would be strong enough to assure the security of all those who embraced its principles?

This might have been—and still is—a franchise for survival which any nation truly desiring peace should be anxious to consider.

This is not intended as an indictment of our political leaders of whatever party. The democratic faith is based not so much on the assumption of leadership from the top as it is upon the wisdom and conscience of the many and the groundswell generated thereby. When this groundswell becomes manifest, there will be a magnificent connecting up, between man and his governors, and, what is more important, between man and man.

*   *   *

The night I returned from the U.N. military cemetery, I slept in an abandoned Korean schoolroom. Many times during the night I could hear, very distinctly, the strong staccato voices of the South Korean soldiers as they sang while marching to the front. The sound and the echoes would die away slowly only to be replaced with the fresh staccato voices of a new unit on its way to war.

The echoes in the distance, like the war itself, seemed to call for new voices and new lives, and the demand was now being met.

I thought back upon the events of the day—the war refugees in front of the railroad station; the American M.P. directing traffic; the U.N. military cemetery, and the ride back. Mostly I thought about the military cemetery and the bodies that had to be buried twice.

Military cemeteries. The day I visited the military cemetery at Taegu was within a few weeks of the anniversary marking fourscore and seven years since Lincoln dedicated the military cemetery at Gettysburg.

Gettysburg and Korea weren't so very far apart. For beyond November 19, 1863, there were to be hundreds of military cemeteries. Words of compassion and resolution were to be spoken over fallen American soldiers on strange battlefields many thousands of miles from home—at Flanders and in the Argonne Forest on the banks of the Meuse and the Seine and the Rhine, at Château-Thierry, Verdun, Maubeuge, and Metz-Lorraine, at Saint-Mihiel and Chemin des Dames; on islands small and large stretching across the Pacific: Pearl Harbor, Midway, Kwajalein, Guam, Tarawa, Tinian, Truk, Iwo Jima, and Okinawa; at places hardly even mentioned in geography books; Guadalcanal, Saipan, Tulagi, Apamama, Salamaua, Rabaul; at Gona, Buna, Makin, Munda, and Bougainville; at places where they waited so long for us to come back, Bataan and Corregidor and Leyte and Manila; at a dozen harbors in North Africa and in the sands of Algeria, Tunisia, and Libya; in Pantelleria and

Sicily and the mainland of Italy, at Salerno and Cassino and Bologna and the beachhead of Anzio; at places in France familiar to fathers and brothers only twenty-five years ago, Dieppe, Calais, Cherbourg, Le Havre, Caen, Rouen, Beauvais, Compiègne, Saint-Quentin, Soissons, Chantilly, Reims, Montmédy; along the long roads to Saint-Lô and Luxembourg and the dozens of small villages blood-locked by the Bulge. Or the thousands of graves of the coasts and far out in the world's oceans, or in planes crashing over Britain and France and Germany and Italy and Africa and remote mountain regions in China and Burma and wherever planes flew.

And then, Korea. It was not even a fresh generation that had been called up; indeed, many of the same men who returned only five years earlier to live out the anticipations of peace were now returned to war. The graves in Korea, like the others, would have their dedications; but the dedications this time were in marked contrast with the life of the nation as a whole. For we were at war and yet not at war. Each day there was fighting and dying at the Korean front, but there was no home front in the sense that there is any real community of sacrifice. The geographical distance to Korea, great as it might be, was far less than the moral distance. There was a strange sense of detachment and compartmentalization. At home, we anxiously followed the war news, to be sure; but it was roped off in a corner of our minds and largely unrelated to the life of a people enjoying the greatest prosperity in human history.

Korea demonstrated with blazing urgency the fact that peace is not an amorphous, drifting thing but has an architecture of its own, requiring clarity in its design, depth in its foundation, strength in its supports. And the founding fathers of world law were not so much the statesmen of Lake Success as they were the individual soldiers in Korea, hammering out a great principle with their lives. This is the principle that the peoples of the world are no longer obligated to acquiesce in anarchy but must meet the responsibilities involved in protecting the welfare of the community at large.

Korea, however, could only demonstrate the validity and the beauty of this principle; it could not by itself cause the principle to endure. If after Korea it would be recognized that the job was not finished but only begun, and that the remaining task was to build a world community under law, then there would be grounds for hope such as our generation until now has hardly dared even to dream about.

History should be able to say that the new birth of freedom for which we fought in Korea was not only for ourselves but for a human principle, and that the new flag which flew over their battlefields was not merely a tentative emblem but a banner of universal hope and substance.

A quarter of a century before Lincoln defined the challenge of Gettysburg, Alexis de Tocqueville concluded his brilliant and affirmative study of democracy in America with these words of prophetic insight for Lincoln's time and ours:

"It is true that around every man a fatal circle is traced beyond which he cannot pass; but within the wide range of that circle he is powerful and free. As it is with man, so with communities. The nations of our time cannot prevent the conditions of men from becoming equal, but it depends upon themselves whether the principle of equality is to lead them to servitude or freedom, to knowledge or barbarism, to prosperity or wretchedness."

"Anciently, the establishment of the frontier-gates was to guard against violence.

"Nowadays, it is to exercise violence."

—MENCIUS, CCS II

* * *

"A sovereignty over sovereigns, a government over governments . . ."

—ALEXANDER HAMILTON

* * *

"To accumulate doubts is the way to ruin your plans; to be idle and indifferent is the way to ruin your government."

—CONFUCIUS

* * *

"Man . . . is the best of all animals, but, when separated from law and justice, he is the worst of all, for armed injustice is the more dangerous, and he is equipped at birth with arms, meant to be used with intelligence and virtue, but which he may use for the worst ends."

—ARISTOTLE

* * *

"The ultimate aim of government is not to rule, or restrain by fear, nor to exact obedience, but contrariwise, to free every man from fear. . . . In fact, the true aim of government is liberty."

—SPINOZA

CHAPTER XI

"AS HONG KONG GOES . . ."

After Korea, Hong Kong.

Within three hours after I arrived, I acquired absentee ownership of a house with fourteen rooms, including four baths, a library, music room, and a thirty-eight-foot living room. The house was furnished. Some of the furniture, I understood, consisted of valuable antiques. Three well cultivated acres went with the house. In addition, there was a gardener's cottage.

The total cost of the house and acreage was $50.

When the deed exchanged hands, the former owner apologized and told me he realized he was getting the better of the bargain. Until the last minute he kept asking me whether I was sure I wanted to go ahead with the deal. He told me in all fairness that I could probably buy even finer homes in the same neighborhood for less money.

Naturally, I bought the house sight unseen. It was in Red China, the suburbs of Shanghai. I bought it in Hong Kong from a well-to-do Chinese lawyer who fled from Shanghai just before the city was occupied by the Communists. Though he had not heard directly from the new city administration, he believed that either his home had been confiscated or that he would be called upon to foot an annual tax bill of perhaps $5,000 or more. In any case, like hundreds of other Chinese who had come to Hong Kong from the interior, he had just about written off his Chinese holdings.

Since Mao's victory, mansions in China had been a drug on the market in Hong Kong. I heard of a small estate consisting of twenty-six acres, three houses, and a modest-sized barn that was offered at

$250 and went for $75. A large concert grand piano that would bring perhaps $3,500 in New York was sold for $7.50 in Hong Kong, subject, of course, to possession in Peking. A Peking parlor sofa could be bought for the price of your morning newspaper.

Despite my friend's concern that he had the better of the transaction, I couldn't resist the price tag of $50 for a palatial residence in Shanghai. It was probably confiscated by the time I bought it, and even if it wasn't I had no intention of paying annual taxes of $5,000 or even $0.50. But modern Chinese history is far from being a closed book. The feeling you got in Hong Kong was that Mao was experiencing a major problem in political digestion. It was no secret that land reform had not gone off as advertised. Political favoritism and privilege had done much to dissipate ideological enthusiasm. In any event, if refugees from Red China, as well as some consular officials in Hong Kong whose governments maintained relations with China, were to be believed, Mao's biggest headaches were ahead of him.

There was surprisingly little surface awareness of tension in Hong Kong over Communist China. With only a twenty-five-mile peninsula to separate them from the Red armies, the people of Hong Kong seemed strangely placid—at least on the surface. There was certainly far less talk and excitement over rampant Communism than there was in New York or Chicago or almost any American city. Indeed, Hong Kong in atmosphere and appearance seemed as far removed from the tide of political revolution as any city I had seen anywhere in the world. The main streets were crowded with well dressed people going about their business, of which there was plenty. Store windows proclaimed the fact that this is the changing center of the East, with everything from electric refrigerators to expensive lingerie. Great banking institutions, as common as beer taverns in Hoboken, were the busiest places of all. The side streets were like country bazaars, thronged with shoppers threading their way past the colorful pushcarts.

Across the street from my hotel a new skyscraper was going up. It was to be a twenty-story bank building, the tallest structure in Hong Kong, which would also make it, I suppose, the tallest building in the Far East. It was fascinating to watch the riveters working on the steel skeleton. My sidewalk superintendent's card was as good in Hong Kong as it was in New York. But I wondered what the foreman of the construction crew reading his newspaper at lunch time thought of the front-page headline proclaiming the announcement that the United States Government had ordered the evacuation from Hong Kong of all women and children and citizens not engaged in vital work. Then I wondered what the foreman thought as he went back to the job of putting up a brand-new building symbolizing capitalism smack in the only part of China not yet taken over by the Communists. I wondered, too, what passed through his mind when he knocked off work for the day and passed the American branch of the Chase National Bank, which had closed operations because of the war emergency.

It may be that Hong Kong was doing some of the fanciest whistling in the dark the modern world has known. Certainly the British, who administered this international settlement, were pursuing an official policy of optimism. I spoke to British consular officials and businessmen, all of whom felt that no Communist move was impending and that there was no reason for American alarm.

"Now that you mention it," one of them said with some irritation, "I think the American evacuation order was downright silly. It was entirely premature. You're beginning to give people the jitters."

This sounded as though he may have had some information on China's intentions that was not generally available, and I pressed him to say just why he thought our move was "premature."

"No, I don't have the foggiest notion what Mao is up to," he said. "But we don't think Mao is going to attack. Why should he? Hong Kong is a convenient trade outlet for him with the rest of the world. He is doing pretty well, and I don't think he just wants a lot of pretty real estate if it means he will be deprived of this valuable access to the world outside the Iron Curtain."

An English businessman rounded out the picture from the British point of view.

"The Foreign Office isn't saying very much about it," he said, "but the fact is that it is burning up over the American evacuation order. We've been in Hong Kong for some years and we think perhaps we know at least a little about the place. We had supposed that the American Government might ask our advice about the feasibility of such a move long in advance. Instead, we were notified about this only twenty-four hours before the official announcement was made.

"We had been trying to calm things down out here," he continued, "because, after all, this is a business community and it just won't do to have things up in the air all the time. Just consider the problem of morale on our own people. We want them to feel secure, and then all of a sudden the Chase National Bank closes and America tells its citizens to start getting out. Most unfortunate."

The natural question you asked yourself after conversations such as these was whether the British actually were as confident about Hong Kong as they sounded. After a while, you began to put the pieces together. You began to realize that there were perhaps two British policies. One policy is open and public optimism, without which a trade and banking community such as Hong Kong might be difficult to operate. The second policy was one of quiet preparedness for instant action, with respect to both the military position and evacuation.

But outer serenity was the order of the day. It seemed clear, moreover, that Britain was proceeding on the assumption that an attack on Hong Kong would precipitate World War III. In that case, of course, Hong Kong would be untenable anyway.

This "as-Hong-Kong-goes-so-goes-the-world" attitude had percolated through to the general population and perhaps accounted for the calm and philosophical approach of most people to the proximity of Red China. A Chinese cab driver summed it up when he said to me: "Me worry about Communists? Not my worry. Your worry. Communists come to Hong Kong. War comes to world. War comes to America. Then comes atomic bombs. No one drops atomic bombs on Hong Kong. Everybody wants own Hong Kong after war."

CHAPTER XII

FOOTBRIDGE TO CHINA

You don't have to be in Hong Kong very long before you want to see where Red China begins.

This was where the Iron Curtain of Asia was slightly parted. I had heard that only a frail footbridge, lightly guarded, separated the peninsula above Hong Kong from Mao's China. Were people allowed to get through? How heavily was the border fortified? What about all the reports that the border was actually a fabulous funnel for all sorts of capitalist goods pouring into Communist China from America and the outside world? Finally, what did it feel like to look across the border at the world's most populous Communist nation?

These were some of the questions in my mind when I applied at the American and British consulates for authorization to make the trip. The authorization came, but not without a few qualifiers. First of all, British patrol protection ceased about two miles from the actual gateway to Red China, and the remaining distance was a strip of no-man's land. Next, if I wanted to do anything beyond that point, I would be strictly on my own. Finally, authorization to get to the border itself would have to come from local village police about one mile this side of Red China.

An American businessman, Julius Stulman, and an interpreter joined me on the trip. We couldn't have picked a worse day. It began to rain shortly after we started; a cold, sharp wind did everything but blow us off the narrow mountainous road up the peninsula. Before we got onto the peninsula, however, we had to ferry across from the city of Hong Kong to Kowloon, where we were to pick up

our car. The ferry ride takes about seven minutes; I was sorry it
didn't last all day, for it seemed to me that this was the most colorful
bay in the world. The white skyline of Hong Kong is sharply contrasted against the deep green and brown of mountains rising
abruptly in bowl-like fashion from the city. Hundreds of ships of
all sorts, sizes, and colors dot the harbor. Chinese junks with their
square-rigged patchwork sails move alongside palatial ocean-going
passenger liners. Sampans dodge out of the path of larger ships.
The impression all this maritime traffic gives you is of a Times
Square on the sea.

Out from Kowloon the road climbs steadily until, three or four
miles out of the city, you are high up on the mountain and are able
to look back on the spectacular panorama of the Hong Kong harbor.
It is a narrow road, winding, twisting, and turning, and you travel
three miles to go one. You have to be careful to hug your own
side and watch out for large trucks from the other direction as
they come shooting at you around the sharp curves.

The passenger cars thinned out rapidly. By the time we had gone
ten miles, we were the only private car on the road, coming or
going. The trucks from the other direction continued to come at a
rate of about two or three every five minutes. Most of them, so far
as we could see, were empty on their way back to Hong Kong.

The countryside was alternately lush and barren. For a short
stretch we would see Chinese farmers working over fertile fields,
then we would come upon a long view of eroded and scarred land
reaching out to brown and bony mountains in the distance. Then the
country became rough and rugged, and you wondered how the
British engineers had been able to carve a road out of such seemingly
impossible terrain. About two-thirds of the way to the border we
began to observe military posts and fortifications. Frequently little
British Bren gun-carriers with tank treads would come scooting
along the road, the faces of their two-man crews red with the wind
and the rain.

We passed several military encampments, but we didn't see many
troops. The general terrain is ideally suited to defensive military
operations, but how long even the best trained and well equipped
troops could hold out against overwhelming numbers was worth
pondering.

The last Chinese town on the Kowloon side of the border was

Sheng-Shi, about five miles from the border. There was nothing to distinguish it from other Chinese towns and villages of the same size. Most of Sheng-Shi was spread out along the main road, with overhead banners lending it a somewhat festive air. The shops were one-story wooden structures with wide-open fronts. Inside might be found almost everything from oriental nuts to wooden water buckets. Most of the people on the street didn't appear to be going anywhere in particular. There was a feeling of remoteness and calm that seemed strangely out of place only a few miles from the Red China border. You wondered what impact this proximity had on the lives of the people, and, judging by appearances alone, you came to the conclusion that it wasn't very much. Just a few miles back on the same road, for example, we had stopped at another village to chat with the people, some of whom had never heard of the war in Korea, the invasion of Tibet, the United Nations, or the advent of atomic energy.

A short distance beyond Sheng-Shi we ran into no-man's land. There were no sentries or road blocks, merely a slab marker on the right side of the road saying simply, "To the north of this road out of bounds." We proceeded to the local police station to apply for a permit to go up to the border itself.

The police were pleasant enough but difficult to convince. Finally they decided to telephone police headquarters at Hong Kong for advice. It took about twenty minutes to put through the call. I went outside and walked around. The police station was a two-story stucco structure with crude gun turrets front and back. The yard was enclosed with a triple fencing of barbed wire. In front of the police station was a water pump. Teen-age girls took turns at filling up large buckets and carrying them on poles across their shoulders. Each load weighed at least one hundred pounds, but the girls carried it without apparent strain.

After a while a young police sergeant of perhaps nineteen or twenty arrived with the permit. He said he had been instructed to accompany us to the border. The reason for it, he said, was that during the previous day there had been some shooting across the border, and two men on this side had been killed. My itch to see the gateway to Red China diminished considerably. But we had cleared every obstacle up to this point, and we were too close to turn back now. The sergeant got into the car and we drove off.

After two or three minutes we came to a sentry post manned by village police, who motioned us on when they saw the sergeant sitting in the front seat. Then we turned off to the right, went up a short hill, and the sergeant pointed in the direction of the hills and said something.

"Those hills over there are in Red China," the translator said.

We made another turn, this time to the left, and then suddenly we saw the gateway. Directly in front of us, almost in the form of a funnel, was the entrance to Red China. The large wedge-shaped strip of land in front of us narrowed abruptly to a footbridge about eight feet wide and forty feet long. The bridge forded a small stream that marked the border. A formidable steel and barbed-wire fence at least eight feet high wound in and out of the hills on the Chinese side of the stream as far as the eye could see.

On the other side of the footbridge was a small detachment of shabbily dressed Chinese Red Army sentries. In back of them was a combination wood-and-tent structure. From the top of a tall bamboo flagpole flew the Red Chinese Communist flag—whipped by a strong wind and slightly tattered at the edges. We were at the vital supply mouth of Red China.

But what really commanded the attention was a seemingly endless array of trucks of all sizes fanned out on our side of the border. A large area had been cleared away on the right side of the road, and dozens of trucks were in the process of unloading. As I walked down to the footbridge, I observed that most of the goods were in large wooden crates, so that it was impossible to tell exactly what was being sent over the border. But I was able to see, from the markings on a few crates, that some of the goods came from Occupied Japan. One truck carried a large consigment of heavy-duty American tires, which were obviously being resold by a non-American trader. Several other trucks, so far as I could see, were unloading wiring and electrical equipment.

No wonder Communist China hadn't overrun Hong Kong. Why should it, when Hong Kong, a free port, was such a productive transmission belt?

Escorted by the sergeant, we walked down to the footbridge. On the left lane were people coming across from Red China. It was explained to me that most of them were small businessmen or farmers trading with villagers on both sides of the border. There were some women and children who were obviously not traders; it was explained that they had been visiting relatives or friends.

Everyone coming over the footbridge in the lane from Red China was thoroughly frisked for concealed weapons by Hong Kong Chinese police. The searching of women was done by the guards with little apparent embarrassment to either. Whenever someone would come over with a large bundle or box, he would be taken over to one side while the guard would go probing for contraband with a long iron rod. I felt sorry for anyone whose box happened to contain eggs.

Few people coming from Red China, however, were carrying bundles. Most of the heavy traffic was going the other way. Coolies carried large crates from the trucks.

I walked out toward the center of the bridge. This was as close as you could get to Red China and yet be outside the spreading Iron Curtain.

As I looked at the Chinese Red Army soldiers staring at me less than forty feet away, I wondered whether the same thoughts were crossing their minds as crossed mine. Not too far away from where we stood, in Korea, Chinese and Americans were killing each other in battle. But Americans had no quarrel with the Chinese people themselves. Historically the Americans had perhaps been more highly regarded by the Chinese than the people of any other Western nation. Now the Chinese people were being told by their new masters that the Americans wanted to use Korea as a jumping-off place for an attack on China itself. They were being told that America was determined to restore the old Western imperialism, and that we would never be content until the white man had firmly established a system of slavery over all of Asia. Along with this went the assurance that only Soviet Russia, homeland of Communism, sympathized with the Asian peoples and would respect and support their historic desire to liberate themselves from Western domination.

A Chinese sentry walked out towards me from his side of the bridge, then stopped ten feet from the center, which was the precise line of demarcation between Red China and the peninsula. He looked at me in my American clothes. Perhaps his thoughts were the reverse of mine; perhaps as he stared at me he toyed with the idea of setting me straight on what he considered to be my own misinformation or ignorance concerning China. In any event, if this is what went through his mind he gave no indication of it. All he did was to look at me, the expression being neither friendly nor unfriendly.

Suddenly I remembered something that happened to me in Berlin during the ominous and explosive days of the airlift. I had run into a Russian Occupation soldier near the border of the Soviet zone in Berlin. He seemed as impassive as Berlin's new mammoth Red Soldier monument itself. I tried without success to get him to unfreeze. Then I tendered a package of American cigarettes. His face warmed up with a big grin. He reached out to accept the gift, then offered me his hand in friendship and gratitude.

Communicating with the Chinese sentry was a tougher problem because he was some fifteen feet away. I reached in my pocket for a pack of American cigarettes—which have an almost magical reputation in the rest of the world, especially among fighting men. I held it up so that the Chinese sentry could see it, then without waiting for any response I tossed it to him. He had no trouble catching it, though for a second I was afraid it would be carried off by the wind. Then came the inevitable grin, which I reciprocated. He said something which I assume meant he was grateful, and I said something in acknowledgment that was equally unintelligible to him.

The sentry made no motion to come closer to me, nor I to him. We stood there in the wind and the stinging rain for a minute or two, looking at one another; then each turned and walked back to the world he came from. I moved slowly up the hill towards the car and looked back over my shoulder. The Chinese sentry was following me with his eyes. He waved casually, and I returned the gesture. He smiled briefly, then walked toward his post.

That was all there was to it. It was a trivial incident, but there came vaguely to mind a scene from *War and Peace* involving Davout, the Frenchman, and Pierre, the Russian. They confronted each other in the smoke-charred ruins of Moscow. Tolstoy refers to the shock of human recognition that took place when suddenly both men were face to face. It was only an instant, but there was communication between the two far more graphic and incisive than all the teachings and conditionings of the separate worlds that fashioned them and to which they owed their first allegiance. There was a magnificent pause as a sensation of kinship ran between them, only to vanish as their external separate worlds quickly moved in again to assert the prior claims.

What had happened to me was far less dramatic and eventful, yet it carried a symbolic quality that stayed in the mind. Months later I kept thinking of the Chinese sentry and the circumstances that made it impossible for two creatures to build on their essential mutuality. Both of them shared the fabulous gift of human existence, both of them were dependent upon the same natural bounties for well-being, both of them were part of the same mixture, part of the same potential.

In that sense—the sense of having something in common far more vital than the differences officially assigned to us—we were members of a leaderless and unrepresented group. Belonging to a nation, we had a nation that could speak for us. Belonging to a religion, we had a religion that could speak for us. Belonging to an economic or political order, we had an economic or political order that could speak for us. But belonging to the human race, we were without a spokesman. Indeed, we could hardly speak to each other.

As I say, it was something that stayed in the mind.

"What our civilization needs today, as a condition for increasing human maturity and for inner renewal, is the cultivation of an exquisite sensitivity and an incomparable tenderness."

—LEWIS MUMFORD

* * *

"Pain is a more terrible lord of mankind than even death himself."

—ALBERT SCHWEITZER

* * *

"What is the life of man? Is it not to shift from side to side—from sorrow to sorrow—to button up one cause of vexation and unbutton another?"

—LAURENCE STERNE

* * *

"Be a philosopher; but, amidst all your philosophy, be still a man."

—DAVID HUME

* * *

"All mankinde *is of one* Author, *and is one* volume; *when one Man dies, one* Chapter *is not* torne *out of the* booke, *but* translated *into a better* language; *and every* Chapter *must be so* translated; God *emploies several* translators; *some peeces are translated by* age, *some by* sicknesse, *some by* warre, *some by* justice; *but* Gods *hand is in every* translation; *and his hand shall binde up all our scattered leaves* againe, *for that* Librarie *where every* booke *shall lie open to one another. As therefore the* Bell *that rings to a* Sermon, *calls not upon the* Preacher *onely, but upon the* Congregation *to come; so this* Bell *calls us all: but how much more mee, who am brought so neere the* doore *by this* sicknesse."*

—JOHN DONNE

CHAPTER XIII

THE HUNGRY CONTINENT

When you travel in Asia, you have to get used to the face of hunger.

I first saw the hungry in a jail on the island of Ceylon, and I know I shall never forget it. They were illegal immigrants fleeing the famine in the south of India, and the Government of Ceylon was detaining them in a prison in Jaffna until arrangements could be worked out for their return to India. They had come by small boat, landing during the night on the north coast of Ceylon, where some of them had been picked up by the police. No one knew how many Indians had fled to Ceylon in this manner.

In the jail at Jaffna I spoke to a woman of fifty-five who looked closer to ninety. I doubt that she weighed eighty pounds. Her face was little more than a bare skull out of which small eyes glowed feverishly. She had come to Ceylon to join her married daughter, who had escaped successfully two months earlier. This much she was willing to tell, but she would not tell the police where her daughter might be found, even though it meant she herself would be returned to India alone.

I next saw the hungry in the south of India, where the suffering was the most acute of any area on the subcontinent. I saw them against a backdrop of parched and browned fields, with pale stubbles where rich rice paddies should have been. The reason for it was that the rains hadn't come that year. They hadn't come the year before or the year before that or the year before that.

"Four years, no monsoon," one of the elders in a village forty miles from Madras told me. "The older people have thought hard, but they do not remember when before the fields have been so dry. The wells are very low."

He looked up at the scudding clouds. "Clouds like this used to bring rain. Now they go out to sea and drop their rain where there is no need of it. The old people can eat little. If they are thin it is no great harm. Gandhi was thin. But the children are thin, and they become sick quickly. Smallpox has killed many of them. Thirty had smallpox in this village. Sixteen died.

"We send men into the cities to work so they can buy rice to bring back to the village. But there is so little rice and the rations have been cut again, and what they bring back cannot fill the bowls of many persons. We eat what we can—bananas and some coconuts—but very many people here are starving."

I next saw the faces of the hungry on the streets of Calcutta. Many of them were homeless. They had lost their homes during the partition of India when Pakistan was created. They were Hindus who feared the Moslems, and they had abandoned their homes in Pakistan and crossed over into India. In India there were perhaps eight million such refugees—it might be many more; no one knows exactly how many. Thousands of them came into Calcutta, the world's most populous city, looking for food and homes. They slept in the street. Wherever you went at night, on the main thorough-fares or in the alleys or in the hallways, you could see the human forms huddled together against the cool night. During the day they waited in lines for Government food or they begged.

Near the luxurious Grand Hotel in Calcutta was a child of eight or nine, with not enough clothes to conceal the bloated, empty belly of hunger. He was looking in the streets for scraps of food. Nearby was a young woman of about twenty, her body covered by the rags of what once must have been a handsome sari. A child of two was on her hip. The child was badly undernourished, and his head rested on his mother's shoulder. His face was empty and expressionless.

I also saw the hungry of Bangalore. They sat against the walls of buildings and waited.

Then I saw them in Delhi. There were more of the hungry and homeless in Delhi than in any other city in the north of India. As in Calcutta, many of them were refugees—perhaps 500,000 or 600,000—and they had crowded into the city, setting up crude wood-and-straw shelters, most of them closet-size. And every day the dead were carried out by men who were little more than half alive themselves. I stood on the corner of a busy street in Delhi and watched the refugees as they passed. Out of thousands who passed by only two would be considered plump by American or European standards.

The Indians were reluctant to talk about themselves or about their hardships. I was able, however, to win over the confidence of the attendant assigned to my room. He told me about his six-year-old son, the one with tuberculosis. He said his son had been praying a great deal recently, much more than usual, and he had asked his son what he was praying for. "My son was praying that he might die. He wanted to die and he wanted God to make him into a crow. I had told him about the crows that fly into the open windows of the hotel rooms and pick up food on the table and then carry the food off. My son said he wanted to be a crow so he could fly wherever there was food and bring it back to our family."

Then the attendant, whose name was Arun, turned away from me and knelt down to fix the fire. "India has been hungry for many months," he said. "They are saying that America has known about this need and that America has not wished to send us food."

I replied that what he had been told was not true. What had happened was that we had been too slow in responding to India's need, and that was bad enough. Americans had to operate through their Government, and often democratic government is slow in doing what had to be done promptly. I asked him to believe that millions of Americans were deeply concerned and were prodding our Government to action.

Then he mentioned the report he had read in the newspapers about the American Senators who wanted to punish India because India did not agree with the United States in the United Nations.

"It is true, is it not, sir, that we may not get the food because we do not say before the world what you wish us to say?"

I had to think a little while before replying, because I wasn't too sure that what he had feared might not turn out to be true. Should I have told him not to pay any attention to the stories in the press about the few members of our Congress who displayed so little conscience on vital matters concerning the human community? Should I have told him that it might take many days before the wheat bill might pass, during which time he would have to watch his youngsters continue to eat out of partially filled bowls?

Finally, I told him that there was no real answer to his question, except to say that we would do our best, our very best, and that the American people would be angry if any attempt were made to deprive other people of food because we might disagree with their leaders.

Arun finished making the fire and left. It occurred to me that what ought to be done was to take Arun to the United States on the very next plane in order to bring him before the Senate of the United States. One had the feeling at that distance that the Congress, in delaying the wheat-gift bill, was dealing not with human beings but with statistics. If the Congressmen didn't want to send wheat to Arun and countless millions of his countrymen, then they ought to have told it to Arun directly. Then they should have listened to Arun talk about his children. Then they could, if they wished, have told Arun exactly why a nation which had a surplus of wheat did not feel that it should put politics to one side when people are starving.

That afternoon, walking through the streets of Delhi, I could recall the emphasis that had been placed in America on the need to speak to peoples and not only to governments. But the most powerful language in the world is food. It is clearly understood. It can build bridges mightier by far than radio broadcasts or published material, especially when people have no radios or cannot read.

My purpose in coming to India was to try to tell the Indian people about America and to try to answer the many lies being told about us. Those lies aimed at splitting America off from the rest of the world. Yet there was nothing deliberate propaganda could say about us that could do nearly the harm that we did to ourselves during the long debate on wheat, when it seemed that we were turning our back not only on India but on the meaning of America itself.

CHAPTER XIV

LIFE AT A BARGAIN COUNTER

Your first impression in India—and it sticks with you—is that the cheapest thing one can buy is people. Let us suppose you live in Madras and decide to move to another part of the city. Your first inclination is to call a moving van, but then you discover that this would be the most expensive way of all to move your furniture. For half the cost of a moving van you could hire two large bullock carts—with four massive bulls and eight men. But there is an even cheaper way than the bullock cart. You could hire sixteen men to carry your furniture and belongings across the city by barefoot. They would make as many round trips as were necessary, and the total cost would still be much less than the bullock cart and only a fraction of what a motor truck would cost.

Suppose you have a small farm in the south of India. The farm requires irrigation. You could buy an imported Diesel engine to pump the water—the most efficient but also the most costly method. Or you could put the great bulls to work on a crude but durable water-drawing pulley device. But human muscle would be cheapest.

In Bombay I spoke to a businessman who is part owner of a firm that bottles natural water. He told me that when he analyzed his costs he discovered that the labor cost per bottle was less than the cost of the water itself. Thus life is cheaper than water.

Another instance. The hotel in New Delhi at which I stayed is as well appointed and modern as almost any fine hotel you might name anywhere in the world. The rates are reasonable, though not especially inexpensive. The attendant who cleaned my room and swept the corridor received a monthly salary of about $15. Out of this he tried to support a wife, three children, and two aging in-laws. For him the term "future" is purely a matter of chronology and not of progress; if he lives to be sixty (highly unlikely) he will never get past the sweeper's job. This is not so much a matter of personal limitations as it is of economic determinism. He was the son of a sweeper; his own place in life, society, and the economy of the nation is as a sweeper.

*   *   *

Confronted with the cheapness of life in India, the outsider too frequently chalks it up to the law of supply and demand. Since people are plentiful and hungry and since machines are scarce and costly, the result, as the outsider sees it, is the inevitable one: people are cheaper than machines. But there are other questions worth asking. Does industrialization fit India? Are the values of Indian village life inferior to those of the large cities that came in with industrialization? Should the worth of man be measured according to his ability to compete with a machine or according to his ability to think, feel, and be part of his culture? Isn't a culture worth pre-serving and developing—even though that culture may not happen to lend itself easily to the operation of factories and congested cities?

In short, are the benefits of an industrial society universal and absolute—under all conditions, for all cultures, at all times?

The fact that an industrial civilization is not easily superimposed upon a society with the culture and traditions of India is no more an unfavorable reflection upon Indians than the inability of Ameri-cans to absorb the superimposition of Indian culture on our own country would be an unfavorable reflection upon us. The de-centralized, non-dynamic, and leveled-off life of the Indian village if thrust upon America would produce the same profound dis-locations and misery that the productive, variable, and volatile life of an industrial civilization has in fact brought to a large segment of India.

If life is cheaper than the machine in India, we can deplore the over-population that highlights the problem; but we can also con-template the fact that the machine is our measuring rod, not theirs.

The West helped to change the basic conditions of Eastern culture and cannot now in good conscience complain that the people have responded poorly to changed conditions.

I tried to argue this point out with an English businessman who was visiting India for the first time. We were in a plane flying from Madras to Calcutta.

"The trouble with most Americans," he said in a friendly manner, "is that you tend to romanticize the Indians. You keep looking for spiritual and cultural nuggets, and then when you fail to find them you imagine them into being. You've just got to accept the fact that you're dealing with a backward, primitive people, most of whom haven't changed their customs for six thousand years and who can't even operate their own government, as we are currently observing.

"Just look at the poverty and the ignorance," he continued. "Annual income per capita not more than $20 per person. Maybe one out of ten knows how to read and write. And did you ever try to teach one of them to operate a machine? The Indians are all right so long as the machine keeps running, but the moment the slightest little thing goes wrong the people go to pieces. And, I might add, so does the machine. In no time at all—whether the people are operating a motorcar or a lathe—they have the entire machine completely dismantled, with no idea of how to put it together again."

As he spoke I looked out from my plane window at the tired, parched Indian countryside. For four years the seasonal rains had failed. I wondered what the fields would look like in America if we had no rains for four years. We would irrigate, certainly, but even irrigation is dependent upon rain. Few countries in the world had more irrigation canals in their agricultural areas than India. But the canals and the wells were now drying up. And people were being hurt. They were measuring out such food as was available. They were thin and getting thinner. Soon their bodies would be too weak to fight the sickness reaching out after them.

From the air the Indian villages looked like clusters of brown serried mounds, seeming like natural growths on the soil. They were connected with each other over somewhat uneven country by thin cart roads. My traveling companion was right about one thing, at least: life in the villages hadn't changed much from what it was a few thousand years ago. In that sense it was primitive; but he was wrong in assuming that this meant the people were backward, ignorant, in need of outside control. Perhaps only a small percentage could read or write, but the overwhelming majority enjoyed the literacy of ear and mouth, rather than that of the eye and hand. Literature was recorded, as Sir George Grierson had written, "not on paper but on the memory. . . . The fleshy tables of the heart are often more trustworthy than birch bark or manuscript paper." The resultant culture is no less real or lacking in substance because of it. The people take pride in that culture, in their handicrafts, in their work in the fields. There is nothing mystical or mysterious about this, and it is not "romanticizing" the Indian people to point it out. It is a way of life which has well defined values of its own— values the Indian people do not ask us to accept or reject but merely to understand.

Yet here was my traveling companion repeating the error of so many people in the West. He was applying his own yardsticks and his own values in examining and describing the East. If a man is less fortunate than oneself, then there must be something wrong with him. If a man is impoverished and hungry, he is probably capable of nothing better. If he can't even read a newspaper headline or sign his own name, he is a helpless ignoramus. If his land has undeveloped re- sources in an age of combustion, commodities, and consumers, then others with know-how and can-do have the obligation and the right to move in, install the levers, and operate them. As for operating a national government—that's a science far beyond the reach of natives.

Was I doing my traveling companion an injustice by associating him with those who reflected such views? I was wondering about this when he remarked that the Indians were now discovering that running a government was far more difficult than denouncing it.

"It's easy enough to demand independence," he said. "But what does independence mean if the country is virtually at the point of collapse because there are no administrators? The steel frame of highly trained public officers which held India together under the British has just about crumbled. They'll be wishing before long that we'd never left."

I was fortunate in being able to pass along to him by way of reply something that the then High Commissioner of the United

Kingdom in India, Sir Archibald Nye, had told me in New Delhi.

"I doubt that any government in the world has a bigger or more complicated job on its hands today than India," Sir Archibald had said. "Four hundred million people or more—perhaps one fifth of the human race. Exhausted land. A difficult, fatiguing climate. A subcontinent suddenly divided into two entirely separate nations, India and Pakistan, at the time of independence.

"Twelve million people lose their homes at the time of partition and become refugees. All this superimposed on the problem of starting up a large nation virtually from scratch."

This testimony apparently failed to impress my traveling companion.

"Sir Archibald Nye, a fine fellow," he said. "But, after all, he does represent a Socialist Government which can be expected to have a bias towards other Socialist-minded states."

This effectively ended the conversation, at least for the moment. I turned to my American newspaper—a real luxury in India even if it is a week or ten days old. It was difficult to get the type before me into focus. I was uneasy and disappointed because of the failure of words. My traveling companion and I spoke the same language, yet there had been no effective communication between us. Both of us could pass literacy tests, yet literacy wasn't enough to convey meaning. The tools of reason had apparently failed us.

I felt completely separated from my traveling companion. In terms of communication and cultural interchange I felt much closer to many of the Indian people I had spoken to—with or without benefit of interpreters.

I was certain, too, that the gentleman at my right was entertaining equally severe questions about me. No doubt he thought of me as a sentimentalist and a softie who didn't understand hard realities or the practical approach to things. I was almost at the point of volunteering the information—apparently the badge of conversational respectability—that I had actually met a pay roll and participated in the operation of a business myself, when my friend cleared his throat.

"Let's be frank, now," he said. "Wouldn't you prefer living in the United States than in this half-civilized, God-forsaken country where you're afraid even to shake hands with people because they may give you some awful disease? Wait until you get to

Calcutta. I understand that you have to step over the bodies of scabrous beggars on the sidewalk in front of your hotel. Would you really prefer that type of life to the conveniences of America? Why, you're the envy of the whole world."

I told the gentleman that I wasn't planning to give up my home or my citizenship, which I valued most highly. No; I didn't prefer the Indian way of life over my own. I was merely trying to suggest that the Indians probably had some good reasons for creating and believing in their own values. Mine was an argument for the recognition of differences as a worthy end in itself, as against the argument that one set of differences was necessarily better than another. Beyond that was always the intriguing possibility that we might be able to learn from each other.

"Very well," he said. "But do you agree that we do a much better job in the West in providing for our people than they do here?"

I winced, then tried to cover up with a smile. There it was all over again. The English language we shared was being used as a medium for the acceleration of misunderstanding.

After an awkward moment of silence we both took refuge in our newspapers. On the front page of my paper I read that a Senate Committee headed by Estes Kefauver was investigating widespread corruption in the United States, indicating direct tie-ups between public officers and gangsters. The entire nation was shocked, apparently, by the extent to which local government was being used as a cover-up for gamblers and criminals who were operating with both immunity and impunity. A photograph atop the story showed three well fed gamblers present at the hearings. They could read and write, presumably. They were obviously up to their ears in big money. Any of the yardsticks we apply so mechanically to the people of the East would have shown them at an advantage.

In an adjoining column, prominently headlined, was the story of college basketball stars who had been bribed by gamblers to throw important intercollegiate games. Several of them indicated that there was nothing unusual about this, that it had been going on for some time, and that most people "in the know" just assumed that some of the games were fixed. One of them deeply regretted betraying his school but said it was difficult to turn his back on that kind of money. He wasn't discarding all values; he was merely putting one set above another. He lived in an environment where one's standing in the community-at-large was more frequently measured by the car you drove, the clothes your wife wore, the liquor you dispensed at your parties, and the clubs you belonged to than by the things you thought and felt deeply about or by your natural talents or your loyalties and ethics. If making $1,000 a week was the big goal and the platinum yardstick, then the important thing was not how you got it but that you had it.

Were these warped values his alone, or was he merely reflecting the values of the community of which he was a part? Once again I wondered whether these boys might not rate high on most of the counts made against the Indian people by the gentleman on my right.

A third story in my newspaper told of the record number of income-tax violators. In particular, the news item mentioned a manufacturer who had hired a battery of lawyers and accountants for the express purpose of finding and stretching loopholes through which the manufacturer could pass. The manufacturer was outraged that the Government should "pick on me." He had done nothing that everyone else hadn't done or tried to do.

And in a sense he was right. We were living in a sort of loophole civilization where almost everyone took loopholes for granted. The moment a law was passed, the job of the lawyer was to get around it.

I was tempted for a moment to cite these three news items by way of suggesting to my traveling companion that the concern of the good society might go somewhat beyond the size of an individual's waistline or his bank balance. Moral standing, cultural standing —weren't these valid yardsticks too? I wasn't being critical of my own country—corruption and greed were not the exclusive problems of any single nation; I wanted to clinch my original argument about the need to break away from the provincialism of making assumptions about a natural superiority or inferiority of one people as against another.

I wanted, too, to make the point that, though one could buy human life more cheaply than almost anything else in the East, this in itself didn't mean that one was dealing with inferior merchandise. Perhaps we were judging the wrong party when we came to harsh conclusions about the person who sold himself at such a low price. Perhaps there was something wrong with the buyer and his values.

As I say, I was tempted to offer these arguments, but the plane was approaching for a landing at Calcutta, and there was too much fussing with safety belts and seat adjustments and random papers to attempt a serious discussion in the short time remaining.

When we got off the plane my traveling companion said goodbye, but not before patting me on the back and renewing his advice about watching my step in front of my hotel. Scabrous beggars, you know.

CHAPTER XV

LITERACY vs. KNOWLEDGE

In a small Indian village less than two hours by car from Calcutta, I spoke to one of the finest conversationalists it has been my pleasure to meet anywhere in the world. He was a farmer of fifty-two, the leading citizen of the village, renowned in the area for his knowledge of Hindu religion and philosophy and for his good-natured humor. We conversed through an interpreter. After about forty minutes of philosophical exchange leavened by the farmer's illuminating witticisms, I got up to leave. I expressed the hope we might be able to continue our discussion by correspondence after I returned to the United States.

The farmer hesitated before saying anything, then looked down at the ground while the interpreter stammered his reply.

"Our friend is deeply honored at the suggestion that you and he correspond but regrets he is unable to do so as he has never been taught how to read or write. He would be glad to correspond through a translator, but there is no one in this village or the next who is qualified for such work. But he is grateful indeed for your kind thought."

In Calcutta itself, following a public lecture, a young man of about thirty-five got up to ask a question about the political organization in America. I did as best I could in the five minutes I had been forced to budget for each question. After the talk, however, I sought him out and offered to send him material from time to time from America. Then I handed him a pad and pencil to write down his name and address.

"If it would not offend you," he said in English, with an accent that revealed some slight Oxford influence at least, "I should be grateful if you would write my name and address down for me. I have never learned how to write—in English or Hindi. I understand and speak English because for eight years I was a bearer for an English gentleman who was kind and patient with me. I am intending to go to adult school so that I may read and write English, and perhaps some day I may be able to read for myself the material you will send me."

Incidents such as these were repeated perhaps a dozen or more times during my visit to India and Pakistan. And each time I had the same feeling of momentary shock. It was difficult to reconcile the ease and frequency with which illiteracy and intelligence went together. When you came from a part of the world where people are considered dolts if they can't sign their own names, you find it difficult to adjust yourself to the idea that people can be well developed intellectually and yet have no contact with the written word.

There are no exact figures, but the illiteracy rate in India must be close to 85 per cent; in Pakistan perhaps slightly higher. Only a scattered handful of persons participate in the regular disseminations of news and ideas. Newspapers are numerous but small in total circulation in comparison to the United States; the total annual consumption of newsprint in India is about 2 per cent of our own, even allowing for the current acute newsprint shortage in India.

Books are an intellectual luxury, though low-priced. The problems of writing and publishing in India are complicated by the lack of a working national language and by the phenomenal cultural disparity of the various regions. The differences in the folkways and social organization between those Indians who live in the Madras area and those who live in the northwest regions are almost as great, let us say, as the cultural differences between the Italians and the Danes. Hindi has been proclaimed the national language, but it may be years before it actually develops into one. Meanwhile, the various regions have their own tongues, the result being that an Indian author to be widely read in his own country has to be translated into several languages, at least. And because of the comparatively small size of the literate community in each language he can consider himself fortunate if his books average two or three thousand copies each in sales. Ten thousand copies sold would indicate a best seller. Getting a book published in most cases depends upon special arrangements that can be worked out with the publisher to lessen the risk and investment. Hence there are few authors, comparatively speaking, and very few publishers. As elsewhere, most of the profitable publishing is in the textbook field, where some degree of mass production is possible in filling advance orders. In any event, writing for the general reader is pretty much of a sideline for people who are primarily engaged in other professions or businesses.

The English language is read and spoken in India by perhaps 2 per cent of the total population. Paradoxically, however, English is the principal language in the political life of the country and in the expression and articulation of public opinion. The most influential newspapers and magazines are written in English. Sessions of Parliament are conducted in English. But not many of the Indian attendants or Parliament employees understand what is being said on the floor. Thus there is the phenomenon of a country's affairs being deliberated by men speaking a language unfamiliar to 98 per cent of that country's people—a language chosen not because it was preferred over Hindi or any of the regional tongues but because it is the only language which all the legislators present could understand. As a result, a session of Parliament more nearly resembles an international than a national meeting. This is but a reflection of the fact that India is less a nation than a common historical experience shared by related cultures.

* * *

The world of the average village is a world apart, a world that draws very lightly for its needs upon the outside; it is primarily concerned with the folkways of family, community, and religion. It pays its taxes though it is never quite sure of the theory and practice of taxation. It is untouched by the political storms and upheavals which animate the cities.

But though it is an inarticulate world, the world of the village represents the *ultimate* power in India. The literate few may decide India's immediate future, but the village will decide India's destiny. On specific day-to-day matters, on government policies concerned with specific questions, and even on the choice of public officers, the village may have comparatively little direct effect. But on the long-term orientation of those policies, the weight of the village will be heavily, perhaps decisively, felt.

Whatever the differences between the various groups in India may be—differences between the literates and illiterates, between the villager and the industrial worker, between one caste and another—all of them share the basic concern for the future of India.

The lack of close contact between the world of events and ideas and the world of the village is not necessarily the result of the widespread illiteracy, but of the fact that the two worlds are separate. When you get thirty or forty miles outside one of the large cities, you observe a way of life as far removed from the life of the city as the pre-Christian tenth century is from the twentieth. This is not by way of passing judgment—for I am beginning to suspect that there are survival values inherent in the Indian village way of life which have so far eluded the Western world. The gap between urban and rural life in India, or between the life and thought of the educated few and the uneducated many, is so wide and deep as to be almost unfathomable. Geographically, historically, and politically the villager is a citizen of India; intellectually, he regards India as more of a universe of which he is a part than as a well defined nation which has jurisdiction over him in many respects and to which he has specified obligations.

An English journalist in Calcutta told me of an experience he had in a village some seventy miles from the city. He was interviewing some people about progress in India since the British had left, and discovered that some of those present didn't even know the British had come. I encountered nothing so extreme as this, but I did go into village after village where the names of Roosevelt, Truman, Stalin, Churchill, Hitler, and Attlee were unheared of. Not far from Madras I spoke to village elders who were completely in the dark about Communism or democracy or atomic energy or the Korean War or the Civil War in China or the United Nations or any of the major issues and events that dominate the times. In one or two instances, incredible as it may seem, I came across men who were unfamiliar with the name of Mahatma Gandhi.

What does this widespread illiteracy and lack of knowledge add up to? It would be a serious blunder for us to conclude that the bulk of the Indian people are backward or unintelligent or ignorant.

The yardsticks of the West for measuring intellectual capacity or cultural standing are completely out of place when applied to India. Many of the Indian people may be uninformed about the ideological struggle going on in the world today and may be unable to read or write, but their personalities are as well integrated as those of any people in the world. Whatever the shortage of information, there is certainly no shortage of intellectual awareness or acuteness. Even more important is the basic fact that there is a highly developed sense of justice and moral obligation which would excite the admiration of theologians and educators both. A discussion about purpose in life or about man's relationship to his fellows can be stimulating and rewarding and, though your companions may be technically illiterate, you are not mindful of any lack of philosophical scholarship.

So far as actual knowledge is concerned, it is futile to speculate whether ours is superior to theirs or vice versa; the levels of knowledge are different, that is all. I should hate to be called upon to pass an examination in all the things that are part of the funded knowledge of the average Indian villager. It is enough to recognize that their knowledge is apparently suitable for their purposes as is ours—we hope—for our own.

Apart from this, there is the very real question whether history may not decide that life in the Indian village was far better adapted to the survival of man than life in the highly advanced and organized world of the West. It has yet to be proved whether Western man can keep his civilization from turning against him. The concept of the dynamic society, the concept of rapid progress, the concept of ever expanding knowledge applied to man's problems, the concept of bigger and better technology to liberate man from drudgery—it has yet to be proved whether these concepts can actually be made to serve human welfare or whether they are beyond man's understanding and control and therefore may be used against himself.

The average Indian is emancipated from modern civilization and its dualism. He is uncontaminated by modern knowledge and its effects. He is largely apart from the tides of his times. No matter what happens in the years just ahead, it is likely that the Indian village will continue as it has for the past two thousand years. It is largely self-contained, and offers no temptation for a conqueror who may be drawn to the cities and the factories but who may have no inducement for carving out roads to reach people who present neither a challenge nor a prize.

This is no glorification of the static. It merely attempts to recognize the fact that any attempt to measure India by our standards must be preceded first of all by substantial proof that we can make industrial civilization and all its works serve the ends of man.

CHAPTER XVI

AN EAR TO GO WITH THE VOICE

W hat would you think," I was asked in Dacca, the leading city of East Pakistan, "if someone sent you a letter marked 'Norwalk, Connecticut, U.S.A., Canada'? You would wonder at the schooling and reading of that person, would you not? You would wonder not only at his ignorance but also at his presumption.

"Here in Pakistan," my host continued, "we receive letters every day from the United States addressed: 'Dacca, Pakistan, India,' or 'Karachi, Pakistan, India,' and so forth. It is always 'Pakistan, India.' Our reaction is not so much wonder as pain. It pains us that in your distinguished and highly literate country people should not know that Pakistan is a fully independent nation, no more a part of India than the United States is part of Brazil, just because they both happen to be in the Americas.

"Yes, we are a young country, and we were once part of the Indian subcontinent. But it is now four years since the partition of the subcontinent, surely enough time for educated people in your country to know that Pakistan has become not only a state by itself, but the fifth most populous nation in the world. It would be different if these letters that we received came mostly from young people who have yet to achieve a broad knowledge of the world. But many letters come from people of standing—officials, educators, authors, writers, editors. If you will forgive me for saying so"—my host seemed reticent almost to the point of stammering—"the small package I received the other day from your office in New York to give to you on arrival was no exception. It came with the inevitable address—'Dacca, Pakistan, India.' "

Somewhere in Byron's *Don Juan* this advice is offered: If embarrassed beyond apparent recovery, scratch your ear. I can bear personal witness to the inadequacy of that advice. Under the circumstances the best I could do was to follow Mark Twain's suggestion to a flustered friend: Swallow hard and say nothing.

My host smiled. "I do not mean to be critical," he said. "But we Pakistani take great pride in our nationhood. Ours is a double independence many generations in the making—independence from Western rule, independence on the subcontinent. We have come into being under extraordinary circumstances. Partition took place so rapidly that we had to start virtually from scratch. The government was like the improvised field headquarters of the high command of an army. We had to use crates for desks and boxes for chairs. We had very little of the facilities of government and not enough people who were trained to use them. And yet Pakistan today is one of the world's most stable governments—our affairs are in order; our problems are severe but they are well in hand; our people are productive; the spirit is wonderful."

My friend paused, then looked at me gravely.

"Yet many of us engaged in the building of this nation are now and then disheartened when the people we admire so much, the Americans, show so little awareness of the things that are important to us. Your map companies rarely even recognize our existence. Hammond's 1948 Library World Atlas doesn't mention us; the new Encyclopaedia Britannica Atlas doesn't list us in the Index of Countries; most of your globe manufacturers apparently never heard of us. These oversights, like the wrong addresses on our letters, are small matters, of course, and we would pay no attention to them if it weren't for the unhappy fact that they symbolize so sharply the lack of knowledge in America about Pakistan.

"Here in Pakistan we have many schools to build and long generations of work before we can have the same high percentage of literacy as you. But at least the educated people here know a few things about your country, your institutions, your religions, your problems. Is it unfair or discourteous to ask whether the same can be said of educated Americans about our country and people? Let's go beyond Pakistan. What of the entire Moslem world? There are almost 250,000,000 Moslems—in lands that stretch all the way from the Pacific Ocean, across Asia, the Middle East, North Africa, and to the Atlantic shores of Spain. What do educated Americans know of the Islamic faith? We have studied Christianity and Judaism; indeed, the Koran embodies many of the tenets of the New and Old Testaments. Can it be said that many educated Americans have a general knowledge of the nature of our religion and know that it actually incorporates a large part of yours?

"What about our literature? Iqbal to us is what Shakespeare and Shaw are to Britain, what Tagore and Kalidasa are to India, what Emerson, Thoreau, and Whitman are to you. Do American schools, in teaching your young people about their neighbors in the world, tell them about Iqbal and our pride in him and why we believe he has meaning for men everywhere? We know you are familiar with the *Rubáiyát*, but that may be because FitzGerald has endowed the translation with the qualities of an English epic. Lacking a Fitz-Gerald, what has happened to Sa'di and Hafiz, who were writing great poetry at a time when European culture was still sleepy from the Middle Ages? Sa'di's *Gulistan* and Hafiz's *Odes* are as rich as the *Rubáiyát*, I assure you, but they may not lend themselves to facile versifying, with all due respect for Mr. FitzGerald."

My friend had stated his case with the utmost tact and, everything considered, with remarkable courtesy and restraint. As he spoke, I had a strong sense of personal inadequacy. I was not equipped, except in the vaguest way, for comprehending the ideas and institutions of the vast world of which he was a part. He helped to dramatize the fact that there are not two worlds which comprise this planet, but four and possibly five. He was part of the Moslem world, but there were also his Hindu neighbors—one-third of a billion of them; also the people in the Southeast Asia complex; also the entire continent of Africa.

At that distance from the United States—in Dacca, Pakistan—it seemed painfully clear that we were rapidly becoming the prisoners of our own oversimplifications. Much of our thinking got as far as Moscow, and abruptly stopped there. Yet there were serious tensions, dislocations, pressures, and issues outside the Soviet. Communism didn't create the issues; it exploited them. Our comprehension of those issues; our ability to see them in relation to the total problem of world peace; our capacity for winning the support and goodwill of peoples—these were as vital to our own future as any conventional measures taken in the national defense.

In any event, we had a big job ahead of us. It involved getting behind and beyond the daily headlines, recognizing and respecting individual and national pride, learning the proprieties.

Apart from this, there was one aspect to my Pakistan host's observations which had special meaning for our information program overseas. It wasn't enough to talk about ourselves; we had to convince peoples we were interested in them. Wherever I went—Asia, Africa, Europe—I discovered I had come only half prepared. Our history, our institutions, our literature—these were some of the subjects I had come prepared to talk about. But many of the questioners wanted to know how well informed we were about them and about our comprehension of their problems. Whether it was the Kashmir question with respect to Pakistan or India, the oil-expropriation question in the Near East, the foreign concessions in Cairo, or the export problem in Great Britain—people were more anxious to find out where we stood on these issues than they were about life in the United States, our standard of living, or our domestic politics. You got the feeling, too, that other peoples wished we would occasionally do less talking and more listening. Perhaps the best thing we could do for the Voice of America is to develop an Ear of America.

CHAPTER XVII

WHAT THEY ASK ABOUT
THE UNITED STATES

Don't Americans ever read books?" was one of the questions asked of me in Lahore, West Pakistan, one of the intellectual centers of the East. "We hear a great deal about your science and invention, we see just about all your movies, and of course we know about your automobiles and your planes and your cities. But we know almost nothing about American culture. Are you interested in books? Do you have any important writers?"

This was at a meeting of writers, journalists, editors, and publishers. I hardly knew where to begin in my reply. I decided it might be a good idea to ascertain whether my questioner's lack of information about reading and writing in America was at all representative of the group assembled. Taking an informal spot poll, I called off the names of about three dozen American writers, beginning with Washington Irving and ending with John Hersey. The names of Whitman, Emerson, Thoreau, Upton Sinclair, and Jack London elicited some slight recognition, but there was only the skimpiest acquaintance with writers such as Hawthorne, Mark Twain, Oliver Wendell Holmes, and Henry James. As for later writers—Ellen Glasgow, Willa Cather, Theodore Dreiser, Sinclair Lewis, William Faulkner, Ernest Hemingway, John Steinbeck, Thomas Wolfe—the poll drew a virtual blank. And even among those who recognized as many as four or five names it was interesting to learn that few of them had actually read books by those authors.

As the discussion broadened out, it developed that this unfamiliarity did not extend to the body of English literature. Indeed, there was abundant expertness in the field of both classical and contemporary English writing.

This was not the first time in my tour of India and Pakistan that I had been asked basic questions about American culture, but never before had the indictment been so sharp and comprehensive. I decided to ask some polite questions of my own. How was it, I asked, that highly educated Pakistani and Indians, themselves engaged professionally in writing and publishing, should know so little about the American literary tradition in contrast to that of the English? I spoke of the university libraries I had visited not only in Lahore but in other cities of Pakistan and India—and how disappointed I was to see that we were represented almost exclusively on the library shelves by works on technology. You could find volumes on engineering, chemistry, geology, physics, agronomy, astronomy, genetics, biology, medicine, transportation, architecture, and metallurgy—but nothing by Howells or James or Thoreau or Melville or Faulkner or Dreiser.

I didn't have to wait for an answer. Three or four members of the group began to speak at once.

"There is nothing mysterious or deliberate about this," one of them said. "The fact is that our education was under the British. Apparently you were never able to convince the British that you had a literature. In the universities here virtually no attention was paid to American writing. If you go back and examine the typical syllabus of the secondary school or the university, you will see that the literary tradition never really crossed the Atlantic. When students asked about American writing they were told that it existed, certainly, but that the university was setting up no compulsory reading requirements in that regard."

"But that's not all," another member of the group chimed in. "How are we to get American books? Even if we had known about them, I doubt that it would have been possible to obtain them. First of all, there's a ban on imports and money leaving the country. Next, how are we to afford the high prices? We can buy books in English or Urdu for one-sixth the price you charge. And we haven't even had the incentive to see whether your books are worth the difference."

An elderly gentleman who had been introduced to me as one of Lahore's leading critics entered the discussion.

"I have had the good fortune to obtain some American novels," he said. "Friends who visited the United States in the past few years have been good enough to bring me, at my request, a few books which enjoyed popularity. But I confess I have not been able to get very far. It is hard work, very hard. I have had to puzzle over almost every paragraph. It is your strange way of writing. American writing is wandering very far from the English language as we speak it and read it.

"In discussing this with one of your consular officials," he continued, "I was told that I might find H. L. Mencken's book *The American Language* useful for translation purposes. He sent me a copy of the book. I was fascinated by it, but I still did not learn enough about the idiomatic use of the American language to make the reading of American novels less of a chore.

"But in what little I did read I found a great difference in thematic treatment between the English and the American novel. American writers seem to be extremely self-centered; they write about their own neurotic problems and about what are, after all, trivial and petty themes. To some extent, of course, you have infected a number of outside authors, but at least we still have a few British writers left who are concerned with universal themes and who speak for the basic problems and challenges that concern most people."

I was interested to hear him use the possessive "we" in speaking of English writers. Whatever the burning resentments against the British were before Independence, or are today, there is a deep respect for, and pride in, the English literary tradition. The emphasis on Moslem culture in Pakistan and on Hindu culture in India apparently has not weakened this feeling of identification with the English cultural heritage among the educated peoples of the subcontinent. This made it all the more surprising that there was so little familiarity with the American contribution, such as it was, to the development of Anglo-Saxon literature.

While I was reflecting on this, a Pakistan journalist began to comment on the remarks of the literary critic.

"I, too, have had the opportunity to examine American books," he said. "The novels I have seen are your shiny paper-covered pocket-size books. Like my friend, I have found the language rather strange. But even stranger was the physical appearance of the books. The drawings on the covers astounded me. They were strongly offensive. They seemed to compete with each other in their cheapness and bad taste. You must realize that our religion—and this would also hold true of the Indian people—makes us extremely sensitive in these matters.

"I am sure you can understand the sense of disgust we must feel when we pick up what are supposed to be reprints of good American novels and see drawings of incredible debauchery and violence. The bedroom is usually the scene of action. A young woman would be sprawled out across an unmade bed, her nightclothes partly ripped off. Then you would generally have either a brutish sot clawing and tearing away at her or a somber creature standing over her with a smoking revolver. As though this weren't enough, the publishers would try to emphasize the vulgarity and the violence by their descriptive matter. One such description comes to mind. There is a quotation under a particularly offensive bedroom scene. 'I stood looking at her body,' a man is saying, 'wondering what had gone on before the knife.' "

*   *   *

I should like to be able to say that it was possible within the confines of an informal discussion to provide the definitive answers to all the questions about American literature or that I succeeded in replacing doubts and criticisms with favorable certainty.

The best that could be done under the circumstances was to indicate that the American people were not as barren culturally as those assembled had found reason to believe, and to put before the audience a friendly and sincere invitation to pursue the matter in a number of ways—one of which perhaps might be a visit to the local United States Information Service Library in Lahore. The literary shelf was not as well stocked as it ought to be, but there were at least a few titles worth consideration. In particular, I suggested the series on American literature by Van Wyck Brooks beginning with *The Flowering of New England*. The style was far from idiomatic or mannered, and the content would provide a well integrated analysis of the literary tradition in America. This might serve as something of a gateway to our writing. They would also find on the USIS shelf a few titles from among the more recent novels; perhaps the works of Willa Cather, Upton Sinclair, and Theodore Dreiser, for example, might have a special appeal with respect to both style and substance. In any event, even a cursory inspection might indicate that not all our books were concerned with neuroses or that they all had dust jackets glorifying cheap love and cheap death.

In saying this I recognized that we had a long way to go—not only in Pakistan but, indeed, throughout the world—before we could answer the questions of people who wonder why America's technological development has so far outdistanced our cultural growth.

Our State Department already has a series of excellent projects in operation, one of them being the United States Information Service centers, the libraries of which have become effective research headquarters in almost very country in which they have been established. The books most in demand are those on modern medicine, technology, and farming. The service afforded by these libraries is abundantly appreciated. But the cultural side of the libraries so far has been underdeveloped—understandably so, perhaps, in view of the basic needs of scientists and scholars. Now that the basic job has been done, however, it is time to pay increased attention in our information services to the life of the mind in America as it is reflected in our serious novels, belles-lettres, philosophy, and historical works.

"Men were one nation once, and God sent Prophets with good tidings, and sent down with them the Book in truth; but none did disagree therein, save those who had been given it after that manifest signs had come to them, through greed amongst themselves."

—THE KORAN

* * *

"Above all things is it profitable to men to form communities and to unite themselves to one another by bonds which may make all of them as one man; and absolutely, it is profitable for them to do whatever may tend to strengthen their friendships."

—SPINOZA

* * *

"We are sons of the earth; and, like Antaeus in the fable, if, in wrestling with a Hercules, we now and then receive a fall, the touch of our parent will communicate to us fresh strength and vigor to renew the contest."

—BENJAMIN FRANKLIN

* * *

"O masters, lords and rulers in all lands,
    How will the Future reckon with this man?
    How answer his brute question in that hour
    When whirlwinds of rebellion shake all shores?"

—EDWIN MARKHAM

CHAPTER XVIII

THE NUMBER ONE QUESTION

At a Junior College in Lahore, I ran into trouble. In the question period following my talk a student of perhaps nineteen or twenty demanded the floor, then leveled a long and accusing finger at me.

"You have come to the wrong place if you expect us to believe your propaganda about America," he said in a tense and angry voice. "We know the truth about America, and we students protest your use of the platform of this college to try to pass off dishonest and untruthful stories about the United States. Since you have already spoken, it is too late to do anything about it. We can, however, enter a protest with the principal of the school for having invited you to speak. And we can demand that a representative or a supporter of the Soviet Union be permitted to come here and talk to us about conditions in that country."

As the student spoke, the head of the college, seated at my right, was visibly disturbed. He got up and walked to the front of the platform, interrupted the student, then began to apologize to me publicly for what he described as an "unfortunate outburst."

"I ask that the speaker ignore this demonstration of bad manners," the principal said. "Here in Pakistan we give honor and not insults to our guests. I am sure I speak for the large majority of the students here in admonishing our ill tempered and ill mannered member."

It appeared from the general applause at this point that most of the students agreed with the principal. I regretted, however, that he had disciplined the student openly. Actually, the student was not to blame. I had set the stage for his protest by expressing the hope that everyone would feel completely free to take issue with anything I said during my talk. My purpose in coming to Pakistan was to have the fullest possible exchange of views. Accordingly, I assured the principal that I didn't feel that what the student said reflected in any way upon the hospitality of the college and that I was anxious to have the student enlarge on his remarks. What, in particular, did he object to in my talk as being propaganda?

The student seemed reluctant to get to his feet, and I asked the principal to assure him that it was entirely in order for him to continue to speak as openly as he did a moment ago. The principal seemed a little dubious at first about my request, then instructed the student to comply with the wishes of the speaker.

"I am sorry if what I said was regarded as an insult," the student began, "and I am sorry if I seemed angry. But you can understand how disturbing it is to hear things that we believe to be false and how unfair it is not to be able to hear at firsthand about the Soviet Union if we are officially assembled to hear about the United States.

"You have asked me what it is in particular I dislike about your talk. Much of what you said about the United States was very general. You tried to give us confidence in America's intentions in the world. Frankly, I believe you to be an apologist for the American people at a time when America is committing great crimes in the world. If you really wanted to be honest with us"—and here his voice took on the same tenseness and harshness it had when he had spoken the first time—"you would have admitted all the ugly things you do to people in America who do not happen to have a fair white skin."

At this point there were staccato shouts of approval and a short burst of applause. This emboldened the student, and he raised his voice.

"In America there are twenty million people who are called citizens but who are not citizens at all. They have been condemned as inferior beings and they are not allowed to participate in what you call your democracy. They do not enjoy the same protection under the laws you give to white people. If a colored person commits a crime, however minor that crime may be, he is apt to be seized by crowds. Your lynchings are the purest form of mob justice in the world.

"If a colored person becomes ill, does he have available to him the same hospital and medical facilities as does the white? If he wants to travel somewhere, is it not true that he is compelled to sit in a specially designated section, so that he will not contaminate the pure white travelers? Can the colored person sit down at the same school desk, at the same dining table, or register at the same hotel? Why do you insult the intelligence of the world by calling yourself a democracy when twenty million of your people are forced because of the accident of skin coloration to live in slums and eat inferior food and go to inferior schools and work at inferior jobs? Is this what you mean when you say that in a democracy the individual must be given every opportunity to develop himself and to fulfill his highest potential? Those are just words. Stupid, dishonest words, and you do no credit to yourself when you say them."

The principal stood up and once again started to reprimand the student when I asked that he be allowed to complete his statement.

"I am grateful to you for your courtesy," the student said, "but I want you to know how I feel. Every one of us sitting here feels the same way about your wicked and cruel race prejudice in the United States"—loud applause from the audience—"and every time we read about a lynching or about that very distinguished American Ralph Bunche not accepting a high position in the American State Department because he would have to live in Washington, where he would have to stay out of the best hotels and restaurants and accept the status of an inferior person in the very capital of the country he was called upon to serve—when we read about this, we shake our heads, sadly, then we shake our fists, because what you do is not only an insult to a great human being like Mr. Bunche, but a direct insult to all people in the world who do not happen to have white skins like yourself.

"Often we read about members of our Government and their families who have gone to the United States on official business and how they are openly insulted in the streets by ignorant and evil Americans and how they are turned away from hotels or deprived of seats in public transportation carriers or made to feel inferior. The chairman speaks of hospitality. You are entitled to it. But no country in the world offends the others with its lack of hospitality as does America. We are fully aware of the embarrassment felt by our people when they visit your so-called great democracy.

"Well, we will tell you one thing. We are not inferior. There is the entire Moslem world that is involved in this. And there are the peoples of India and China and Indonesia and Japan and South America. One day you are going to discover that you and your stupid prejudices are alone in the world and that the overwhelming majority of the world's peoples have decided that they have put up long enough with your fancy talk of superiority and your fancy airs and your evil discrimination."

The atmosphere in the small auditorium seemed supercharged. Under the whiplash of the student's emotional outburst the audience was being transformed into an angry entity. He had touched off something powerful and harsh in the group, producing a mass countenance of vengeful bitterness. The principal saw it and moved quickly to head it off.

"A question period is for questions," he said strongly. "If you have a question, ask it, but no speeches."

"I intended what I said to be a question," the student said. "Does the speaker deny that race discrimination and prejudice exist in the United States, and if so, how does he reconcile it with his general statements about democracy in America?"

The student sat down and smiled triumphantly in response to the murmuring approval of his fellows. Though the majority of the students may not have agreed with the tone and temper of his remarks, they seemed to be generally sympathetic to his basic argument.

This did not surprise me. By the time I came to Lahore I had spoken perhaps fifty times at various public meetings in the Far East. And each time I had spoken, without exception, the issue of race prejudice in the United States came up. Out of the countless hundreds of questions that were asked me everywhere, this was by all odds the one asked most frequently. Indeed, you could almost count on it to lead off any general question period, no matter what the particular subject matter of the talk happened to be. If I spoke about education in the United States or about journalism or about books or about American foreign policy, the first question was apt to be about lynchings or segregation. Nor did the auspices under which I spoke make much difference. Whether it was a gathering of conservative businessmen at a Rotary session in Bombay, or a small meeting of Government officials in New Delhi, or a confer-

ence of editors, writers, and publishers in Calcutta, or a teachers'
college for women, or a convention of theologians, the question
unfailingly came up. Generally, of course, it would be asked with
far more tact and moderation than had just been shown by the
young Lahore student, but it was just as deep and insistent.

Before leaving the United States, I had been warned that this
was something I could expect to encounter almost everywhere I
went, but not until I had to contend with it day after day was I able
to comprehend how strong and basic it is in the thinking of the
Asian peoples. I had thought from what I had read that our identification with the British in Asia or our own Far Eastern foreign policy would be the chief targets of criticism. These were of concern,
certainly, but they were small matters compared to the criticism
against us on color grounds.

You were conscious of it in almost everything that happened.
Day after day the local newspapers would play it up prominently
on the front pages. Frequently the news would be distorted or exaggerated, and sometimes news items ostensibly having nothing to do
with the problem of the Negro in America would carry some
strained reference to it. The question would come up in polite and
sometimes not so polite conversation. People seemed to have all the
details about the exclusion of a colored applicant from a Southern
university the day before, or the complete account of what happened when Indian or Pakistan individuals appearing in American
public thoroughfares in their own national dress were insulted or
accosted as freaks or dangerous foreigners.

Not infrequently these critics claimed a great deal more information about the color problem than actually existed. I was astounded
at the weird misconceptions of the nature and extent of the color
problem in America. It was not unusual to find well educated persons thinking in terms of the problem as it existed perhaps fifty years
ago, making generalizations about the whole of the United States
that were only true regionally.

It should be obvious, of course, that color is the biggest telling
point in Communist propaganda against America. The revolution
in Asia today takes different forms in different places, compounded
generally of the struggle for freedom from outside domination, of
the longing for basic justice and opportunity, of the so-far losing
fight against disease and enfeeblement.

But through it all runs something constant and powerful. It is the quest for self-respect, a revolution of pride. It is the deep determination to end the Age of Indignity. This is a mighty and growing natural force which the Communists are putting to their own use. Forget everything else the Communists are doing or saying about us in their propaganda. Forget for the moment the absurd charges of atomic diplomacy, warmongering, aggression, and all the other stereotyped nonsense. All this is easily enough answered. The one argument we have yet to meet effectively is the one that touches Asian peoples where they are most sensitive and where they have a personal sense of involvement. Color.

I should have been very much surprised, for example, if there was no direct connection between the patent pro-Soviet feeling of the Lahore student and his mountainous resentment against America on color grounds. One might suppose that the natural antagonism between Communism and the deeply felt religion of the Moslems would act as a bar to Communist propaganda activity. Yet in Pakistan I found a surprising disposition in some quarters to accept at face value many of the rosy interpretations of life and politics in the Soviet Union, with a corresponding tendency to believe the worst about America. Behind these attitudes was usually the conviction that the Soviet was the champion of equality while the United States was the global headquarters of race prejudice.

What do we say when we are confronted with these attitudes and arguments? In my own case, during the early part of my trip I was overly circumspect, overly cautious and diplomatic, overly concerned about stepping on sensitive toes. After a while, however, I realized I would have to be completely direct and blunt, almost to the point of seeming militant. By the time I got to Lahore, I was pretty well tuned up for the challenge.

I began my reply to the student's detailed question by saying that, certainly, race prejudice exists in the United States. Having said that, it was important to make a distinction between the problem as it actually existed and the problem as presented by Soviet propaganda and as generally reported in the press, not excluding the influential _Times_ of Pakistan. The condition of the American Negro was bad enough, but it did not even remotely resemble the deliberate exaggerations and distortions that were concocted for propaganda purposes and that were, unfortunately, so widely accepted.

Yes, race prejudice existed, I said, but did the students suppose that nothing was being done about it? Did they suppose that the overwhelming majority of the American people were not aware of the problem and were doing nothing about it?

Did they know anything about the work of such organizations as the National Association for the Advancement of Colored People under Walter White, a Negro himself and one of the most respected and influential American citizens?

Were they familiar with the reports of the N.A.A.C.P., which made it clear that greater progress had been made in the past fifteen years than in the previous fifty?

Were they aware of inspiring advances which indicated that America was well on its way toward eliminating the evil of segregation? A slow but steady integration was taking place—without widespread violence?

Educational opportunities were increasingly in evidence.

Many states had prescribed penalties against job discrimination on racial grounds.

The hideous denial of the ballot box to colored American citizens was being abolished.

In town after town throughout the South Negroes were being elected and appointed to public office.

Old taboos against Negroes in professional sports were practically extinct.

The nation's finest prize fighters were Negroes. In baseball the man who was probably the most popular player in the game today was a Negro.

In literature, science, philosophy, religion, music, the dance, Negroes were making outstanding contributions and enjoyed the esteem of their fellow Americans.

Now this progress wasn't fast enough or deep enough—admittedly—and it could never be fast enough to suit many millions of Americans who were aware of the challenge and who had been working for many years to meet it and who would not be content until it was completely solved. But the important thing was that they *were* at work on it, that historic progress was being made. The important thing, too, was that the Government itself was not a party to the crime or the party behind the crime, as happened in Germany with respect to race and religious prejudice under Nazism. Indeed, the executive branch of the American Government had been in the role of prodder to get action by Congress and the States in removing racial barriers.

But the problem of prejudice, I went on, was not a uniquely American problem. It was a human problem. It existed inside people. It was the problem of inferiority and superiority. It was that corrupting and corroding experience that took place inside a person when he arrogated to himself certain privileges which he denied to others on the basis of what he liked to think were nature's own laws. I was deeply disheartened, for example, by the prejudice and discrimination I had seen on the Indian subcontinent. Among Indians themselves I frequently found discrimination according to color and caste as severe as any I had observed in the United States. National laws had been passed against the inequities of Untouchability, yet many of the evils persisted. What was worse, many of the Untouchables were willing parties to the social contract of prejudice. In Pakistan, and I said I hoped that those present would correct me if I was wrong, I had found evidence of religious intolerance and prejudice. This was nothing official, so far as either state or theology was concerned, but it was there just the same. There was an unfortunate attitude of superiority of religion that inevitably made for prejudice. So far as minorities were concerned, there was a distinct prejudice against Sikhs.

I brought this up, not by way of admonition, nor even by way of using the glass-house theory to obtain immunity from criticism. I brought this up only by way of indicating that the problem of prejudice knew no national boundaries. To a large extent it was a common problem. Perhaps all peoples working together inside the United Nations might be able to contribute to the self-understanding that would have to go into the making of any basic attack on the problem of prejudice—racial, social, religious, economic, political. Perhaps such a common effort might be more constructive than the destructive and often ill informed criticism that served only to enlarge misunderstanding and therefore prejudice.

This was my attempt at an answer which would be neither apologetic nor self-righteous. I was gratified by the response of the students, especially when it led to a friendly post-lecture discussion with the student who had asked the question in the first place. He said he was satisfied with the answer but felt that we were at fault for not making our story known all over the world.

There was certainly no argument about that.

CHAPTER XIX

THE PRIME MINISTER

A return visit to New Delhi was my last stop on the Indo-Pak subcontinent. By this time there were many questions growing out of the tour that I was anxious to put before Prime Minister Jawaharlal Nehru.

Much of what I had seen deeply disturbed me. I had expected to find some deterioration in relations between India and America, but I was not prepared for the growing misunderstanding, and in some instances, severe hostility, toward the United States. This was the result of many factors, not least among which perhaps was America's delay in sending wheat to India at a time of widespread hunger and approaching famine. Apart from this, however, I found some astounding misconceptions about life in America and about our purposes in the world at large that were not far removed from the stereotyped pictures generally associated with deliberate propaganda.

The situation was alarming, but fortunately it was not yet critical. There was still a considerable, though diminishing, carryover of goodwill from those long years during India's struggle for independence when she enjoyed the moral support of the American people. This was nothing that could be destroyed in a short time. We could—the peoples of both countries—build upon that ground of long friendly association and in so doing create a profound force for world peace.

In pointing to Indian misunderstandings about America, I was not overlooking for a moment the misunderstandings of at least equal seriousness in America about India. The Indian press was sorely pressed for paper, but it at least managed to carry a fair amount of news about the United States—however exaggerated or strained some of that news might be. The American press as a whole, however, carried very little news about India outside of news of our disagreements with the Indian leaders. Apart from the resultant lack of current knowledge about India, there was also a widespread ignorance in America about the historical record in India. Education in the United States paid some attention to the history and culture of Western peoples, but very little to the Orient. All this resulted in a poor American background for an approach to the Indian people.

The basic question, however, was not whether we or the Indians were primarily to blame. What was important, it seemed to me, was the need for an honest exploration and understanding of whatever differences there were between the countries. There was nothing wrong or dangerous in having differences so long as there was also some recognition of a framework within which these differences can be faced without resulting in hostility.

In any event, these were some of the things I was anxious to talk to Prime Minister Nehru about when I arrived in Delhi. Mr. Loy Henderson, then our Ambassador to India, made the request for an appointment. Later that day, a messenger arrived with a note from the Prime Minister inviting me to lunch the following day.

At the luncheon, which took place in the garden of the Prime Minister's House, as the executive mansion is formally known, the discussion veered from Indian and American affairs to philosophy, religion, and government in the modern world. Mr. Nehru expressed great concern over the individual in the twentieth century, pulled and tugged and mauled in all directions by competing forces and pressures and subjected to all sorts of inner and outer tensions. If the purpose of society is to provide the individual with the conditions of creative development, then there was a very real question whether those conditions were not now shrinking. He was disturbed about the "de-individualization and brutalization of individual man" in the modern world.

"More and more the individual is giving way to the crowd," he said. "When he is by himself, he can be approached and he is responsive to reason. You can appeal to the good that is inherent in him; he has a sense of responsibility. His conscience, if not always in absolute control, is at least a factor in his decisions and actions.

"But then he is attracted to the crowd and strange things begin to happen. The crowd seldom places the reins on itself that the individual often feels compelled to do. The crowd dominates the individual but lacks a conscience of its own.

"Almost everywhere today the individual is giving himself over to the crowd or is being seized by it. The crowd is a brute. The crowd terrifies me."

As he spoke, I thought of the early days following independence, when India was partitioned and Pakistan was created. I thought of the mass bloodletting that took place as crowds swept up and down the streets bent on random murder. It was Hindu against Moslem and Moslem against Hindu. In a people deeply influenced by Gandhi's philosophy of non-violence, there was human destruction on a scale and of an intensity astonishing even in an age of violence. Lifelong friends turned on each other with psychotic fury. A chain reaction of terror and retaliation had set in, spiraling upward in retaliation and counter-retaliation. The sense of brotherhood preached by two religions was engulfed in a blood bath. In areas that were predominantly Moslem few Hindus were safe; in areas that were predominantly Hindu few Moslems were safe.

In New Delhi, which was predominantly Hindu, the Prime Minister had rushed unguarded into the streets in an attempt to stop the violence. He ran to Connaught Circle, the principal shopping center, where Hindus were looting Moslem shops and killing Moslems who tried to resist. A Hindu himself, Nehru pitted himself against the crowd and ordered police, who until that moment had been inactive bystanders, to shoot the Hindu looters.

That act broke the back of the violence in New Delhi.

I thought of all this as Nehru spoke because I felt certain that the hideous memories of what happened to otherwise rational individuals in the blood riots of 1947 inevitably came to his mind when he thought of what happens to man when he becomes part of the crowd. And when he said the crowd terrified him, he certainly could not have meant that he was lacking in personal courage when confronted by a mob. I doubt that the official home of any head of state in the world today is so lightly guarded as is the Indian Prime Minister's. Shortly after the assassination of Mahatma Gandhi by Hindu religious fanatics, a detail of 250 armed guards was assigned to the executive mansion without Nehru's knowledge. They were promptly discovered and dismissed by the Prime Minister.

Members of the government openly express concern at the Prime Minister's disdain for adequate personal protection as he moves about the city and the country. They fear that the same militant religious Hindu organization that set itself up to combat the Moslems and that killed Gandhi might for similar reasons make an attempt on Nehru's life. Nehru is opposed to the transformation of India into a religious state. He has offered full protection to the forty million Moslems who stayed behind in India at the time of partition, when Pakistan became a Moslem state. The militant Hindu radicals see Nehru as their only real obstacle to the formation of a Hindu religious state. Despite this, and not in a spirit of false bravado, Nehru has refused to move less freely than he did before he became head of the government. One of his favorite quotations, whenever the subject of his accessibility came up, is President Roosevelt's now famous aphorism, "The only thing we have to fear is fear itself."

Indeed, this fear of fear itself is seldom absent from Nehru's thoughts or his conversations. At our luncheon, and at dinner the following evening, the discussion centered largely in the causes of fear in the modern world. This served as perhaps the chief point of difference between us. Mr. Nehru believed that before the world could reasonably expect to avoid a catastrophic war and before any real peace program inside or outside the United Nations could be made to work, it was necessary for people everywhere to liberate themselves from the prison of their fears. These fears, he said, prevented man from thinking rationally. This time of all times required the utmost in human reason and intelligence if peace and justice were to be achieved.

My argument was that these fears did not exist in a vacuum. Fear today was in large measure the result, I contended, not of political and economic insecurity alone, but of the raw threat of aggression and war in a world that had failed to face up openly to the bold challenge of creating the mechanism of world law. The certainty as to what a new war would bring and the absence of any real hope that war might be averted were perhaps two of the leading causes of fear in the modern world. Not until we changed the conditions producing fear could we expect to cope with it.

The Prime Minister said that even if he agreed that this were true, it did not answer the larger question: Are the world's peoples ready for the creation of the type of world structure that might enjoy the powers of world law? How far could a state go in proposing or supporting certain projects if the people of that state were not prepared for them or if they withheld their support? This brought up the question of man's relationship to the state.

I asked Mr. Nehru whether he would agree that the function of enlightened leadership was to accelerate history, raising the sights of people and enabling them to sprint toward objectives if there was a danger that crawling might never get them there in time. To come back to the problem of the crowd, I asked him if leadership was not the means by which the crowd was able to find a collective conscience and to act upon it.

Mr. Nehru's answer was that such leadership was to be desired under all circumstances, but even the most enlightened leadership had to contend with the unique history of a particular people. Acceleration of history had to be seen against the historic pace of peoples. They were limited to what could be expected of leaders—even of the greatest leaders. What about the need for greatness in the people themselves, he asked. A great people can generate the qualities of leadership in the men they select to represent them; but the greatest leadership may fail if the people themselves lack the ability to recognize a necessary challenge and rise to the occasion.

He was speaking, he said, not of any particular people, but in terms of historic principle.

This furnished what seemed to me to be an excellent opportunity for bringing up a question that I had pondered ever since I arrived in India and began to observe the effects of centuries under a caste system.

Let us accept as a working hypothesis, I said, the principle that good government or the good society was largely the result of constant prodding by the individual himself, and that democratic government was the product of popular pressure for the rights of man. Now assuming all this, was it at all possible that India's own history was working against the creation of such a democracy? What about the determinism in the prevailing philosophy or religion of India? What about the fatalism that would dull the sharp edge of protest for the individual, convincing him that his misery was necessary and even holy? Wasn't it difficult to interest an individual in democratic reform and in the right of protest if he felt he was paying for the sins of a previous incarnation? In short, was determinism or fatalism consistent with democracy?

Mr. Nehru replied that there was nothing inconsistent between Indian philosophy or religion and democracy. Hindu religion, he pointed out, had within itself an impressive universalism: it could adjust itself to change; it was large enough to encompass different and even conflicting beliefs. It might take a little time, but religion in India would undergo whatever reorientation was necessary to have it reflect the general welfare of the people. Many times before Hinduism had digested great changes.

As for the age-old debate between free will and determinism as it concerned the Indian people, he said he believed there was ample scope for the exercise of free will in his country. Month by month he was able to observe public opinion shaping itself and getting stronger all the time. People were making up their minds, and seemed to be under no fetters in declaring themselves. Members of labor unions seemed to have no difficulty in exercising free will as it concerned the right to demand better conditions or to go on strike by way of giving added point to the scope of free will of the employer in meeting their demands.

It would be a mistake, the Prime Minister said, to eliminate completely the factor of free will in the philosophy or attitudes of the Indian people. Actually, there was a blend of both determinism and free will.

"Naturally," he said, "it is difficult to say precisely what role there is for determinism and precisely what role for free will, whether with respect to the Indian people or human beings in general. Not long ago I heard a good definition of the relationship between free will and determinism. Someone compared it to a game of bridge. When the cards are dealt and you pick up your hand, that is determinism; there's nothing you can do except to play it out for whatever it may be worth. And the way you play your hand is free will."

No, there was no real debate between free will and determinism. India could never get away from itself, but there was still a great deal it could do within itself and for itself. Then, smiling slightly, he said that perhaps more important than determinism at this time was the determination of the India people to consolidate their independence and protect it.

*   *   *

This, in rough outline, covered the main points discussed at the first three meetings. There remained, however, a wide area yet to be discussed. India's position inside the United Nations, particularly on those matters involving major differences of opinion with the United States; the place of India in the vast historic upheaval now under way in Southeast Asia; the question of "neutralism" in the present ideological and power conflict in the world; the internal and external stability of the nation—on all these I was anxious to hear the Prime Minister's views. And because of the importance of these subjects, I asked Mr. Nehru whether he would be willing to have his answers released in full to the United States. For this purpose, I suggested the use of a tape recording machine. Mr. Nehru was at first apprehensive about this proposal, saying he generally had a tendency to tighten up in front of a microphone. I was anxious, however, to get on the record for the American people a fairly complete statement of the Prime Minister's position in his own words. He concurred with my suggestion that we at least give it a trial.

Several days later I brought a tape recorder with me and set it up behind the couch of the main living room on the second floor. The microphone was placed on a coffee table in front of us. At first Mr. Nehru seemed somewhat inhibited by the microphone, but after a few minutes he managed a complete adjustment.

In all, approximately two and one-half hours of conversation, spread over two afternoons, were recorded. It is important to emphasize that the Prime Minister had no advance knowledge of the nature or form of the questions I put to him. The questions, in fact, flowed out of the discussion rather than out of any prepared outline. The Prime Minister was given the opportunity of correcting the text of the transcript for publication purposes but declined to do so, approving it in the precise form in which it was recorded.

I began the recorded interview by asking Mr. Nehru about his objectives for India. His reply made it clear that he refused to take a narrow view of India's place in the world.

"Our objectives—our ultimate objectives," he said, "are human rather than geographical. For the moment, however, and here I am speaking only about India, we are—well, in search of our soul. That sounds rather metaphysical, but I am not, of course, discussing metaphysical matters. We are groping and trying some kind of adjustment—integration, if you like—of our national life with our international life, and with our lives as individuals."

Mr. Nehru lit a cigarette, then resumed.

"Having passed through periods of transition and very rapid change, we have to find some equilibrium. Well, normally this would have been difficult enough; but in the present state of affairs, after all that occurred since the war in India—the partition, independence, and so on—all this has shaken us up a good deal. And so we are trying to search to find out what our objectives are. Some of us may have vague notions; others try to look at things without any fixed ideas as far as possible. So when any—shall I say slogans or fixed concepts—are put, we use them in a measure, but we are rather suspicious, too, because slogans are apt to petrify a man's thinking."

Several times previously, in our discussions, he had referred disparagingly to the slogans of the times. I asked him what slogans or fixed concepts he had in mind.

"Every slogan, every word almost, that is used by the Socialist, the Communist, the capitalist," he said without hesitation. "People hardly think nowadays. They throw words at each other. They talk about democracy, but when we sit down and think about democracy all kinds of aspects of it appear.

"An Englishman may think of democracy in terms of his system; an American in terms of his. Russia talks about the people's democracy, which is completely different. They all use the same word."

He was leaning forward now. I could tell that there were probably numberless meetings and discussions during which he had chafed under the imprecise use of the word "democracy."

"What is your own definition of democracy?" I asked.

"Now, I told you just now that definitions are very difficult." He smiled. "I do not presume to define anything, because to define anything that is as big as democracy is to limit it. Nevertheless, if I may vaguely suggest something, I would say that democracy is not only political, not only economic, but something of the mind, as everything is ultimately something of the mind.

"It involves equality of opportunity to all people, as far as possible, in the political and economic domain.

"It involves the freedom of the individual to grow and to make the best of his capacities and ability.

"It involves a certain tolerance of others and even of their opinions when they differ from yours.

"It involves a certain contemplative tendency and a certain inquisitive search for truth—and for, let us say, the right thing.

"Democracy is a dynamic, not a static, thing, and as it changes it may be that its domain will become wider and wider. Ultimately, it is a mental approach applied to our political and economic problems."

It was an impressive definition but I was anxious to have him establish the relationship of one type of equality to another. Granted that democracy was the combination of political, social, and economic equality, was any one of these imperative in advancing the others? Would he agree, perhaps, that political equality was the means through which the other equalities would be achieved? The right of protest, for example. If this right were forbidden, were the other equalities secure? Could any country really call itself a democracy if it did not guarantee this right of protest?

He crushed his cigarette and lit another.

"Yes," he said, "political freedom or political equality is the very basis on which you build up other equalities. At the same time political equality may cease to have meaning if there is gross economic inequality—however noisy the protest. Where, let us say, people are starving the vote does not count. They are thinking in terms of the next meal and not of the next vote.

"But leaving that out for the moment, political equality is the basis for other equalities."

The question that might then follow, I said, was whether the most effective form of protest wasn't a free election.

Mr. Nehru said he accepted that principle completely. But he added that the people can be preyed upon so much by propaganda in rousing their passions that "you may get some entirely wrong decisions and wrong policies. But you must take this risk. It is far better to take this risk than the other risk of no election."

He agreed, then, that the individual must be protected in his right to change the state?

"The individual has to be protected in that right," he replied. "Also, the social organism has to be protected against the predatory individual. So the process of protection is twofold. And it is just possible—in fact, not only possible but it has taken place innumerable times—that a group may gain power and may manage for some time, at least, to stay in power not merely by physical force but by deluding the individual."

I gathered from this, I said, that he believed that the state was made for man and not man for the state. The individual, of course, did have obligations and responsibilities to society at large, but the state basically was created to advance the welfare of the individual.

"The individual is uppermost in my mind," he said, slowly. "But in a social organism an individual cannot be separated from the rest. The rights of the individual must be balanced by the obligations of the individual to the social organism. Without obligations there can be no real rights."

I began to ask him to define these "obligations" when he cut me short, but not without a smile.

"This business of definitions rather embarrasses me," he said. "I am not a professor or a philosopher or even a very effective politician. I have dabbled in various things. But I am interested in such questions. I have given a great deal of thought to these matters because they interest me.

"A state's obligations to the individual or the individual's obligations to the state must necessarily have varied during different periods of history. The original state was a very, very simple state in which, practically speaking, all that the state had to do was to protect the individual from a foreign enemy or another tribe.

"Then, from that developed the concept of what might be called, without being offensive, a police state. It preserved law and order, protected its citizens from foreign enemies, and took taxes to carry on its business. For the rest, it was left to the individual or the group.

"The present idea of the state has grown far beyond that. Every state—I am not talking about any particular state right now—every state is trying to do ever so much more for the individual than has ever been attempted previously.

"So the state becomes more and more of a socially functioning organism—for the good of society or the individual, as you like. And the more it becomes that, the more benefits it confers on the individual; the more, in a sense, the individual has obligations to that state.

"So the two things, the rights and the obligations, march together. If the state and individual are properly integrated and organized, there is no conflict. Otherwise, if one side goes ahead of the other there is a lack of balance."

"Within that general framework," I asked, "what would you say an individual has the right to expect of a state—not only as a matter of protection against a foreign power but in his everyday life?"

Mr. Nehru began his reply by saying that the state, apart from protecting the individual from foreign enemies or internal disorders, had the duty to undertake to provide him with opportunities for progress, education, health, sanitation—"generally, everything that would give him the opportunity to fit himself for such work as he is capable of doing."

"And, you see," he continued, "the state, as everything else today, has grown more and more centralized. The deep problem of today, to put it in this way, is this: how to escape centralized authority, whether of the state, the big corporation, the trade union, or any group.

"Now all centralization is an encroachment on the freedom of the individual. We want to preserve the freedom of the individual, and at the same time we cannot escape centralization in modern society. How to balance the two?"

And his own answer to that question? How was he answering it for India?

Once again the cigarette.

"The general idea is that we—the state, that is—try to function in a way, first of all, to provide for the primary needs of our people. It is inevitable that in India, where private resources are not great, any project must be a state project. Our river-valley schemes must be state schemes. No one else can do them. Any other really big project can either be a state project or jointly owned by the state and private enterprise with a measure of state control, leaving a large field for private enterprise.

"Thus we get what I would call a public sector of our economy and a private sector and maybe a sector where the two overlap, with part state control and largely a private sector managing under state control.

"So we have these three branches of our economy. There need not be any rigid lines between them, and we can see which functions better and more successfully and allow them to develop. Our approach is experimental and not dogmatic."

And the rights and the needs of the individual when confronted by such centralization?

"So far as political rights are concerned, I suppose that our Constitution has gone as far as any constitution can go toward safeguarding the political rights of the individual. So far as economic questions are concerned, it is a question of a state interfering for purposes of protection rather than intrusion. In rather undeveloped economies there is a tendency in certain groups of vested interests to override the interests of the large groups by whatever methods they have.

"Now, we are, very largely speaking, an agricultural agrarian country. And one of our first programs is land reform; that is, to change the old big-landlord system here—rather semifeudal in its nature—in favor here and there of cooperative farms, which we wish to encourage.

"That removes one out-of-date system—the big-landlord system —which came in the way of our growth. The change-over has been complicated because we have done it by Constitutional means and by giving compensation to the landlords, which is a heavy burden. Nevertheless, that is clearing the way for other reforms—plans for industrial growth, agricultural growth—in many ways combining the two as far as possible and thus bringing about some kind of a balance between industry and agriculture today.

"There are far too many people on the land. We have to draw some of them into industry—big industry or small industry or both."

Could or should the United States help?

"It is obvious," he said, "that a highly industrialized and technologically efficient nation like the United States can give the greatest help to any underdeveloped country like India. After all, industrialization is limited, as it must be by various factors. There is the factor of the resources we can apply to it, which ultimately means, let us say, annual savings to be put into future growth. There is also the factor of the technical personnel that we can train.

"At the same time, we know that progress cannot be superimposed —it has to grow in the country, carrying the people with it. It is not teaching somebody at the top or just putting up a machine. We must grow up to it.

"The United States can help us in terms of capital goods and technical personnel. After all, in the nineteenth century a good deal of the development of both North and South America took place with help from Europe. That process to some extent can be applied to Asia now."

Now that we were on the subject of America and India, I was anxious to get his views on the misunderstanding between the two countries.

"Reading the press of India and also reading clippings from newspapers in the United States," I said, "I have had reason to be concerned about the relations between these two peoples. It is upon them to such a large extent that the burden of world peace rests. How do you account for this growing misunderstanding, which in many instances seems actually to approach hostility?"

I had the impression that the Prime Minister didn't think very much of that particular question. He shifted in his seat, then put it squarely up to me.

"You have been here now some weeks or months," he said. "There are many Americans who have visited India during the last few months and have met all kinds of people—members of Government, our officials, our people in the fields and factories, peasants, and the rest. I should like to think of your own experience here. Have you in your individual capacity experienced—shall I say— any hostility toward you yourself or toward Americans as individuals?"

There was only one answer to that.

"Mr. Prime Minister," I said, "here in India I have been made to feel as much at home by the Indian people as I would be in my own country. I have received the warmest hospitality.

"Yet at the same time I have observed, especially during the question period following my talks, in the comments that came to me from the audiences, and in reading some of the newspapers,

I have observed misunderstanding about the United States that could result in hostility.

"I know this," I added, "that if I were a citizen of India and my impressions of the United States were derived mainly from the newspapers, I am afraid I would have a rather distorted idea of the United States. I know that I might then be increasingly vulnerable if someone came at me with propaganda against the United States. I might feel that what he said would be correct, because I would have been conditioned in that direction.

"So I would say, based upon my experience, Mr. Prime Minister, that while I have nothing but the warmest feeling for the Indian people who have offered their hand in friendship wherever I have gone, I am, as an American, disturbed at what I have read in the press and what I have heard here about America and the American people as a whole."

"I asked you that rather personal question," Mr. Nehru said, "because I wanted you to appreciate a certain difference between what might be called personal reactions toward you and reactions in regard to some vague impersonal group or policy.

"Now, look at our history vis-à-vis England. For 150 years or more there was a great deal of hostility, as was natural, against the British occupation of India. To some extent that was transferred to the Englishman or the English officers here, too. But—not too much. Now, after this change in India to independence, you have no doubt found that there is very little hostility—practically none —to England and certainly none to any individual Englishman."

There was no doubt about that. One of the miracles of independent India, in fact, was the evidence of the popularity not only of Great Britain but of British institutions in general. And yet I had the feeling at times in India that Americans were being held accountable for all the colonial and imperialistic abuses of the English during the period of their rule. Was it wrong to say, I asked, that America might have replaced Great Britain as a villain in the eyes of some Indians, at least?

Mr. Nehru thought not—at least not in that sense. "The Englishman," he explained, "came in contact as an officer with the masses of our people. The Americans don't. America is something distant about which our newspaper readers may read and talk. They don't know much about it.

"But what I had in mind was this: that one must differentiate between what might be called the basic feeling of difference in outlook or policy, which for the moment may be expressed strongly but which does not represent any basic hostility. So far as India is concerned, I do not think we are very good at keeping up hostility for very long.

"Apart from that, for at least thirty years or more we have been conditioned by Mahatma Gandhi. He was continually telling us that we were fighting against British imperialism but that we must treat the Englishman as our brother. Well, we did not learn this lesson very well, perhaps, but it did affect our minds and ways of thinking.

"Anyway, the whole point is this—that I do not think there is any basic hostility against America or, for that matter, against any country here in India. Certain things, certain policies, which may not be clear or which may conflict with our own policy, may create criticism—which is a completely different thing.

"Now our policy, I should like you to remember, our present general world policy is the natural outgrowth of all our thinking during the last thirty years or more. If you read the resolution our Congress passed—twenty-five years ago, thirty years ago—you would find a certain way of thinking which we repeated again and again. It was quite natural for us to carry that thinking on—varying it, of course, adapting it to changing conditions in the world.

"Then came our independence. Again, the reaction of a newly independent country is not to get entangled; to keep going itself; to protect its own interest in terms of its larger friendship in the world. So much for the background.

"In general, then, we have felt all along that the right approach for us as a nation must be as far as possible an approach of friendliness. Not appeasement. We make distinction between the two. One must not appease evil, but we have to convert evil as far as possible.

"Therefore we have to be firm and yet courteous and friendly. The evildoer may not be converted, but remember there are vast numbers of people who are not evil but are conditioned by the evildoer."

It was my guess, I said that the American people would thoroughly agree with him in what he had to say about appeasement. In our own relations with the rest of the world today, we, too, felt that we were confronted with a matter of principle which it was difficult to put aside or ignore. We believed these principles to be related not only to American security but to the security of free peoples everywhere, for the two are interdependent.

"I agree with you entirely when you say that there should be no appeasement of evil," he interposed. "Having said that, it depends how you deal with evil. It depends also what is evil and what is not and to what degree a thing is evil. Very few things are 100 per cent evil—just as very few things are 100 per cent good—and if condemning something which is mixed good and evil you condemn the whole thing you might get slightly entangled in condemning the good, too."

"But what happens when you are threatened by the whole thing?"

"Well, when you are threatened by the whole thing you resist that threat. But you try to distinguish between the elements of good and evil nevertheless. Otherwise, you confuse people's minds and make them think that you are against the good, too."

"So far as the need to distinguish between the whole thing and its parts is concerned," I said, "we in America do try to make distinctions. We make a distinction, for example, between the Russian people and the Russian Government. I don't think there is any hostility in the United States toward the Russian people. We regard the Russian people as human beings who are entitled to the same fair share of the good things of life as we want for ourselves. But some peoples in the world today are harnessed by their governments to purposes which threaten the peace. Under these circumstances would you agree that even if we do make distinctions the threat to world peace can continue? How are we to deal with this threat—again, without uncertainty or appeasement?"

"Well, that is a big question that you have raised. I should have said that the basic threat today in the world was fear. And fear is the most dangerous companion for any individual or for any country to possess. Fear clogs the mind, and fear leads often to impassioned action.

"As you have said, we must not give in to evil, but we must also remember that evil is not surmounted by wrong methods which themselves produce more evil.

"Therefore, the method becomes very important. It may sound—well, shall I say—like preaching a sermon. I have felt more and more that the basic lesson that Gandhi taught was right, and that was that means should never be subordinate to ends.

"I know that these sayings cannot easily be translated into life. A politician or statesman cannot function like a prophet, whether it is in a democracy or any other type of government. He has to limit himself to people's understanding of him and people's appreciation of what he says, otherwise he cannot function at all. Nevertheless, this basic idea seems to be most important: that the right means should be employed and firmness should be allied always to a spirit of friendliness and conciliation, not of appeasement. I do make a distinction."

We had arrived at the point in our discussions when it seemed appropriate to bring up my favorite subject—revising and maintaining a structure of law above nations. Did the U.N. have this potentiality, I asked. Did it offer the means of creating an atmosphere of reason?

"The United Nations was formed with an objective defined in its charter," he said. "It is essentially an instrument for peace. The whole idea of the United Nations, in the minds of President Roosevelt and others, was that people in countries of different ways should come together around the table, and that, in fact, every country in the world should come there and hammer out solutions instead of fighting on the battlefields. But it does seem that the effectiveness of the U.N. is diminishing."

"Yet isn't it possible," I asked, "that the existing structure of the United Nations is such as to make it difficult for all the nations of the world to sit around the same table? If one nation can set aside the will of the others through the veto, for example, then there is not much inducement to sit around a table for the purpose of coping with fairly fundamental problems. Then too, so long as there is no workable security system, isn't there a tendency for nations which feel insecure to strengthen themselves through armament programs or military alliances? Doesn't this, in turn, make it difficult for one bloc to see the other bloc attempt to build up its position?"

I decided to take the plunge on China. "Much has been said," I continued, "about the refusal of the West to admit China. Yet Russia has consistently opposed the admission of Ceylon, which is certainly a representative government. Russia takes the view, no doubt, that to admit Ceylon would add strength to an opposing bloc in the U.N. For perhaps some of the same reasons and a great many others, shouldn't the West feel justified in opposing the entry of China? Isn't there some way of resolving the problem by making the United Nations stronger than any possible combination within it? In such a United Nations, built upon clearly defined rights and obligations, might we not have the basis for the universal design you seek?"

I knew I was talking too much; but this was one of the key issues on which there was so much misunderstanding between the two countries.

"Doesn't what you have said mean a change in the basic conception and structure of the United Nations?" Mr. Nehru asked. "Wouldn't it lead up to a United Nations which represents, by and large, countries of one way of thinking?"

There would be no point, I agreed, in having a U.N. if it reflected only one way of thinking. Indeed, the challenge was to strengthen the U.N. so that it could deal with diversity—not only the diversity of political philosophies but all the major diversities that could produce major frictions.

Mr. Nehru reverted to the question of China and the U.N.

"Surely the United Nations cannot claim two things at the same time," he said. "One is to ignore a country within its counsels and at the same time try to impose its will on that country which has been ignored. The two are contradictory. The United Nations by keeping out some countries, whether China or Ceylon—both I think are equally wrong—in a sense denies itself the moral right to deal with that country.

"If you cannot deal with a country within the form of the United Nations, then the only alternative is to deal with it outside, ultimately by force of arms.

"When you talk about blocs, it is rather difficult to define what a bloc is. Any military alliance is a very close bloc. Any two or three or four countries joining together is a bloc—whether for military or other reasons. So either on the one side you must put an end to any association of two countries for any purpose— other than maybe cultural—or some kind of alliance will take place **ultimately.**

"Such things have to be met by an improvement of the world situation; because much of this is due to fear—whether fear of oppression, fear of other countries spreading out and attacking the interests and privileges of their neighbors. The basic way to move is to create conditions of lessened fear. Having done that, you can then build up that type of United Nations you have suggested."

In that case, wasn't the challenge to create a world organization which could rise above blocs? In such a U.N., would not the big job be to get all the nations to come in?

"That is true," he said. "But, again, I repeat that if the United Nations itself in the minds of large numbers of people does not represent the world as a whole, it becomes a part of the world and the other part is out of it. That part of it, then, is not subject to its jurisdiction, and you can only bring it in or deal with it by the policemen's methods—which countries resent. So that instead of assuring peace you are gradually drifting to greater conflicts."

I brought up the possibility of calling a Revision Conference under Articles 108 and 109 of the Charter for the purpose of a world consideration of all these questions. Wouldn't it be a good idea to have a fresh start?

"The objectives of the U.N. are still sound," he said; "but still, if a revision is required, certainly we should consider it to make the United Nations more of a universal body. That would no doubt help."

Our meeting ended at that point. So far as I was concerned, it ended happily. We had come together at the end, after all. The common goal was universalism in world organization. The differences between us concerned the circumstances under which universalism was possible or desirable. But at least there was agreement on the value of a general inventory of the U.N.'s assets and liabilities.

*   *   *

When we resumed our discussion the following afternoon, the Prime Minister picked up the trend of our talks. He spoke of the complexity of the causes of war in the modern world. Any world organization, to be successful, must comprehend these complexities.

"The League of Nations failed for a variety of reasons—chiefly because, I suppose, people and nations and governments were not wholly trained up to that idea. The United Nations came into being after that rather unfortunate experience. They tried to build it on solid foundations. The United States came into the picture, which made a very great difference for good. I have no doubt that in the long run the world must go on toward some idea of what is called rather vaguely 'one world.' "

"What kind of 'one world'?" I asked.

"What form it will take, I cannot say—probably fairly close cooperation between autonomous nations for the preservation of world order, something more than the United Nations represents today.

"Anyhow, we have to grow up to it. The United Nations—or rather the idea behind the United Nations—was a very big step toward that. Obviously, one of the essential features of any world government or the United Nations must be the prevention of aggression by one country over another, one people over another. It should also be the promotion, actively and positively, of better relations between countries, cooperation in various branches of activity.

"Now the world as we find it today is unbelievably varied, and various parts face different problems.

"In Asia the primary problem is, let us say, food or raising terribly low living standards. The people lack the necessities of life. They think primarily in those terms. They have just come out of the colonial stage and they have a certain vital purpose in life. They have a certain resistance to any attempt to reimpose that colonialism, and they are strong enough to resist any imposition of any form of foreign domination.

"One cannot think in terms of imposing anything on Asia today against the will of the people. No solution which is not accepted by large masses of people can have any possible enduring quality.

"In Asia today, the party or the idea that represents any kind of liberating force appeals to the people. That liberating force when applied to the political domain might be called nationalism. It may be applied to the economic domain when it deals with, let us say, land problems or others that appeal to people. And so the right appeal to the people should be connected with their idea of liberation—either political or economic."

Was it possible, I asked, that some nations and parties were dishonestly using the nationalist goals and the need for land reform? The Soviet, for example, was appealing to the people on every possible level, exploiting local issues to accomplish nationalist and imperialist aims of her own. Russian expansion in Asia, particularly in China, went back to 1896. She wanted control of Asia—an ambition that antedated the Communist regime itself. Was there general awareness of the imperialism behind the ideology?

Mr. Nehru agreed concerning the imperialistic aspects of Russia's program, but he pointed out that for a time, early in Russia's Communist phase, she appeared to be breaking away from the Czarist expansionist program. "At that time," he said, "Russia spoke to many countries in Asia on anti-imperialist lines and appeared to be a kind of liberating force. There is no doubt that the measure of sympathy—a large measure of sympathy—that Russia a quarter of a century ago obtained in Asia was because of that. That is, it allied itself to the nationalism of various peoples.

"In recent years there has been a very marked difference in approach. The Communist tendency has come into conflict with the nationalist tendency in many countries—India, Indonesia, Burma, and some other countries. Where this has happened thus far, the nationalist tendency has proved the stronger—provided always that the nationalist tendency does not support reactionary social tendencies, because reactionary social tendencies come in the way of the economic change that is so urgently desired—more especially in regard to land, but in other matters too.

"Communism in India right up to the beginning of the Second World War had very little importance except as a vague idea which appealed to some people in support of the national movement. Therefore it was a very small fringe of the national movement, which didn't count for much otherwise. It did count for a little among the industrial workers then.

"But in the larger scheme of things it was not important. It was really in the later days of the war that Communism became more important, partly because of the opportunities given to it in wartime to build itself up, because it was supporting the war; that is, after the Soviet Union came into it. It built itself up at the cost of breaking away from nationalism.

"It did gain something in organization, but it lost a good deal in its break with the nationalist movement and therefore in the hostility it aroused among the members of the nationalist movement.

"Today in India, Communism is definitely opposed to our nationalism. It can give us a lot of trouble in local areas, either industrial or agricultural areas, but that is somewhat limited.

"Now the question is: How far can the nationalist movement go forward in solving some of the urgent economic problems? If it fails, naturally that is an encouragement to Communist ideas. If it succeeds, then Communism or Communist ideas in India shrink."

Could India move forward at a pace which would make it possible to resist Communism?

"When you talk about Communism," he said, "you must distinguish between certain ideological, economic bases of Communism which we vaguely call Socialism in its various aspects, and the particular tactics employed by the Communist party, say, in India. By mixing the two together some confusion is created in the mind because there are certain things about Socialism rather than Communism which attract large numbers of people in India. But there is very great resentment and opposition to the tactics of Communism in India. Communism here really has become purely terroristic, and challenges not only the government but most things in India.

"Therefore, I think that unless any government in India completely fails to satisfy the economic urges and wants of the people Communism will not gain very much hold here."

"If Communism, as you define it, through terrorism or otherwise, does not take hold in India ideologically, is it at all possible there may be an attempt to take hold more directly—by overt action or aggression? How do you interpret the invasion of Tibet?"

Mr. Nehru seemed determined in the way he replied.

"No, I am not afraid of any external threat to India of that kind. And I certainly am not afraid of any threat from the Tibetan side for a variety of reasons, which I needn't go into now. But the real reason and the basic reason is that I do not think that India and China are going to behave in that way toward each other."

But wasn't it possible that China, because of her connection with Russia, might be persuaded that her interests lay more in the direction of fulfillment of Russia's ideological and national aims than in the direction of the type of United Asia Mr. Nehru espoused?

"I don't think so," he said, lighting up the inevitable cigarette. "China is closely allied to Russia in many ways, but in the final analysis it decides for itself what it has to do and what it has not to do. I do not see how it can possibly profit China or even, for that matter, Soviet Russia to think in terms of taking India.

"In the present state of affairs there can either be a continuation of peace or there might be general war. If there is war on a world scale, then the chief theater of war which will make a difference to the final outcome of the war will be situated elsewhere, not in India. It may be situated in Europe. That is the most important theater. It may be situated in the Far East. India does not come into the picture at all as an important theater, and it is perhaps imperiling the final result of the war to indulge in such adventurous schemes."

"Well, if the showdown comes—if the war does come—what role do you think India would play?"

"India for the present is trying her utmost to prevent such a showdown—not because India thinks she can make too much difference to the world's destiny but because she is absolutely convinced that a war on the scale that is imagined now will mean a total destruction of every idea and objective that civilization stands for. In fact, the very things one might fight against, while defeated in battle, may triumph because of the general ruin that may come to the world. Therefore, it becomes of essential importance to prevent that war and get a period of peace which might permit us to establish some kind of world equilibrium.

"I am quite convinced that people in every country, wherever they may be, generally desire peace. Now if war comes, it is a little difficult to imagine what its cost may be, but one thing is clear —it will mean large-scale destruction, and it may be a very lengthy war.

"India will try to do her best to prevent that war from happening, or, if it does happen, from spreading, just as she has tried to the extent of her capacity to limit the Korean war. If a large area of the world can keep out of the war, it may be able to help in bringing about peace a little sooner than otherwise."

"Yes, there can be no doubt," I said, "that the world's peoples want peace. But do all the world's rulers want peace? And do we have today in the world the means by which aggression, for example, may actually be prevented? Aren't these two factors largely responsible for the fear of which you spoke earlier?"

"May I just tell you the background in which I have been trained?" he said. "When Gandhi came on the scene in India, his message to us all was, 'Do not be afraid of British imperialism.' They had all the armies, all the apparatus of the state, all the resources at their command. We had nothing except our bare hands and, if you like, a certain spirit.

"It was odd, his telling us 'Do not be afraid' and telling that, not to people like me, but to the poor, downtrodden peasant in the field who had always been kicked about by everybody. And yet, strangely enough, something of his message caught, and we did shed our fear and we found a great release.

"Ultimately, as you know, it was very largely through Gandhi's tactics and methods that we obtained our independence. Now, one may not apply that exact parallel to the world's state, for conditions are different. But I think basically there is a great deal in it which can be applied.

"Today, fear is almost all-pervasive. The strongest countries are afraid—not afraid of any one country—but afraid of the consequences of what might happen. And I think if we could possibly lessen this great tension and strain, that by itself would be a great gain and give us some chance, some opportunity of working more constructively for peace.

"So I would suggest that the first step should be this attempt to lessen the strain and tension in people's minds and the minds of governments. I cannot suggest a definite thing to be done in regard to that, because it depends on circumstances and on steps to be taken to fit in with those circumstances.

"I think it can be done, and I am quite sure that the reaction of the peoples would be tremendous. Then the next step would immediately become a little easier. That is why we were anxious that this Korea affair should be settled, if possible, quickly, because for the moment that seemed to be the one thing most likely to lead to wider hostilities, ultimately even on a world scale."

Would he agree, I asked, that the goal was not only to avert war, but to avert it without sacrifice of justice or moral values?

Yes, he emphatically agreed. "In fact," he said, "one of the most painful things that we have seen in the last thirty or forty years, partly owing to the big wars that have taken place, is the degradation of moral values in the world. After all, the greatest force in favor of degradation is war. Human beings function in wartime as they never function in peacetime. So from that point of view, also, war is a hateful thing; and if we are to preserve any kind of moral values in the world we have to avoid war."

I pointed out that some American newspapers had questioned his policy of neutrality as a turning away from the moral questions involved. The point had been made that India today was not really neutral but was actually inclined toward Russia and China.

He took the question in his stride.

"The word 'neutrality,' of course, is not a correct word to describe our policy.

"Normally neutrality can only be used as opposed to belligerents in time of war. In time of peace the question does not arise—unless one is always thinking in terms of war.

"Our policy is simply this: We wish to judge every issue on the merits and the circumstances then prevailing, then decide what we consider best in terms of world peace and our other objectives. We do not wish to adopt a policy or be against a country merely for the sake of being against the country.

"Now to meet your earlier question. So far as India is concerned, I have not a shadow of a doubt that any kind of aggression against India will be met by resistance. India will not tolerate it. I do not expect it, but I've made it perfectly clear that we will not tolerate any aggression."

"Will you be ready for it if it comes?"

"Absolutely, at any time, from any direction."

Once, earlier in our talks, the Prime Minister said with a smile that the frequency with which I reverted to the need to strengthen the United Nations was perhaps suggestive of a needle stuck in the same groove of a phonograph record. I hated to put the needle to work again, but—

"Would you agree," I asked, "that India's and the world's last best hope of peace, then, is a stronger United Nations—to return to an earlier point in our discussion?"

He took it in good grace—needle, groove, and all.

"If you want the United Nations really to be great," he said, "not only powerful in the material sense but a power affecting the minds and spirits of men, then it must function in a particular way to capture the minds and spirits of men.

"It is quite inevitable that something in the nature of the United Nations has to take charge of the world in the wider sense, not of compulsion so much. Compulsion can ultimately only be exercised over a small evildoer if society believes in a certain fundamental moral principle. If that principle itself is challenged by a great part of society, then there is conflict.

"Ultimately, the United Nations must not only be of course universal but must, shall I say, deprive to a certain degree other nations of some phases of their sovereignty. That is to say, it will have to develop the international order into an international government, in the largest sense of the term and without interfering with national autonomy.

"The world today is a curious mixture of some degree of uniformity and a great variety—a great variety in the sense that there are differing historical backgrounds, cultural methods, ways of living, economic conditions. Some countries are very backward, some are underdeveloped, some are highly developed. There is the difference of cultural backgrounds. Of course, we do come nearer to each other because of rapid communications and transport, and so forth. But basic things such as racial backgrounds remain. How are we to deal with this variety? It is no good trying to make them uniform and regimented, and I don't think it would be a good thing to try to do this.

"So it comes to this: giving as much freedom as possible for each way of life to develop along its own lines, helping it where possible without too much interference, understanding its ways, and, of course, neither interfering with it nor allowing it to interfere with others.

"That is, in the world as it is we have to adopt the principle of live and let live, but always with an ever growing cooperation which gradually integrates the world more and more closely together.

"One has to balance these factors all the time; one has to have more and more cooperation developing into a world order, and at the same time more and more autonomy in respective regions for the people in those regions to function as they like."

It was a good working definition of federalism. Once again, we could close our discussion on common ground. In the morning I would take the plane westward. Was there anything in particular Mr. Nehru wanted to say to Americans?

"Yes. All I can say is this, and I am speaking with absolute honesty. When I went to the United States a year and a half ago, I knew something about American people. I had read about their history, their Constitution, their progress, their literature, so I looked forward to that visit very greatly. I went there, and I saw large numbers of people in many fields; I saw many famous places.

"And the more I remained in America and the more people I saw, the more I got the impression of an essential friendliness, of frankness, of forthrightness—qualities which I value very greatly —and I returned with the feeling of great friendship and gratitude to America and her people."

My own feeling about India could not have been better stated.

PART TWO

Ideas and Decisions

"*There is not a good work which the hand of man has ever under-taken, which his heart has ever conceived, which does not require a good education for its helper.*"

—HORACE MANN

* * *

"*Nations are the citizens of humanity, as individuals are the citizens of the nation.*"

—GIUSEPPE MAZZINI

* * *

"*My country is my world; my countrymen are mankind.*"

—WILLIAM LLOYD GARRISON

* * *

"*Where liberty dwells there is my country.*"

—BENJAMIN FRANKLIN

* * *

"*The world is my country,
All mankind are my brethren,
To do good is my religion,
I believe in one God and no more.*"

—THOMAS PAINE

* * *

"*By far the greatest obstacle to the progress of science and to the undertaking of new tasks and provinces therein, is found in this—that men despair and think things impossible.*"

—FRANCIS BACON

* * *

"*There is no disease more hopeless than want of wisdom.*"

—ALI IBN-ABU-TALIB

CHAPTER XX

PERSONAL INVENTORY

This book began with the story of one man's re-education. There is yet another phase of my re-education that I ought to write about here—as a postscript to the account of the personal odyssey just completed, and as a prelude to this section on Ideas and Decisions.

My conventional education had prepared me superbly for a bird's-eye view of the world. It taught me to recognize easily and instantly the things that differentiate one place or one people from another. Geography had instructed me in differences of terrain, resources, and productivity. Comparative culture had instructed me in the differences of background and group interests. Anthropology had instructed me in the differences of facial bone structure, skin pigmentation, and general physical aspect. In short, my education had protected me against surprise. I was not surprised at the fact that some people lived in mud huts and others in bamboo cottages on stilts; or that some used peat for fuel and others dung; or that some enjoyed music with a five-note scale and others with twelve; or that some people were vegetarian by religion and others by preference.

In those respects my education had been more than adequate. But what my education failed to do was to teach me that the principal significance of such differences was that they were largely without significance. The differences were all but obliterated by the similarities. My education had by-passed the similarities. It had failed to grasp and define the fact that beyond the differences are realities scarcely comprehended because of their shattering simplicity. And the simplest reality of all was that the human community was one—greater than any of its parts, greater than the separateness imposed by the nations, greater than the divergent faiths and allegiances or the depth and color of varying cultures. This larger unity was the most important central fact of our time— something on which people could build at a time when hope seemed misty, almost unreal.

As I write this, I have the feeling that my words fail to give vitality to the idea they seek to express. Indeed, that the idea itself is a truism which all peoples readily acknowledge even if they do not act on it. Let me put it differently, then. In order to be at home anywhere in the world, I had to forget the things I had been taught to remember. It turned out that my ability to get along with other peoples depended not so much upon my comprehension of the uniqueness of their way of life as upon my comprehension of the things we had in common. It was important to respect the differences, certainly, but to stop there was like clearing the ground without any idea of what was to be built on it. When you got through comparing notes, you discovered that you were both talking about the same neighborhood, that is, this earth, and the conditions that made it congenial or hostile to human habitation.

I said a moment ago that my education had insulated me against surprise. That is only partially right. I did experience wonder and surprise. But it went the other way. It grew out of the ease with which communication among different peoples was possible— despite all the pother that is made out of linguistic difficulties and semantic obstacles. Once the conversation moved away from immediate local issues and problems and onto a higher level where basic problems common to people everywhere were discussed, there was a rapid traffic in meaningful ideas. The contemplation of human destiny is a powerful solvent for separativeness.

There is a form of illiteracy far more baneful than the one having to do with the inability to read and write. The illiteracy of which I speak has to do with survival knowledge, or rather the lack of it. It is the illiteracy of those who can read and write but who are unprepared for the building of a world community.

Whatever the uncertainties about the future may be, of one fact we can be sure. The present generation of Americans and the next generation and the generations after that will have to be citizens of this human community. They will have to be at home in many lands and among many peoples. They will have to talk many languages and comprehend many philosophies, psychologies, and approaches which are now uncharted in much of present-day education. They will need a special knowledge, certainly; but they will need something far more important—an intense awareness of common human values and of the conditions under which those values can be created and maintained.

Only a few years ago an education in differences fulfilled a specific if limited need. That was at a time when we thought of other places and peoples largely out of curiosity or in terms of exotic vacations. It was the mark of a rounded man to be well traveled and to know about the fabulous variations of human culture and behavior. But it wasn't the type of knowledge you had to live by and build on.

Then overnight came the great compression. Far-flung areas which had been secure in their remoteness suddenly became jammed together in a single arena. And all at once a new type of education becomes necessary. The new education must be less concerned with sophistication than with compassion. It must recognize the hazards of tribalism. It must teach man the most difficult lesson of all: to look at someone anywhere in the world and be able to see the image of himself. The old emphasis upon superficial differences must give way to education for mutuality and for citizenship in the human community.

In such an education we can begin with the fact that the universe itself does not hold life cheaply. Life is a rare occurrence among the billions of galaxies and solar systems that occupy space. And in this particular solar system life occurs on only one planet. And on that planet life takes millions of forms. Of all those countless forms of life, only one, the human species, possesses certain faculties in combination that give it supreme advantages over all the others. Among those faculties or gifts is a creative intelligence that enables man to reflect, anticipate, and speculate, to encompass past experience and also to visualize future needs. There are endless other wondrous faculties the mechanisms of which are not yet within the understanding of their beneficiaries—the faculties of hope, conscience, appreciation of beauty, kinship, love, faith.

Viewed in this planetary perspective, what counts is not that the thoughts of men lead them in different directions but that all men possess the capacity to think; not that they pursue different faith but that they are capable of spiritual belief; not that they write and read different books but that they are capable of creating print and communicating in it across time and space; not that they enjoy different art and music but that something in them enables them to respond deeply to forms and colors and ordered vibrations of sounds.

These basic lessons, then, would seek to provide a proper respect for man in the universe. Next in order would be instruction in the unity of man's needs. However friendly the universe may be to man, it has left the conditions of human existence precariously balanced. All men need oxygen, water, land, warmth, food. Remove any one of these, and the unity of human needs is attacked, and man with it. The next lesson would concern the human situation itself—how to use self-understanding in the cause of human welfare; how to control the engines created by man that threaten to alter the complex conditions on which life depends; how to create a peaceful society of the whole.

With such an education, it is possible that some nation or people may come forward not only with vital understanding but with the vital inspiration that men need no less than food. Leadership on this higher level does not require mountains of gold or thundering propaganda. It is concerned with human destiny; human destiny is the issue; people will respond.

CHAPTER XXI

THE PROVINCIALISM
OF THE SCHOLARS

This chapter is about provincialism. It is a provincialism built on a paradox, for it exists where you would least expect to find it—among a large number of philosophers and scholars.

In particular, I have in mind those thinkers and writers who perform a disservice to the human community by placing peoples and civilizations in two big bundles neatly marked "East" and "West." Having created these rigid entities, they proceed to exalt one at the expense of the other. For example, scholars in Europe and the Americas who should know better, who should understand the implications of a superiority complex in the modern world, talk and write about the "destiny of Western man" or the "mission of Western man" or the "prospects of Western civilization" or the "survival of Western values." Scarcely a month passes that an article or a book does not appear with Western man as the central and awesome figure of modern history.

What do these philosophers and scholars mean when they talk about the "West" or about "Western" man? What is it that makes him different from "Eastern" man? Is it philosophy or literature or political science or a common yardstick of values? Is it Christianity that defines the oneness of the West? Is there a magic biological fluid that circulates through his body, creating a natural kinship between Europeans and North Americans and South Americans?

First, let us consider the origin and distribution of the species. A not uncommon error here is to confuse anthropology with philosophy. "Western" man is Greek and Roman, but he is also German and Scandinavian and English and Portuguese and Spanish and Polish and Russian and much more. If you go back far enough, there is a common stock, of course, but by going back just a little farther you can also include the people of Asia and Africa. Does living in Europe endow a person with a special chemical attraction for anyone who lives in the Americas? And what part of the Americas are you talking about? Canada? Puerto Rico? The United States? Argentina?

Is there a biological oneness felt between Germans and French that either party cannot possibly feel for, say, the Egyptians? And how would you classify a substantial part of the Mexican population, with Spanish and Negro and Indian blood flowing together? Are North American Indians to be considered East or West? They are authentic Americans; in fact, they once owned the place, but the anthropologists relate them to Eastern races. When we talk about the destiny of Western man, then, do we include the Indians of North and South America?

Or perhaps we are thinking of our political heritage. Classical Greece, in particular. True, Greece was the vital ground in which the political roots of democratic government were planted. It was here that the operation of society became a political science. The concept of constitutional government, separation of powers, limitation of tenure, direct responsibility of officeholders to the people, rights and duties of citizens—in all these respects Greece made a towering contribution to history. When we add to this the Roman science of laws, we have a legacy that is deeply felt, deeply valued, deeply expressed—and rightly so.

Yet even this is not enough to tie the West together and enable us to talk of Western man as a recognizable and complete democratic entity. The history of the West shows far longer periods of monarchy, autocracy, oligarchy, and totalitarianism than it does periods of democratic government. It may be argued that the true lessons of Greece did not begin to be learned for two thousand years; yet even if we confine our scope to recent history we can see that the principal threats to democratic institutions have come from within the West itself. Nazism and Communism, with their nihilism and authoritarianism, their iron heels and their iron curtains, are prime disorders within the body of the West. When we think of the citizen as a mighty source of freedom, are we thinking of the individual German under Hitler or the Argentinian under Perón? The fact is that there is neither a political compact in the West nor even a general grouping around commonly accepted values.

If the case for the uniqueness of Western man moves from the political to the intellectual, here again we can pay our debt to the Greek teachers, philosophers, historians, and theoreticians. And we can pay an even greater debt to their disciplined rational intelligence than we do to the actual results of those intellectual labors. If more attention had been paid to Aristotle as an example of the creative thinker rather than as the sovereign monarch of all knowledge, perhaps there would have been less intellectual stagnation after the fall of Rome. As for Plato, it should also be recorded that many of his ideas on the perfection of man were to become distorted by numberless self-appointed Platonists, and that some of these ideas were to be used against man himself. The fact that versions of neo-Platonism played into the hands of advocates of a master race and brutalitarians is not to be held against Plato, of course, but it at least indicates that there is no firm agreement in the West about what he tried to say or about the practical application of his thought.

Long before Plato ideas on the need for perfection in man and his institutions were being voiced and heard in Asia—especially in China, India, and Persia. The moral code of Zoroaster, aiming at the triumph of virtue not only over the material world but over the spiritual world as well, actually helped to fertilize Greek thought. Confucianism is almost synonymous with individual virtue and applied ethics, and has influenced far more people in the East than have been influenced by affirmative Platonism in the West. Similarly, it is doubtful whether the logic of Aristotle has made a more profound impact on any nation than it has upon Persia, possibly not excluding Greece itself.

The only generalization worth making about East and West is that there is far more cross-fertilization of ideas than has been generally acknowledged. A few Western scholars, such as Gilbert Chinnard, H. G. Creel, John Dewey, Lewis Mumford, George Sarton, Charles Farnsley, Horace Kallen, Irwin Edman, Jacques Barzun, Arnold Rowbotham, Bertrand Russell, Ralph Turner, and F. S. C. Northrop, have been concerned with the cross-currents and cross-penetration of ideas that have been associated with geographic East and West. But too little of this has percolated through to the general body of our knowledge of scholarship.

More ought to be said about the mission of the Jesuits to China in the sixteenth and seventeenth centuries, and the impact upon them of Confucianism. They were accused in Europe of having been converted themselves. The favorable accounts of Confucianism they sent back made an important contribution to the development of the French ideas of equality. The Jesuit Le Compte was especially impressed by the absence among the Chinese of hereditary nobility and the absence of caste or other distinctions. The Physiocrat School, so important in the making of the French Revolution, formally acknowledged its great debt to Confucianism, as interpreted by the Jesuits. In turn, Benjamin Franklin and Jefferson acknowledged their debt to the Physiocrats.

It is unimportant whether such influences were primary or secondary. What is important is that neither East nor West held any monopoly, as Jefferson himself pointed out, on the concept of equality. It is interesting, too, to observe the basic similarity in the thinking of Jefferson and Confucius, especially in their concern for the farmer, their cordial disdain for mysticism, their belief in the natural rights of man, their strictures against authoritarianism, their emphasis upon education as a proper function of government, their belief in the full development of the individual's potential, and their unending search for public and private virtue.

*   *   *

Those who are accustomed to making pronouncements about the "mission of Western man" or the "destiny of Western man" will claim that we have so far slighted one fact of mountainous importance: Christianity. Isn't Christian civilization, they will ask, synonymous with Western man? Isn't this what gives Western man the right to think of himself as different and special?

The main trouble with this line of questioning, of course, is that it assumes that Christianity itself is an entity. Is there general agreement about the meaning of Christ and the teachings of Christ in the West? Is there common acceptance of the same articles of faith? Indeed, are not Christians divided by their beliefs into numberless and occasionally opposing denominations? In a certain sense this is inevitable. So long as men will be confronted with new problems, so long as they have the capacity for creative interpretation, so long as they can exercise the right of free choice, they will be unable to devise and stay within any single institution or credo. This is natural and right. There is strength in such diversity. But this strength is misapplied if it tries to segregate or compartmentalize humanity into Christians and non-Christians, Eastern and Western man, or make something unique of one man as against another. The province of Christianity is not the ennoblement of Western civilization but the ennoblement of man.

The greatest paradox of all, however, is that the truest expression of Christianity today is to be found, not in the West, but in the East. In India countless millions of people are living out the ideals of Christ, though they do not call themselves Christians and are unfamiliar with Christian theology. They are the poor and the meek and the merciful and the pure in heart. They regard life as sacred and will not harm it in any of its forms. They practice renunciation. They believe in non-violence and they worship the memory of a human being who perhaps has come closer to enacting Christianity than anyone in modern history. Interestingly enough, Gandhi's struggle was directed against a Western Christian nation.

Are we to overlook the basic unity of most religions? The code of Hammurabi, the Koran, the Talmud, the Analects, and the Bhagavad-Gita have many of the same fundamental tenets defined in the Sermon on the Mount. What we call the Golden Rule has its parallel expression in almost all other religions. The Islamic faith is as closely related to the Hebrew and the Christian faith as the latter two are to each other. It is astonishing to find how little is known about the Islamic religion in otherwise well educated circles in Europe and the Americas. The extent to which the Mohammedan belief incorporates many of the fundamentals of Hebraism and Christianity is overlooked in the frequent references by many Western thinkers to "Judeo-Christian" traditions or civilization. This is properly regarded by the peoples of the Near East as another example of our philosophical and theological provincialism.

"When will the West understand, or try to understand, the East?"

asked the Japanese philosopher, Okakura-Kakuze, more than fifty years ago. "We Asiatics are often appalled by the curious web of facts and fancies which has been woven concerning us. We are pictured as living on the perfume of the lotus, if not on mice and cockroaches. It is either impotent fanaticism or else abject voluptuousness. Indian spirituality has been derided as ignorance, Chinese sobriety as stupidity, Japanese patriotism as the result of fatalism. It has been said that we are less sensible to pain and wounds on account of the callousness of our nervous organization!"

The East, of course, is no more a political or cultural or anthropological entity than is the West, although those who talk with such careless ease about Western man generally juxtapose him against Eastern man. What common center fuses an Afghanistan Moslem with a Filipino Catholic? Or a Ceylonese Buddhist with a Chinese Taoist? The religious Hindu is as appalled by the paganism of some of his Chinese neighbors as are the Episcopalians by Jehovah's Witnesses. Conversely, some Chinese are as baffled by Indian mysticism and Theosophy as many of us are, though it must be recorded that Theosophy is a product of the West. And the biggest ideological threat in Asia today, Communism, is not an Eastern idea but a Western one. What all this adds up to is not an Eastern entity but a vast complex inside a complex, with no single unifying thread.

The Asians—one and one-half billion of them—happen to share a continent which is a formal geographic unit only by human designation and not by divine insistence. To make grooved and rutted generalizations about these people is to commit a sin against good scholarship and the human community at a time when a vast expansion is needed in man's awareness and comprehension of man.

It is astonishing to see how often university conferences in Europe and the Americas on the problems of philosophy or politics in the modern world will allow stock references to Asian peoples and cultures to go unchallenged. One hears about the "disdain for action" or about "lack of systematic thought" or about the "Oriental love of vagueness" or about the "Eastern mentality" or about "typical Eastern mysticism" or about the "propensity for negation."

What is most unfortunate about these remarks is not so much the polite arrogance which assumes that failure of communication is necessarily the fault of the next fellow, but the unscholarly technique of placing "Eastern" philosophers inside a single academic enclosure. Anyone who has attended a philosophical meeting, whether in Japan or China or Indo-China or India or Pakistan or Turkey, is able to bear witness to the same spread of ideas and approaches, the same display of argumentation over ends and means, the same contrasts of soaring thoughts and plodding trivia which enliven similar meetings in Paris, London, or New York. Imagine, then, a meeting of Filipino, Japanese, Chinese, Indians, and Pakistani being characterized as though the ideas of only a single philosopher were being examined.

It must also be said that the East has its own provincial philosophers and scholars who lack an adequate background for an understanding of Europe and the Americas and who make the error of dealing in stereotypes and non-existent entities in writing about the "iniquitous and materialistic West." Even when they are friendly, they excuse our "rashness" and "impulsiveness" because of our youth. We are "precocious," "mechanistic," "frivolous," "irresponsible," "ambitious," lacking in "perspective," "wisdom," "insight." As yet, however, Asian scholars have not proclaimed any missions for Eastern man, nor have they endowed him with a special claim on human destiny.

What an Eastern philosophical conference has most in common with a Western philosophical meeting, perhaps, is an apparent disposition to invest geographical entities with fixed cultural, ideological, or philosophical components. Thus it is not unusual to hear Western philosophy criticized as lacking in sufficient appreciation of the "vital intangibles" or "elusive but central values." Along with this is the criticism of "Western thought" as being overly concerned with systems and techniques and not enough with the domain beyond man's limited intelligence. This criticism, of course, is merely the Asian manifestation of a philosophical provincialism which is not centered in or confined to any single area.

So far as the overriding needs and purposes of man today are concerned, it is irrelevant to attempt to determine which set of stereotypes came first or which is more unscholarly or unfair—that of the West against the East or vice versa. What is important is that a major effort be made by all concerned to get away from the entity complex. It would be well, perhaps, if the world of scholarship would enter into a sort of compact on specificity. It should be made clear whether when we use the term "East" we are thinking of everything from the Bosporus Straits to the Bering Sea, or whether we have a specific area or culture in mind. Proper distinctions should be made between Japan and China and India and Pakistan and Indonesia and Siberia and Iran and Syria and Israel. Similarly, when Asian scholars comment on Europe and the Americas it would be helpful to know whether they are thinking primarily of the Balkans or Scandinavia or South America or France or Canada or whatever.

Something else we can do is to liberate ourselves from some of the harmful misconceptions that are so much excess baggage. Consider, for example, the frequent remark mentioned above, that the East has a "disdain for action." It is said that it is virtually impossible for Asians to get beyond opinions and into operations. Thus we have heard about Chinese lethargy, Indian passivity, Balinese serenity, and so forth. In the light of recent and current history, that picture can stand some revision. The Civil War in China, stretching over fifteen years, was conspicuous for its lack of lethargy on all sides. Indeed, the missing ingredient appears to have been, not action, but thought. Japanese aggression in concert with the Axis only a few years ago was sharply in contrast to the prevailing conception of an Oriental nation as lacking in drive or dynamics. It is worth noting, incidentally, that industrialization, militarization, mobilization, aggression, and colonization—all of which dominated Japanese life for perhaps a quarter of a century —had previously reached advanced development in the West. So far as India is concerned, the widespread outside impression of an almost universal passivity or impassiveness must be modified in the light of observable facts of life in India for at least fifty years. Passive resistance and non-cooperation were the most vital parts of a real *action* program. After independence, intense political activity on the extremes of both left and right—activity from which Indian men of learning and letters sought no immunity or exemption— made India one of the least passive places on the face of the globe. Bali, too, more closely resembles a hotbed of Balkan intrigue than it does the glamorous, languorous land of Covarrubias's sketches.

As for the complaint of "Oriental vagueness," I have searched my memory but I can recall nothing more tangible or more vividly conveyed than the needs and hopes of Asian peoples I was able to meet. Most memorable of all was the emphatic detail with which they documented their desire to maintain their freedom and self-respect, and their deep resentment at being regarded as inferior beings fit only for servants or subjects. Exclusion acts and humiliation by legislation leave them with no vague reaction. If anything, the response is severely normal—almost to the point of being terrifying. True, some Asian writers and philosophers may have cultivated vagueness for vagueness' sake, but it ought not to be difficult to draw up a list of Western writers and philosophers who have some fairly well developed abilities in that direction themselves.

Then, of course, there is the matter of the "mystical, mysterious, spiritualistic and occult East." This is becoming more and more of a travel-poster slogan for tourists and less and less a description with any substance behind it. The most populous nation in Asia has had more disdain for the popular conception of mysticism and the occult than perhaps any country in the world. The intensely practical and down-to-earth philosophy-religion of Confucius and Lao-tzu has little scope for higher metaphysics.

Is there nothing, then, that distinguishes the peoples of Asian countries from the peoples of Europe and America? Such differences as exist cannot be separated into two large spatial bundles conveniently tagged "East" and "West." Many of the distinctions are national rather than continental, and even here it is important to take into account whatever pluralism may exist inside the nations themselves. In addition to the pluralisms are the paradoxes. Indeed, not until the paradoxes are located and defined does the essential nature of a culture begin to reveal itself. The finest observers, historians, and anthropologists have all been paradox hunters. Hunting and comprehending paradoxes, moreover, is infinitely more challenging and rewarding than the pursuit of incredible entities.

We may live in the two worlds of "East" and "West," but we have only one planet to do it in. As L. L. Whyte has written in *The Next Development in Man*, the "separation of East and West is over, and a new history opens rich in quality and majestic in scale."

"*Different creeds are but different paths to reach the Almighty. Various and different are the ways that lead to the temple of Mother Kali at Kalighat. Similarly, various are the ways that lead to the house of the Lord. Every religion is nothing but one of such paths that lead to God.*"

—SRI RAMAKRISHNA

* * *

"*A land at peace gives heaven its due.*"

—AESCHYLUS

* * *

"*The purpose of religious controversy should be, not to 'convert' the opponent, but to persuade him that his religion is essentially the same as our own.*"

—ANANDA K. COOMARASWAMY

* * *

"*The surface of the earth is soft and impressible by the feet of men; and so with the paths which the mind travels. How worn and dusty, then, must be the highways of the world, how deep the ruts of tradition and conformity.*"

—HENRY DAVID THOREAU

* * *

"*When we survey the whole field of religion, we find a great variety in the thoughts that have prevailed there; but the feelings on the one hand the conduct on the other are almost always the same, for Stoic, Christian, and Buddhist saints are practically indistinguishable in their lives.*"

—WILLIAM JAMES

CHAPTER XXII

ANTIDOTES TO PROVINCIALISM

This chapter began as an essay on the basic unity of the great religions. It was intended to show that differences between religions in the modern world are less theological than psychological. In the course of writing the chapter, however, it quickly became apparent that no interpretation was necessary: the great writings of the great religions speak for themselves.

Hence the following selected quotations drawn from some of the universal themes of religious belief. It is hoped they may serve as a gentle reminder that it may be a disservice to the community of faith in the world to lay exclusive claim to any special destiny in behalf of any faith—even in the name of so exalted an edifice as "Judeo-Christian civilization" or "Western Christendom"—or, equally, "Hindu universalism" or "the mission of Islam" or any other. As suggested in the previous chapter, the sudden emergence of a single geographic neighborhood in the world holds perhaps even more profound significance for the great religions than for other aspects of human thought and activity.

The threat to moral and spiritual values today is not uniquely against the "West" or "East" but is world-wide. The frame of reference is human, not geographical. The disorders of our time are lodged within the body of man and cannot be effectively treated if they are to be regarded as an external and local growth. "The purpose of religious controversy," observed Ananda K. Coomaraswamy, the eminent Indian-American philosopher, "should be, not to 'convert' the opponent, but to persuade him that his religion is essentially the same as our own."

The following excerpts are necessarily limited by space. It would be possible—and highly useful—to compile a separate volume of many hundreds of pages illustrating the basic affinity and unity of the great religions—with particular reference to man's relationship to the Deity, his relationship to his fellow man, and the moral values and spiritual beliefs which give enriched meaning to life.

THE GOLDEN RULE

BAHAI CAUSE: If you look toward justice, choose for others that which you choose for yourselves.

*   *   *

BUDDHISM: One should seek for others the happiness one desires for one's self.

*   *   *

CHRISTIANITY: Therefore, all things whatsoever ye would that men should do to you, do ye even so to them.

*   *   *

CONFUCIANISM: What you would not wish done to yourself do not to others.

*   *   *

HINDUISM: The true rule is to do by the things of others as you do by your own.

*   *   *

ISLAM: Let none of you treat a brother in a way he himself would dislike to be treated.

*   *   *

JUDAISM: Whatever you do not wish your neighbor to do to you do not unto him.

*   *   *

ZOROASTRIANISM: Do as you would be done by.

SHINTOISM: Do unto others as you would be done by.

THE GOLDEN MEAN

CONFUCIANISM: What are the nine virtues?
Affability combined with dignity;
Mildness combined with firmness;
Bluntness combined with respectfulness;
Aptness for government combined with reverent caution;
Docility combined with boldness;
Straightforwardness combined with gentleness;
An easy negligence combined with discrimination;
Courage combined with sincerity; and
Valor combined with righteousness.

* * *

BUDDHISM: Putting away slander, man abstains from calumny. What he hears here, he repeats not elsewhere to raise a quarrel against the people; what he hears elsewhere, he repeats not here to raise a quarrel against the people there. Thus he lives as a binder together of those who are divided, as encourager of those who are friends, a peacemaker, a lover of peace, impassioned for peace, a speaker of words that make for peace. Putting away bitterness of speech, he abstains from harsh language. Whatever word is humane, pleasant to the ear, lovely, reaching to the heart, urbane, pleasing to the people, beloved of the people—such are the words he speaks.

Putting away foolish talk, he abstains from vain conversation. In season he speaks; he speaks that which is; he speaks fact; he utters good doctrine; he utters good discipline; he speaks, and at the right time, that which redounds to profit; it is well grounded, is well defined, and is full of wisdom.

He refrains from injuring any herb or any creature. He abstains from food at the wrong time. He abstains from tricks with false weights, alloyed metals or false measures. He abstains from bribery, cheating, fraud and crooked ways. He refrains from maiming, killing, imprisoning, highway robbing, plundering villages or obtaining money by threats of violence.

JUDAISM: Behold, God will not cast away a perfect man, neither will he help the evil-doers.

The eyes of the Lord are upon the righteous, and his ears are open unto their cry.

*   *   *

HINDUISM: Let him never turn away a stranger from his house. This is the rule.

*   *   *

ISLAM: The liberal man is near to God, near to Paradise and near to man; but the miser is far from God, far from Paradise and far from men. The unbelieving, liberal man is more beloved of God than the miserly, believing worshipper.

O ye who believe! Enter not into houses which are not your own houses, until ye have asked leave and saluted the people thereof.

*   *   *

ZOROASTRIANISM: At the beginning both these Mentalities became conscious of each other, the one being a mentality better in thought and word and deed than the other mentality who is bad.

Now let the just man discriminate between these two, and choose the benevolent one, not the bad one.

Now will I speak out: At the beginning of life the holier mentality said to the opposing mentality who was more hostile: Neither our thoughts, doctrines, plans, beliefs, utterances, deeds, individualities nor souls agree.

*   *   *

TAOISM: The difficult things of this world must once have been easy; the great things of this world must once have been small. Set about difficult things while they are still easy; do great things while they are still small.

*   *   *

BAHAI CAUSE: To advance always; to achieve some new service every day; to hourly widen the horizon of intellect—these three rules must become the program of their lives.

CHRISTIANITY: But be ye doers of the Word and not bearers only, deceiving your own selves.

For if any be a hearer of the Word and not a doer, he is like unto a man beholding his natural face in a glass.

For he beholdeth himself, and goeth his way and straightway forgetteth what manner of man he was.

But whoso looketh into the perfect law of liberty and continueth therein, he being not a forgetful hearer, but a doer of the work, this man shall be blessed in his deed.

For what is a man profited, if he shall gain the whole world and lose his own soul? Or what shall a man give in exchange for his soul?

THE NEED FOR FAITH

TAOISM: He who has no faith in others shall find no faith in them.

. . . . .

The great rulers—the people do not notice their existence:
The lesser ones—they attach to and praise them;
The still lesser ones—they fear them;
The still lesser ones—they despise them.
For where faith is lacking,
It cannot be met by faith.
Now how much importance must be attributed to words!

* * *

SHINTOISM: Take care that Faith does not grow old in your Heart. Faith with a Weak Heart is worthless.

* * *

CHRISTIANITY: For we are saved by hope. But hope that is seen, is not hope; for what a man seeth, why doth he yet hope for? But if we hope for what we see not, then do we with patience wait for it.

Now, faith is the substance of things hoped for, the evidence of things not seen.

* * *

BUDDHISM: Faith in this world is the best property for a man. Dhamma, well observed, conveys happiness. Truth indeed is the sincerest of things; and that life they call the best which is lived with understanding.

*   *   *

JUDAISM: But there is a spirit in man, and the inspiration of the Almighty giveth them understanding.

*   *   *

HINDUISM: A being is full of faith; and whatever is man's faith, that is man himself.

THE FAMILY OF MAN

HINDUISM: "Is this one of our tribe or a stranger?" is the calculation of the narrow-minded; but to those of a noble disposition the earth itself is but one family.

This mankind is the honey of all beings, and all beings are the honey of this mankind. Likewise this bright immortal Person is mankind, and that bright immortal Person existing as man in the body, He indeed is the Self—that Immortal, that Brahma, that *All*.

And verily, this Self is the lord of all beings, the king of all kings. And as all spokes are contained in the axle and in the felly of a wheel, all beings and all those selfs are contained in that Self.

*   *   *

BAHAI CAUSE: That all nations should become one in faith and all men as brothers; that the bonds of affection and unity between the sons of men should be strengthened; that diversity of religion should cease and differences of race be annulled—what harm is there in this? Yet, so it shall be; these fruitless strifes, these ruinous wars shall pass away and the Most Great Peace *shall* come.

Do not you in Europe need this also?

Is not this that which Christ foretold?

Yet do we see your kings and rulers lavishing their treasures more freely on means for the destruction of the human race than on that which would conduce to the happiness of mankind.

These strifes, this bloodshed and discord must cease, and all men be as one kindred and one family.

Let not a man glory in this—that he loves his country; let him rather glory in this—that he loves his kind.

*   *   *

BUDDHISM: As a mother, who at the risk of her life watches over her only child, so let everyone cultivate a boundless friendly mind towards all beings. And let him cultivate goodwill towards all the world, a boundless friendly mind, above, below and across, unobstructed, without hatred, without enmity, standing, walking, sitting or lying—as long as he is awake, let him devote himself to this mind.

*   *   *

SHINTOISM: Whether you call it God or Buddha, the Living-Thing which dwells within the Truth of Heaven and Earth is meant.

The voice of all people is the voice of God.

*   *   *

CHRISTIANITY: There is neither Jew nor Greek, there is neither bond nor free, there is neither male nor female, for ye are all one in Christ Jesus.

And they shall come from the East and from the West, and from the North and from the South, and shall sit down in the Kingdom of God.

And all that believed were together, and had all things common.

*   *   *

ISLAM: God's is the East and the West, and wherever ye turn, there is God's face! . . .

Your God is one God; there is no God but He, the Merciful, the Compassionate.

God, there is no God but he, the Living, the Self-subsistent. Slumbers take Him not, nor sleep. His is what is in the heavens, and what is in the earth.

*   *   *

JUDAISM: The Lord is gracious and full of compassion, slow to anger, and of great mercy. The Lord is good to all, and his tender mercies are over all his works.

MAGNANIMITY

SHINTOISM: A soft answer turns away wrath.
Requite evil with kindness.

*   *   *

JUDAISM: A soft answer turneth away wrath; but grievous words stir up anger.

*   *   *

TAOISM: Recompense injury with kindness.

Even if a man is bad, how can it be right to cast him off?

*   *   *

CHRISTIANITY: Be ye therefore merciful, as your Father also is merciful.

Love your enemies; bless them that curse you; do good to them that hate you, and pray for them which despitefully use you and persecute you—that ye may be the children of your Father which is in heaven. For He maketh his sun to rise on the evil and on the good, and sendeth rain on the just and on the unjust.

For if ye love them which love you, what reward have ye? Do not even the publicans the same? And if ye salute your brethren only, what do ye more than others? Do not even the publicans so?

*   *   *

ZOROASTRIANISM: Treat thy enemies with equity. With a friend proceed with the approval of friends. With a malicious man carry on no conflict, and do not molest him in any way whatever. With the foolish make no dispute. With a drunken man do not walk on the road. From an ill-natured man take no loan.

*   *   *

BUDDHISM: A man is not called just if he carries a matter by violence; no, he who distinguishes both right and wrong, who is learned and leads others, not by violence, but by law and equity, and who is guarded by the law and by intelligence, he is called just.

CONFUCIANISM: When one by force subdues men, they do not submit to him in heart. They submit because their strength is not adequate to resist.

When one subdues men by virtue, in their hearts' core they are pleased and sincerely submit. . . .

The *people* are the most important element in a nation.

* * *

ISLAM: How excellent is mercy conjoined with might.

* * *

BAHAI CAUSE: We must look upon our enemies with a sin-covering eye and act with justice when confronted with any injustice whatsoever; forgive all; consider the whole of humanity as our own family, the whole earth as our own country. . . .

The most urgent requisite of mankind is the declaration of the *oneness of the world of humanity*.

* * *

HINDUISM: This world is not for those who perform no sacrifice. . . . Pleasing each other, you will attain the highest good.

THOUGHT, WISDOM, TRUTH

ISLAM: There is no disease more hopeless than want of wisdom.

* * *

TAOISM: Great knowledge is wide and comprehensive; small knowledge is partial and restricted.

Great speech is exact and complete; small speech is merely so much talk.

* * *

JUDAISM: For, as he thinketh in his heart, so *is* he.

* * *

BUDDHISM: All that we are is the result of what we have thought; it is founded on our thoughts, it is made up of our thoughts. If a man speaks or acts with an evil thought, pain follows him, as the wheel follows the foot of the ox that draws the carriage.

If a man speaks or acts with a pure thought, happiness follows him, like a shadow that never leaves him. . . .

It is good to tame the mind, which is difficult to hold in and flighty, rushing wherever it listeth. A tamed mind brings happiness.

If a man's thoughts are unsteady, if he does not know the true law, if his peace of mind is troubled, his knowledge will never be perfect.

Truth is verily immortal speech. In what is true, in what is good and in what is right, the just stand firm.

*   *   *

HINDUISM: The mind must be restrained in the heart till it comes to an end that is knowledge, that is liberty; all the rest are extensions of the ties which bind us to this life.

Thoughts alone cause the round of birth; let a man strive to purify his thoughts!

What a man thinks, that he is. This is the old secret.

By the serenity of his thoughts a man blots out all actions. Dwelling within, with serene thoughts, he obtains imperishable happiness. . . .

Mind alone is the cause of the bondage and liberty of men; if attached to the world, it becomes bound; if free from the world, that is liberty.

*   *   *

CONFUCIANISM: The senses of hearing and seeing do not *think*, and are obscured by external things. When one thing comes into contact with another, as a matter of course it leads it away.

To mind belongs the office of thinking. By thinking, it gets the *right view of things;* by neglecting to think, it fails to do this. These —the *senses* and the *mind* are what Heaven has given us. Let a man first stand fast in the supremacy of the nobler part of his constitution and the inferior part will not be able to take it from him. It is simply this which makes the great man.

ZOROASTRIANISM: Of the benefit which happens to men, Wisdom is good, because it is possible to manage worldly existence through Wisdom, and it is possible to provide also the spiritual existence for oneself through the Power of Wisdom.

In and of contingencies among men, wisdom is good; in the advancement of business and justice, complete mindfulness is good; in the statements of those who confess with a bearing on the custom of the law, truth is good. . . .

Wisdom is better than the wealth of every kind which is in the world.

*   *   *

BAHAI CAUSE: The greatest gift and the highest blessing in the primary station is *wisdom*. It is the protector of existence and its support and helper. . . .

Wisdom is the first orator in the city of justice. . . .

Knowledge is like wings for the being (for man), and is as a ladder for ascending. To acquire knowledge is incumbent upon all; but of those sciences which may profit the people of the earth, and not such sciences as begin with mere words and end with mere words. The possessors of science and arts have a great right among the people of the world. Indeed, the real treasury of man is his knowledge. Knowledge is the means of honor, prosperity, joy, gladness, happiness and exultation.

*   *   *

SHINTOISM: Wisdom and virtue are always inseparable.

When our hearts conform to the Way of Truth God will protect us though we fail to pray.

*   *   *

CHRISTIANITY: Ye shall know the truth and the truth shall make you free.

"*If there is one principle that has proved its validity throughout the centuries, it is that only a free people with a clear hope of freedom will fight in defense of freedom.*"

—CARLOS P. ROMULO

* * *

"*The love of liberty is the love of others. The love of power is the love of ourselves.*"

—WILLIAM HAZLITT

* * *

"*The end of law is not to abolish or restrain, but to preserve and enlarge freedom. For in all the states of created beings, capable of law, where there is no law there is no freedom.*"

—JOHN LOCKE

* * *

"*The proposition is peace. Not peace through the medium of war; not peace to be hunted through the labyrinth of intricate and endless negotiations; not peace to depend on the juridical determination of perplexing questions, or the precise marking the shadowy boundaries of a complex government. It is simple peace; sought in its natural course, and in its ordinary haunts.*"

—EDMUND BURKE

* * *

"*This is true Liberty when free born men
Having to advise the public may speak free,
Which he who can, and will, deserves high praise,
Who neither can nor will, may hold his peace;
What can be juster in a State than this?*"

CHAPTER XXIII

TWO MEN

When he died, not only a nation but a civilization seemed to measure itself for the grave. When he died, a burden under which he had somehow stood was necessarily shifted to the generality of men, but the burden was too heavy even for the many, and they let it fall. That burden was the burden of a progressive humanity, yet even its benefactors were unable to see it maintained.

He died during a struggle of a civilization torn in two, between Athens at the head of an alliance of democracies and Sparta at the head of an oligarchic coalition. And although Athens survived the war after the death of Pericles, it swiftly descended to a tragic mediocrity in leadership. The building of a peace called for genius, but Athens responded with mental ciphers. And when, within a few years, Athens found itself in war again, it was not surprising that the military should have seized the state by default. Nor was it surprising that Athens should have lost not only the war but its civilization as well.

The virtuous historian regards speculation as the original sin of his profession, but almost every historian of early Greece has yielded to the opinion that the death of Pericles not only symbolized but was directly related to the death of the greatest period of Athenian history. It was under Pericles that Athens had reached the summit of both her power and glory. It was under Pericles that democratic institutions had come into their own, to be exercised for the many rather than for the few. It was under Pericles that men had experienced a vast emancipation from locked chambers, being ushered into a vast plain where they could discover and exult in the powers of creative intelligence.

There was little in Pericles' background or training to indicate that he would identify himself so forcefully with the fight to broaden the base of Athenian democracy—economic as well as political. Pericles himself, through his family, belonged to the small but tight platinum circle that controlled the state. Whatever aristocracy had to offer its youth had been his. Very early he came into an inheritance that made him one of the wealthiest men in all Greece.

Just where or how the deep sense of democratic purpose developed it is difficult to say. Plutarch seems to feel that Anaxagoras, who looked to science and reason as the only bases for philosophy, may have provided the spark.

But whatever the cause, there is no mystery as to the effect—even though the distance between the two may have been considerable. It wasn't until he approached his middle years that he became involved with public affairs, but once in office he acted with a certainty and a boldness that bewildered those of his friends who had never known him to have deep convictions on social and political questions.

Nor could it be said that he had become the willing funnel of strong men behind him. Pericles had put together his political philosophy piece by piece by himself, and he could see it whole. He could see it, too, in relation to the needs of the people. And from this philosophy he never departed.

It was a philosophy built on humanity and humility—not the humility of the weak but the humility of the strong. It was built —almost magically—in such a way that what seemed to be short-range expedients actually fitted into long-range objectives. It was built to serve the individual, but it also recognized that individuals must serve principles. It was built on resilience—a springy quality which enabled it to bounce back after it seemed that all the coils were played out or tied down.

As this philosophy became translated into tangible reality, the members of the circle from which Pericles had come became increasingly incredulous and then increasingly bitter, their attitude finally developing into congealed hate. They referred to him contemptuously as a betrayer of his family and of a tradition, as a subversive and dangerous schemer, as a reckless fool who would bankrupt the nation, and as being personally immoral and depraved. This bitterness met no bitterness in return; only a combined amusement and a determination not to depart from fixed objectives.

One of these objectives was the liberalization of the Areopagus, a counsel of elder statesmen holding broad powers which became broader and more cemented with the years. It was answerable not even to the popular assembly, and constituted itself as the supreme court and council of the land. Members of the court were former high government officials with aristocratic or oligarchic backgrounds. They sat in authority for life, responsible only to their own views of legislative and social propriety.

Pericles lent his active support to a plan by Ephialtes to deprive the Areopagus of the ultimate power over the state and to place it in the hands of the people. The plan also sought to eliminate the powers of censorship which enabled members of the Areopagus to pry into the lives of citizens, then unprotected by a bill of rights.

Despite the opposition of the aristocracy, which saw in the proposed reform a blow at itself through the destruction of a body it had come to regard as its chief protector, Pericles and Ephialtes succeeded in revamping both the form and functions of the council. Thereafter the Areopagus was to have specific and limited functions. Its punitive power was gone; it could not instruct the administration concerning policy; it could not inquire into the private lives of citizens; its jurisdiction over law enactment was removed. And as the Areopagus was reduced, so was the popular assembly raised in scope and authority.

A parallel reform involved a tremendous broadening of the base of participation in government. Qualifications for public office were to be based not on holdings but on citizenship. A definite schedule of pay for public office replaced the old system whereby only the wealthy could afford to serve under the no-pay plan. Moreover, there were specific increments in the new salary plan, with the amount increasing with the responsibility, from a small sum for jury duty to a fair amount for chief executive.

Whatever opposition all these measures provoked was as nothing compared to the upheaval caused by Pericles' public-works projects, involving large expenditures of public funds. A large percentage of Athenians joined the public pay rolls, for the Periclean projects were not restricted to buildings or monuments but extended to the broad range of culture, with the government aiding artists, writers, and musicians.

The unemployment problem, such as it was, was not to be met by having "people sitting around, doing nothing," as Plutarch describes it, but by having them make an actual contribution to the making of a city and to the betterment of the general citizenry. Thus were employed, adds Plutarch, "smiths and carpenters, moulders, founders and braziers, stone-cutters, dyers, goldsmiths, ivory-workers, painters, embroiderers, turners, merchants, mariners, ship-masters, conveyors, cartwrights, cattle-breeders, waggoners, rope-makers, flax-workers, shoemakers, leather-dressers, roadmakers, miners. . . ."

Thus it was that Athens became the most beautiful city the world has ever known. There rose within a few years some of the most magnificent structures to have been built anywhere. The Parthenon, the Temple of Athena, the Odeum, the Propylaea, the Erectheum—these were only a few of the architectural marvels erected during what is now known as the Golden Age of Pericles.

And as the Periclean Era unfolded, so did the human mind seem to unfold, developing fast under conditions of freedom and growth. The intellectual illumination produced by that period was to throw a light across centuries.

Pericles had been in office almost thirteen years when the great war broke out between Athens and Sparta. Nominally, his tenure was to be for the duration of a single year, and there were nervous protests that he sought a one-man state as year after year he was reelected. But democracy under Pericles had broadened and had reached its fullest growth.

Yet this democracy was now threatened by Spartan oligarchy. It was threatened from within, too, by Spartan sympathizers and native oligarchs who not only accused Pericles of war-plotting but who tugged at the sleeves of the nation as it took up its arms. There was little doubt that these efforts were carefully coordinated with those of the enemy. For years, in fact, Sparta had attempted to destroy Athenian democracy and install an oligarchic regime in harmony with its own.

Far from seeking war, Pericles had done everything possible to avoid it. But he correctly assessed the factors generating a war momentum and warned the Athenians that war might come whether they wished it or not. He warned against temporary concessions that could gain temporary delays but that would actually make a potential enemy stronger. "If you give way, you will have to meet some greater demand, while a firm refusal will make them clearly understand that they must treat you as equals. Let us make our decision immediately—either to submit without fighting, or to fight against submission."

War came—a war which exceeded in destruction and devastation anything that history had recorded up to that time. It was a war that proved—for Athens at least—that the vital spark in a democracy can go out unless its people are not only worthy of leadership but can generate new leadership when the occasion demands.

For Pericles never lived to see the outcome of the war. He had fallen victim to the plague which had swept over Athens, although he had seen the nation through the worst of it. One third of the population had perished, but Pericles, with his great genius as an orator, and with his tremendous talent for taking the people into his confidence and telling them the worst while inspiring them to their best, went before them and reunited them in support of the war. "You should know," he said, "that liberty preserved through our efforts can yet give us the means of restoring what has been lost. But if we are ever brought to our knees, we may never be able to stand on our feet again as free men."

After Pericles' death, a tanner named Cleon came into office. He was aggressive in carrying out the prosecution of the war, but undistinguished and tragically unequal to the biggest job Athens as a nation had faced. The little things, the little problems, he could understand and cope with. But problems of state were mountains.

Still, Cleon was not to blame. He was doing his job as he understood it. The real blame belonged to the Athenians themselves. They lacked purpose. They lacked a sense of vital achievement. They lacked conscience. The nation split up into factions, each seeking power and privileges for its own ends. Thucydides tells us that these factions were "engaged in projects unjust to Athens— projects whose success meant that they alone would be the gainers, but whose failure meant near disaster to the entire nation."

Lacking a moral center, which could hold the people together, and lacking a system of security among nations that could eliminate the fear of aggression, the citizens began to turn on one another. "Every form of iniquity took root in the Hellenic world," Thucydides wrote. "The ancient simplicity in which honor was so important a factor was laughed down and so disappeared; and society became divided into camps in which no man trusted his fellow." Finger-pointing became the rule. Even those who thought it impossible, because of their reputation and position, that charges could be brought against them successfully, says Thucydides, "thought it unnecessary to defend themselves and so were the first to be numbered among the victims."

The Athenian problem was not unique: how to obtain strong, dynamic leadership in time of crisis to cope with strong, dynamic forces, and yet retain the ultimate power in the hands of the people. There was need for a leader who was strong but not a strong man, a commander yet a servant, someone who could unite all factions yet favor no single one; someone who could act in the interests of the majority yet not cater to its whims; someone who could keep his head in the presence of an acute crisis and help the people to keep theirs; someone who was courageous and daring but not irresponsible; someone who regarded democracy as a means to democratic and not personal ends; in short, someone who had an understanding of, and a feeling for, the broad struggle for larger freedom.

But such leadership does not spring into being automatically. Sometimes it can be generated only out of the quality of leadership in the people themselves. This quality the Athenians lacked. Disunited, weak, they inevitably drifted into the control of the military. An adventurer named Alcibiades rode into power. Democratic constitutions he regarded as acknowledged folly. He had respect only for ambition—in this case, self-respect. He was vastly ambitious, for himself and for Athens—in that order. He believed in uniting the Greek world—by force and conquest. He believed in peace—a peace kept by the sword with the sword in his own hands.

Pericles had warned Athens against conquest and against acts born out of temper. And it wasn't that the advice was disregarded; it hadn't even been remembered. At a time when the life of the democracy depended upon the day-by-day wisdom of the people themselves, there was not even enough wisdom to invoke the memory of greatness.

The fall of Athens need not have been inevitable. It could have been saved at almost any point—if only the people could have seen themselves as history later saw them; if only they could have sensed their purposelessness.

How do you fashion a full-length mirror for a nation?

II.

On September 25, 1919, Woodrow Wilson made his last public speech. He was fighting to win over the American people to the cause of the League of Nations, for he was convinced that the war just ended would become merely the opening episode of a continuing tragedy if the nations failed to establish world law. And the biggest test was right here in America. Public opinion was slow in seeing the connection between world peace and world law. Traditionally, too, the American people had been accustomed to waiting for a problem to come to a boil before doing anything about it. Wilson's case rested on the need to anticipate crisis as the best means of crushing it.

Imagine the unutterable anguish of the man who had managed to convince millions of people all over the world of this, only to return home to find that leaders of the opposing political party had been capitalizing on the desire of Americans to forget about the war, forget about Europe, forget about foreign involvements. And the campaign against the League was succeeding. Hence Wilson's decision to carry the fight for peace to the people. It was to be a tour that would attempt to crack open the isolationist heartland. The compressed schedule called for about one hundred speeches before audiences in almost every state stretching from Ohio to the West Coast—all in a few short weeks.

The best account of that trip—Wilson's last public trip—is to be found in a compelling and evocative book, *Woodrow Wilson as I Know Him,* by Joseph P. Tumulty, his confidant and friend who served as private secretary for eleven years.

Tumulty wrote that the small group around Wilson resisted the idea of the trip as soon as it became known. The President had returned from Europe showing the effects of his exertions. He was suffering from violent headaches and was easily fatigued. When an attempt was made to postpone the trip, Wilson would have none of it. He told Tumulty that he knew he was at the end of his tether, but insisted that a desperate effort had to be made to win over the American people in time.

"If the Treaty should be defeated," he said, "God only knows what would happen to the world as a result of it. In the presence of the great tragedy which now faces people everywhere, no decent man can count his own personal fortunes in the reckoning."

Tumulty suggested a compromise. Set aside one week in the tour for a rest at a quiet place in the Grand Canyon. Even this the President rejected. "This is a businesss trip, pure and simple," he insisted, "and the itinerary must not include a vacation of any kind."

The trip got under way. As it progressed, Wilson seemed somehow to find a magical second wind that enabled him to speak three, four, or even five times a day, seven days a week. Tumulty and the President's staff marveled at his ability to mask his fatigue while talking. Never had they heard him more eloquent or more convincing. Many of the talks were extemporaneous, but they all reflected Wilson's great talent for clarity and precision of thought and expression.

And Wilson's message was getting across. It was hard work, but you could see the people responding to the call for sanity and the need to put decency to work in dealings among nations. There were hopes in the President's party that the encouraging early reactions would reach a crescendo by the time the tour ended.

When the President spoke at Pueblo, Colorado, on September

25th, he was more impassioned and effective than ever. It was a longer talk than usual, and it almost seemed that Wilson realized it might be his last.

As he spoke, the audience was deeply moved by what he said, but they were also moved by his frail appearance. It was easy to see that something was wrong; his face clearly showed the effects of the constant strain not only of the trip but of his labors overseas for the League.

He began his Pueblo talk by saying that he had come to speak in behalf of his clients. Those clients, he said, were the next generation. He wanted to be sure that the measures would be taken here and now that would make it unnecessary for that next generation to be sent on another war errand. He spoke of the hundreds of American mothers who came up to grasp his hand during his trip—mothers whose sons had been killed in France. They had said, many of them, "God bless you, Mr. President."

"Why, my fellow citizens," he asked, "should they pray God to bless me? I advised the Congress of the United States to create the situation that led to the death of their sons. I ordered their sons overseas. I consented to their sons being put in the most difficult parts of the battle line, where death was certain, as in the impenetrable difficulties of the Argonne forest. Why should they weep upon my hand and call down the blessings of God upon me? They do so because they believe that their boys died for something that vastly transcends any of the immediate and palpable objects of the war. They believe that wrapped up with the liberty of the world is the continuous protection of that liberty by the concerted powers of all the civilized world.

"These men were crusaders. They were going forth to prove the might of justice and right, and all the world accepted them as crusaders. Their achievement has made all the world believe in America as it believes in no other nation in the modern world."

The President spoke of his visit to a hillside near Paris, at the cemetery of Suresnes, where American soldiers were buried. He then referred to the many men in Congress and public life who were now opposing the creation of a world society which, if all nations joined in giving it real authority, might be able to crush the causes of war, and he said he hoped these men might have been with him to see those graves.

"I wish," he said, "that they could feel the moral obligation that rests upon us not to go back on those boys, but to see the thing through, to see it through to the end and make good the redemption of the world. For nothing less depends upon this decision, nothing less than the liberation and salvation of the world.

"Now that the mists of this great question have cleared away, I believe that men will see the trust, eye to eye and face to face. There is one thing that the American people always rise to and extend their hand to, and that is the truth of justice and of liberty and of peace. We have accepted that truth and we are going to be led by it, and it is going to lead us, and through us the world, out into pastures of quietness and peace such as the world never dreamed of before."

As the President spoke, Tumulty looked around and could see the impact of his words. Hard-boiled newspapermen who had sat dry-eyed through the previous speeches were now visibly stirred. He looked at Mrs. Wilson and saw tears in her eyes. The thousands of people in the large amphitheater were responding to moral leadership.

But the tour was never completed. Late that night, the night of the Pueblo speech, Dr. Grayson, the President's physician, summoned Tumulty. The President was seriously ill. His left side was paralyzed. One side of his face was limp and expressionless. His left arm and left leg failed to respond to stimulus. The searing headaches that were an old story throughout the tour now held the President's mind in a steel-like grip.

The Western trip was over. Woodrow Wilson had fought and lost.

For at least fifteen years Americans gave little thought to his defeat. All during the twenties and into the thirties it was fashionable to view Wilson kindly but somewhat skeptically. He was a great idealist, we said patronizingly, a great idealist who never realized we lived in a practical world. The word "impractical" became his epitaph.

But during the Second World War and, indeed, in the years immediately preceding the war, the realization grew that Wilson was perhaps the most practical man of his time, for he had addressed himself to the basic needs of America and the world. He spoke of ideals, certainly, for he believed that ideals were our natural assets and, in time of emergency, our finest weapons. Our failure to act on those ideals in time resulted in countless thousands of Woodrow Wilson's "clients" going on another war errand.

And what about Woodrow Wilson's ideals in our time? There is a United Nations, and the United States has accepted the responsibilities of membership. But there are also signs that the United States is still hypnotized by the false slogans of sovereignty, still willing to shelter the fallacy that world law can operate without compulsory obligations and commitments. We are reluctant to talk about the ideal of world citizenship, though it could be the most effective salient there is against totalitarian ideology. When we talk about ideals we mumble them somewhat incoherently, as though they are uncomfortable on our lips.

When Wilson spoke ideals he was not self-conscious, he did not stammer, he was not apologetic. He was representing the strength of America as he understood it and as history had confirmed it. We do not honor his memory unless we also honor his convictions. At the heart of those convictions was the belief that vision—vision with spaciousness and moral grandeur—is not only the solvent of potential danger but the natural setting for a human community at peace.

"*What is government itself, but the greatest of all reflections on human nature? If men were angels, no government would be necessary. If angels were to govern men, neither external nor internal controls on government would be necessary. In framing a government which is to be administered by men over men, the greatest difficulty lies in this: you must first enable the government to control the governed; and in the next place oblige it to control itself.*"

—JAMES MADISON

* * *

"*The United States will be secure in an absolute sense only if the institution of war itself is abolished under a regime of law . . . We will not be rid of war until the nations arrive at the agreement to live together in peace and to this end give to the United Nations the legal and physical powers under a regime of law to keep the peace.*"

—U.S. AIR POLICY COMMISSION REPORT TO
THE PRESIDENT, 1948

* * *

"*. . . General government shall do all those things that pertain to it, and all the local governments shall do precisely as they please in respect to those matters which exclusively concern them.*"

—ABRAHAM LINCOLN

* * *

"*When a people says: 'There shall be no war among us, for we will unite to form a State; i.e., set up a supreme legislative, executive, and judicial power, which shall settle our disputes peacefully,' the decision is perfectly comprehensible. But when a State says, 'There shall be no war between me and other States, although I recognize no supreme legislative power who secures my right and whose right I secure,' it is quite comprehensible on what it imagines that it bases its confidence in securing its right, unless it is on the expedient of the civic confederation of societies, viz., the free federalism, which reason must necessarily add to the conception of the law of nations, if there is to be any meaning whatsoever in the conception.*"

—IMMANUEL KANT

CHAPTER XXIV

ANSWERING THE ARGUMENTS

One of the happiest days of my life was the day following the election in November, 1948, when I learned that the people of Connecticut, my home state, voted to give the United Nations the powers of a limited world federal government. In an official state-wide referendum they had voted by a margin of almost twelve to one for a resolution passed by the State General Assembly calling upon the United States to take the initiative inside the U.N. in bolstering it with authority to enact, interpret, and enforce world law.

Connecticut thus became the second state—Massachusetts was the first by a vote of nine to one in 1946—in which the national campaign to strengthen the U.N. was carried directly to the people. In both states—indeed, in fourteen other states in which world-government resolutions have been passed by the state legislatures—the question cut across all party lines.

Let no one suppose that the Connecticut and the Massachusetts popular vote for world government through the U.N. was of the I'm-agin-sin-and-war variety. In fact, the strongest opposition came, not from die-hard isolationists, but from many sincere, world-minded persons. Such persons tend to say Yes to world government as an ideal, but don't believe in it as a practical or attainable reality. They say Yes to the basic arguments which point to the need for enforceable world law, but don't see exactly how it is to be achieved.

Isn't the campaign for world government, they ask, actually harmful to world peace in that it diverts people's attention from the needs of the United Nations? Shouldn't we first try to make a success of the U.N.—which at least has the advantage of being in existence even if it isn't too much of a going concern—rather than by-pass it or scrap it in an idealistic but dangerous short cut to some political utopia? In short, if the U.N. doesn't work, what right have we to expect that anything more ambitious will?

What are the specific steps, they want to know, leading to world government? Since a government could not be established except through the cooperation and consent of the world's statesmen, who obviously cannot now agree on matters of lesser consequence, what reason is there to believe that they will agree on nothing less than the abrogation or destruction of that great untouchable, National Sovereignty? Wouldn't those statesmen be called upon, in effect, to repudiate their own authority and their own careers? And if, by some cosmic miracle, you could get them to agree, wouldn't that very act of agreement make world government unnecessary? In short, you can't get world government without agreement; and if you could get agreement, why would you need world government? Wouldn't world government, then, be as superfluous as a referee in an empty ring after a fight has been called off?

Finally, what about Russia?

In asking these questions before they would support the world-federation resolution, the people of Connecticut were actually reflecting, it seems to me, the general popular attitude about world government everywhere. For while most people accepted the need for world law, their doubts followed the general lines of the questions listed above.

Let's begin with the argument that world federalists seek either to by-pass or scrap the U.N. This argument has its source, I suppose, in some of the early doubts over the effectiveness of the Charter. When the tale of two cities, as written at San Francisco and Hiroshima, clearly revealed the inability of the U.N. to deal with a revolutionary new situation brought about by an absolute weapon, some federalists called for the immediate scrapping of the United Nations and for a full government to take its place.

But most federalists were then, and still are, opposed to any and all efforts to undermine the U.N., to scrap it, to by-pass it. They believe, and rightly so, that a really functioning U.N. represents our best chance for peace.

I can say sincerely that nowhere have I found any deeper or more real concern for the United Nations than among believers in world federation. Their program is to save the U.N., to give it blood and bones, to give it something to work with, to make it in fact a world organization capable of keeping the peace. But this cannot be done through dodge, drift, or delay. It can be done only if there is a supreme popular effort to invest it with appropriate authority.

What is the threat to the U.N.? Is it the demands of the federalists for giving it the required strength? Or is it the fact that it has become—even if it was never intended so to become—an adjunct to the foreign policies of the great nations instead of a central agency with power to avoid the inevitable collisions of those foreign policies?

There is a curious atmosphere of unreality in which public campaigns are being conducted in America and elsewhere to promote popular faith and support in the U.N. If a serious crime wave were suddenly to sweep down upon an American community—a wave of murder, arson, theft, and kidnaping—and it became instantly clear that the town constable and his three assistants were inadequate to meet the threat, it is doubtful that posters would be distributed about the importance of maintaining a constabulary. It is doubtful, further, that resolutions of confidence in the constable would be considered sufficient. Faced with a crime wave, the citizens would build up the constabulary into a police force large enough and strong enough to do the job, pronto.

No one can quarrel with the effort to make the American people conscious of the basic importance of the U.N. But the cause of the U.N. is not served through advertising acceptance alone. This can only result in creating disillusion and severe reaction against the very concept of world organization as it becomes increasingly obvious that the U.N., like the local constabulary, is unequal to the job of keeping the peace.

If the U.N. is to become in fact what the preamble of the charter says it is to be; namely, a world agency charged with the responsibility for averting war, then the first order of business will be to put an end to the double standard governing the relations of the nations to the U.N. Under this double standard the large nations proclaim that their first line of defense is the United Nations, but put about four hundred dollars into armaments for every dollar they put into the U.N. Under this double standard we condemned the use of the veto, but soft-pedaled the fact that we ourselves proposed the veto at San Francisco, or that in the summer of 1948 the State Department opposed a congressional resolution calling for a strengthening of the U.N.

Why, then, it may be asked, didn't the United States announce publicly and flatly that it regarded the U.N. as secondary in its foreign policy, that it did not want to see the U.N. become a lawmaking and law-enforcement agency on a world scale? The answer is that the resultant public outcry would have had an earthquake effect in Washington. Hence the double standard—proclamations in favor of collective security but an actual policy of unilateralism and coalition-building inside the U.N.

The decisive factor, of course, is public opinion. The President will have to be convinced that the American people are not frightened by the idea of modifying their sovereignty in favor of a higher security than is obtainable through national military supremacy alone.

American federalists are attempting to convince the American people of the need for a U.N. with jurisdiction and powers confined to matters affecting the common security. They believe that control of armaments must not be limited to atomic weapons but must include all weapons adapted to mass destruction. They believe that armament control must proceed out of a definite body of law, executed by an enforcement agency with clearly defined powers.

Such an enforcement agency would necessarily represent preponderant force over the individual nations; only under those conditions should the United States feel secure in relinquishing its own military program. In order to be effective in terms of averting crises instead of coping with crises, the strengthened U.N. should have authority over individuals—again limited to those matters affecting the common security.

The principle here is the same as laid down at Nuremberg; what the federalists propose is that acts leading to war be made the basis for determination of individual guilt—before rather than after the damage is done.

It will be observed that the powers of law here are fairly well restricted to the security area. The broader aspects of world citizenship represent the long-range objectives. Nothing could be more harmful to the chances for world federation than to attempt to impose upon it at the start all the attributes of a common citizenship. Once the peace is secured, there will be a magnificent opportunity—made attainable by the revolution in communication and transportation—for the peoples of the world to release their energies in the building of a world community. But such a community cannot be legislated into being overnight; what the federalists seek to do is to lay the foundation for it through a world-security organization represented by a federation of the United Nations.

This brings us to the next question: How do we get it?

In 1947, the then Foreign Secretary Bevin announced that His Majesty's Government was ready to sit down with representatives of other governments to explore the requirements of a world organization with effective powers. The new French Constitution contains a specific provision authorizing France to become part of a world government. Pandit Nehru, during his visit to the United States, spoke for the need of world government. General Carlos P. Romulo, former President of the General Session of the U.N. Assembly, has been perhaps the most eloquent orator of all on the need and possibilities of world government. At San Francisco, China actually proposed world government, but the United States and Russia, in their role as leaders, were too intent upon establishing the U.N. as subordinate to their own sovereignties to permit even serious consideration of the Chinese proposal.

All these points bear considerable emphasis. They help to answer the question: What about the rest of the world? They indicate that the world-government movement is something more than an "American fad." They make it clear that it is absurd to say that *all* the world's statesmen are concerned only with protection of their own national sovereignties. Indeed, it is possible to assert that America and Russia are actually holding back the natural political evolution of the nations into a higher unit.

The proposal for giving the U.N. the powers of world law can only come, if it is to have any real chance for acceptance, from the United States or Russia. Obviously no move to revise the U.N. could even be attempted without the active leadership of either or both of the two great nations. Proposals for world law have already been made inside and outside the U.N. assembly by delegates of other nations.

Some of the main reasons for America's opposition to a strong U.N. we have already discussed; in another chapter we shall speculate on some of the Russian reasons. But whatever Russia's reasons may actually be, one thing seems certain: the proposal for world government will not come from Moscow—which, indeed, has already characterized world government as an imperialist plot. That leaves the United States as the only possible effective proposer for U.N. revision—in fact, it leaves the United States as the one nation to which the peoples of the world are looking, and have been looking since the end of the war, for vital leadership in building world law.

Let us assume that the President and the Congress are convinced not only that they have the popular support for American initiative in revising the U.N. but that public opinion actually demands such initiative. What, then, specifically, do we do? Our first job, obviously, is to attempt to establish the atmosphere in which our proposals can be seriously considered, and to leave no doubt of our sincerity in attempting to create a real system of collective security through the U.N.

Article 108 of the Charter provides the principal means for U.N. revision. Under Article 108 a review conference for amending the structure and functions of the U.N. can be called whenever two-thirds of the member nations decide to do so. Such a call is not subject to the veto. We should make clear in proposing the calling of the conference that our aim is solely to examine whatever weaknesses may have developed in the operation of the Charter, and to remedy those weaknesses in keeping with the spirit of the preamble.

The United States should point out that the fundamental danger of the U.N. as presently constituted is not only that it is too weak to cope with an actual crisis but that this very weakness tends to create crises. For the inability of the U.N. to guarantee security has made it necessary for the larger nations to take security measures of their own which frequently overlap or are in direct conflict with each other. Since most of the world outside the United States and the Soviet Union is a power vacuum, and since almost every spot in the world is now of strategic military significance, the struggle for security has meant an inevitable competition between America and the Soviets for predominant influence inside that vacuum. Thus security means expansion, and expansion means conflict.

The most constructive first step for the review conference would be to undertake a security inventory of the nations. Just as an economic inventory of the European nations prepared the ground for the Marshall Plan, so a security inventory would assemble the facts on which a strengthened U.N. could be built. Let each nation state under what circumstances or conditions it would feel secure, first in reducing its armaments, then in disarming. Let the nations define the basis of their geographical security. Then let them state what guarantees of security each would require from the U.N. before giving up their unilateral security programs.

It is not unreasonable to suppose that such an inventory would reveal that most nations, including the United States, would be willing to undertake armament reduction so long as there were enforceable guarantees against secret violations by other nations. With respect to atomic weapons and other weapons adapted to mass destruction, for example, the United States would logically restate and re-emphasize the provisions of the Baruch Plan calling for a comprehensive system of inspection and control. This time, however, we would not be advocating, as we did under the Baruch Plan, the establishment of a separate agency that actually had greater powers than the U.N. itself—an agency to control weapons but not an agency to control war.

It is to be hoped that this time we would make clear that the problem of inspection and control is not to be separated from the problem of world law; that possible violations can be dealt with only against a definite background of statutory law, with due process, and with a law-enforcement agency equal to the job. Anything short of that could not possibly guarantee that the mechanism of inspection and control was being fairly administered, and was not the means by which one nation would seek to prevent another from making full use of the industrial application of atomic energy.

These would most likely be some of the questions considered at a review conference, which would then be faced with the problem of recommending the machinery for implementation. If decisions of the U.N. in those matters clearly related to the common security are to be exempt from the veto, precisely what is to be the machinery for compulsory jurisdiction? And if compulsory jurisdiction is to be effective, what would be needed in the way of preponderant force to back it up? Of what would such preponderant force consist? And what would the basis of representation be in the revised Assembly? One nation, one vote? Or weighted representation according to population, industrial capacity, and other relevant factors? And if the U.N. is to have authority over the individual in certain matters, what rights will the individual have in return?

These problems, it will be observed, go to the heart of the making of government. No more complicated and delicate problems have ever faced any group of constitution-makers in the past. But the difficulty is dwarfed by the necessity; and the important thing is that at least and at last we address ourselves to those problems. At the same time we need not intimidate ourselves by the size and scope of the job. For the conference will not be venturing into entirely uncharted territory. Responsible studies pertaining to representation, for example, have already been undertaken by such well qualified international-law experts as Grenville Clark. On a more ambitious level, there is the draft of a world constitution worked out by a group of distinguished political scientists brought together by Robert M. Hutchins, when he was chancellor of the University of Chicago.

In any event, the most serious difficulty of all is not represented by a definition of compulsory jurisdiction, or by the creation of a preponderant force, or by the relationship of the U.N. to the individual. All these can be worked out—assuming there is general agreement on their necessity. The most serious difficulty, perhaps, has to do with misconceptions on the nature of sovereignty in the modern world.

*   *   *

The right and ability of a nation or a community or an individual to make its own decisions is sovereignty in its purest and finest form.

The principal threat to sovereignty arises not from those who are working for effective world organization. The principal threat arises from the absence of effective world organization. Because of this absence, it was possible for Japan to make the decision that brought the United States into World War II. Our sovereign right to get into war or stay out of it was nullified by that action. Because of the absence of effective world organization, it was possible for the Soviet world to make the decision that caused America to suffer more than 100,000 casualties in Korea. And it is possible today for most of the essential rights that make up the bundle of national sovereignty to be frittered away or seized as the result of external decisions.

How much a nation decides to tax its citizens is a sovereign right. But the decisions made in the Kremlin have determined what American taxes are to be; our lawmakers have not acted but reacted. The decisions made in the Kremlin have been primarily responsible for inflationary pressures arising from the vast sums being spent on non-consumer goods. The nation's business and, indeed, the nation's future, are no longer ours alone to develop or determine.

The question before the world's peoples, therefore, is not whether sovereignty should be surrendered to a world organization, but rather what can be done to restore the essential sovereignties that have already been destroyed. A nation should have the right to shape its own institutions and culture, maintain its own values, have jurisdiction over its own people—so long as it does not thereby interfere with the similar rights of other nations.

These rights or sovereignties can be restored only through the creation of an instrument strong enough to prevent sovereignty-destroying acts by nations bent on aggression or penetration. This, then, is the primary purpose of world federation. By enjoying enforceable powers in those matters clearly related to a common security, by creating the conditions necessary for self-determination of nations, and by enabling the nations to release for purposes of peaceful development the vast energies now going into war preparations, world federation can make the world safe for meaningful sovereignty.

But before this can be done, the old and dangerous misconceptions of sovereignty will have to be recognized for what they are.

At the heart of sovereignty throughout history there has been security based on the advantage of geography or military might. For sovereignty has been inseparable from power. But by the end of World War I, the validity of national sovereignty had sharply changed. The development of air power alone, apart from all other aspects of the world's inexorable trend toward close interrelationship, outdated traditional concepts of independence among nations. Yet we preferred to believe that there was no connection between a world being locked into a single piece and its over-all organization. Unfortunately, our unreadiness or unwillingness to see this connection did not cause the connection to disappear.

So much did this connection exist that it led to World War II. Despite six years of that new war, despite jet planes and rockets, despite the abrupt telescoping of a thousand years of human history in the release of atomic energy, despite the loss of millions of lives, we still act as though sovereignty can function as it did a hundred years ago.

Can it be that we do not realize that in an age of atomic fission and hydrogen bombs the foundations of the old sovereignties have been shattered? That no longer is security to be found in armies and navies, however large and mighty? That in an Atomic Age all nations are now directly accessible to each other—for better or worse? That in the erasure of man-made barriers and boundaries all peoples of the world stand virtually unarmed in the presence of one another? That they are at the mercy of one another, and shall have to devise a common security or suffer a common cataclysm? That the only really effective influence between peoples is such influence as they are able to exert morally, politically, and ideologically upon each other?

All these questions have been in the making for centuries, but the triumph over the invisible and mighty atom has given them an exactness and an immediacy about which there can be no mistake.

The need for world federation was clear long before August 5, 1945, but Hiroshima and Nagasaki raised that need to such dimensions that it can no longer be ignored. And in the glare brighter than sunlight produced by the assault of the atom, we have all the light we need with which to examine the new world that has come into being with such clicking abruptness.

Thus examined, the old sovereignties are seen for what they are—vestigial obstructions in the circulatory system of the world.

Much of the attachment of old concepts of sovereignty, as well as the reluctance to face squarely its limitations in the modern world, grows out of apprehension concerning the control a world authority might have over the internal affairs of the individual state. There is the fear, for example, that the individual constitutions would be subject to central control. There is the fear that institutions built up over centuries would exist only at the pleasure and discretion of a superstate.

Natural and understandable though these concerns may be, they have their source in confusion over a distinction that should be made between world *sovereignty* and state *jurisdiction*.

A common world sovereignty would mean that no state could act unilaterally in its foreign affairs. It would mean that no state could have the instruments of power to aggress against other states. It would mean that no state could withdraw from the central authority as a method of achieving its aims. But it would *not* mean that the individual state would lose its *jurisdiction* over its internal affairs. It would *not* mean the arbitrary establishment of a uniform ideology all over the world. It would *not* mean the forcible imposition of non-democratic systems on democratic states, any more than it would mean the forcible imposition of democratic systems on non-democratic states.

This, then, is the essence of federation. Its powers are clearly defined, its authority clearly limited. It has compulsory jurisdiction only in those matters concerned with the common safety. It is in the exercise of this compulsory jurisdiction that it is able to underwrite the essential sovereignties of the states. Lincoln put it succinctly when he said that "general government shall do all those things which pertain to it, and all the local governments shall do precisely as they please in respect to those matters which exclusively concern them."

But all this is theoretical—as is everything else concerned with world federation—until we face up squarely to the question which begins the next chapter.

"*The leaders of the nations . . . are obliged to reach agreements that will insure to the world a peace for which they, in honor, may assume responsibility and all peoples may find bearable, even though these agreements mean the curtailing to some degree of their several sovereign rights.*"

—POPE PIUS XII

* * *

"*What hope can there be for the future of the world unless there is some form of world government which can make its effort to prevent a renewal of the awful struggle through which we have just passed?*"

—WINSTON CHURCHILL

* * *

"*So far, war has been the only force that can discipline a whole community, and until an equal discipline is organized, I believe that war must have its way.*"

—WILLIAM JAMES

* * *

"*We live in an age of crisis. One crisis follows another; and, even when there is some kind of peace, it is a troubled peace, with fear of war and preparation for war. Tortured humanity hungers for real peace, but some evil fate pursues it and pushes it further and further away from what it desires most.*"

—JAWAHARLAL NEHRU

* * *

"*Nobody can say that government will work. All one can guess is that it must be given an honest try, otherwise our science will have won the day, and the people can retire from the field, to lie down with the dinosaur and the heath hen—who didn't belong here either, apparently.*"

—E. B. WHITE

CHAPTER XXV

WHAT ABOUT RUSSIA?

What about Russia?

By what political hocus-pocus do world federalists propose to eliminate the vast and terrifying differences—differences of ideology, religion, philosophy—now separating America and the Soviet, to say nothing of the rest of the world? Isn't the capitalist-Communist struggle too basic to expect both systems to co-exist within a common government? By its own definition, world government means all nations. If Russia doesn't accept, what then? These questions highlight an important fallacy about Russia and about world federation.

The purpose of world government is *not* to bring Russia and America together; the purpose of world government is to keep them *apart*. It is precisely because both large power systems are coming together—moving toward a catastrophic collision—that some means must be found to head it off. In the absence of a superior force, each seeks the security that can be obtained only at the expense of what the other regards as its own security. And the job of a U.N. with powers of government will be to insert itself between the two, to keep the differences that separate the two from becoming combustible.

World government, in theory or practice, is no steam roller designed to flatten out the differences, however great, that for better or worse are the lot of the human race. It doesn't seek to impose a stifling uniformity but to make the world safe for diversity. But no part of that diversity must be greater than the whole.

The gap—ideological, philosophical, economical, historical—between America and Russia is too profound today to expect that any conceivable formula could be worked out for a unified social system immediately acceptable to both. A world organization which had this as its objective would succeed only in precipitating a civil war. But an organization strong enough to eliminate the competition for security between the two, that could assure both America and Russia a free hand in the development of their internal economies, would provide the best possible proving grounds for the peaceful competition between democracy and Communism.

Deprived of the economic hypodermic of war or armaments races or military-aid programs, American economy will have to prove itself capable—as I am confident that it can—of avoiding the bust that follows the boom; it will have to prove there is nothing inconsistent between a comprehensive program of social welfare and the preservation and, indeed, enlargement of political and economic liberties. Similarly, Russian Communism, deprived of the excuse that a hostile outer world is forcing it to pour most of its industrial, political, and emotional energies into war preparation, will have to prove its ability to raise the living standards of its people.

No one knows whether in a world with the war factor removed, and with something better than quicksand for a foundation, the vast ideological gap between America and Russia may ultimately be narrowed. Whether or not the gap eventually disappears is a matter of speculation. What is of central importance in the interim is that a basis for enforceable peace be defined and established; and if there is a better way of doing it than through a world agency stronger than either nation it has yet to be advanced.

All these considerations should figure largely in the effort to get Russia to go along with us in revising the U.N. Our aim should be to make it as difficult as possible for Russia to refuse, although some circles advocating U.N. revision seem primarily interested in making only those proposals which they are certain Russia couldn't possibly accept.

It has become a cliché to say that Russia respects only strength. The fact that it is a cliché, however, does not mean that the statement is not essentially true. Yet it is important to have a clear idea of what strength is. Strength in this case is not confined to actual or potential military strength. Russia respects and is impressed just as much by political strength. Those who advise against the effort to strengthen the U.N. use as a principal argument their fear that such an effort will drive the Russians out of the organization. There is no assurance, of course, that such may not be the case. Yet the only real chance we have of keeping Russia inside the U.N., it seems to me, is precisely in the direction of a vastly strengthened world body.

It seems clear that Russian policy has tried to straddle two apparently contradictory objectives: One objective is to block every attempt of the rest of the world to come together under a set of guiding principles which carry real weight with the preponderance of the world's peoples. Hence Russia's delaying tactics inside the U.N., its frequent use of the veto and abstentions, its piece-by-piece campaign to acquire or control large populations.

The second objective is to keep itself from being isolated from the world community.

The apparent contradiction is resolved, of course, in the matter of timing. There is Russian concern about being isolated only during the period when the preponderance of the world's peoples is being courted or conquered. But if the preponderance is both determined and strong enough to resist Communist influence and acquisition, then the Soviet, if recent history is a guide, may be forced to shift gears. It may be forced, as in the case of Korea, to continue its participation in a world body because non-participation in a functioning organization having the power of world law would represent a major political defeat.

In any case, in initiating a call for a revision conference under Articles 108 and 109, in calling for a security inventory, in drafting a basis for world law under the revised Charter, and in taking the moral and psychological offensive on a world scale, we can be sure we are putting the pressure on Russia where she is most vulnerable.

The one thing the Soviet leaders dread is the danger that she will be cut off from the mass of the world's peoples; every important Soviet move since the end of World War II has been accompanied by the most painstaking effort at justification before the bar of world public opinion.

This is understandable enough, for the Soviet leaders know, even if we do not, that the fate of both Russia and the United States may very well be decided by the 1,500,000,000 people outside the two nations. And any really sincere and constructive attempt by America—clearly recognized as such by the world's peoples —to bring some measure of sanity and moral leadership to the world at large would shift to Russia the burden of demonstrating her own good faith. After all, we would not be asking her to give up anything or to do anything we aren't ready to give up or do ourselves.

We would be making it clear that what we propose is not the legalizing procedure for a coalition but the genuine basis for mutual security.

If the Soviet's actions since the end of the war have been motivated primarily by fear, and if, as has often been suggested, she has been "reacting" rather than acting, then nothing could be better calculated to allay those fears than a world organization which alone could guarantee her requisite physical security.

But if Russia's actions have been motivated primarily by ambition, then only a world organization possessing an organized preponderance backed by the moral weight of justice and duly constituted law, could provide adequate means of containing such ambition.

In either case—whether Russia is motivated by fear or ambition—by proposing world law, we make the only move which adequately covers both contingencies.

Let us suppose, however, that despite the sincerity of our approach and the reasonableness of our proposals, Russia decides to stay out. What do we do then?

I believe it is our responsibility to go ahead with as many others as are willing to join with us in investing the U.N. with powers of government. We would still work in good faith for Russian adherence, for the goal is a government of the whole. In so doing, we would have the day-to-day opportunity of demonstrating the advantages of participation in the world body. We would know, too, that it would be difficult for any nation or bloc of nations to remain indefinitely outside an otherwise integrated world community possessing both physical strength and a firm moral sanction of the popular will.

Yet speculation as to what Russia will do is futile. The only way to find out is to put the question. And right now the big job is to get the United States to do the asking. Not until we put the question will we get, or be entitled to, an answer.

Russia has been operating on three separate though related levels.

The first level is the nationalist one. Her objectives on this level are historical rather than purely ideological, going back to the nationalist aspirations of the czars: control of the Baltic and the Black seas, a shock absorber or military cushion running through Central Europe; a senior partnership with China. The second level is that of the Comintern and the Cominform, involving world revolution and infiltration. The third level is that of opportunism and exploitation, waiting for, and accelerating and reaping the benefits of, depression in the West, or making use of native populations, as in Berlin or Korea, to commit forces of her opponents without committing any of her own.

It seems apparent that Russian strategy against the United States is to cut her off from the non-white peoples of the world, or the preponderance of mankind. She recognizes that no side could win either the war or the peace unless it is able to attract or control most of the world's two billion people.

Economically, this strategy is designed to weaken America by detaching her from vital sources of raw materials.

Militarily, it is designed to pit America against populous nations on which the atomic bomb would not be decisive—nations that are predominantly agricultural rather than industrial, and against which all the vaunted American technology would be of little avail without armed man power that would have to be measured in tens of millions.

Ideologically, it is designed to identify America with feudalism and against long-overdue land reform and social reform. The purpose here is to discredit democracy as a doctrine that can advance and champion rights and aspirations of underprivileged peoples.

The reasons behind Russian strategy are related to the fact that the world has become a single geographic unit and is fast becoming a single economic unit. But economics cannot be separated from politics. And Russia is unable to deny the pulling power of democracy wherever it has actually made itself felt. Hence she has lost no time in appropriating the word "democracy" for her own use, even as she concocted opprobrious terms to convince the world that America represented, not democracy, but "reactionary imperialism"—a combination of words that hold a specially bitter meaning for the world's colonial peoples in general and the people of Southeast Asia and the Near East in particular.

So far as the United Nations is concerned, Russian policy is to keep it as weak as possible—just short of killing it, for which she is anxious to avoid responsibility.

In line with this policy, Russia has served notice that she would resist all efforts to limit her sovereignty. This was to be expected, for only a strong United Nations could cope with Russia's tri-level strategical approach to a dominant position in the world. It is possible, too, that Russia realizes that it would be difficult for her to remain outside a truly integrated world community. Hence, she has preferred to stay inside a weak U.N., using secession as a threat to block efforts at revision. She is anxious to avoid being confronted with the unhappy choice of becoming part of an organization having the powers to block her expansion, or pulling out of the U.N. and cutting herself off from the rest of the world—thus jeopardizing the three levels of her strategy.

* * *

We have neglected thus far to consider what is offered as a fairly simple way of disposing of the Russian problem—usually advanced by those who are impatient with complicated problems. For example, a Congressman, testifying before the Senate Committee on Foreign Relations, declared that we should "take our power spokesmen and tell them to stick their chins under those of Stalin, Molotov, and Vishinsky. We should tell them to shove their stomachs right up against these gentlemen, physically, and tell them either to disarm or we'll proceed."

And how would we proceed? By dropping the atomic bomb, of course, said this particular Congressman. The argument is not complicated. Since a showdown is inevitable, sooner or later, it might be wise to have it sooner rather than later.

What we are witnessing in all this is the collapse of intelligence and conscience—a collapse of such mountainous dimensions as to blot out the sight of reality. Does anyone think for a moment that moral values can be abruptly annihilated without injury to the annihilator? Does anyone dare dream that democracy as we have known it could survive the deliberate murder of millions of human beings—even though carried out under the pretext that we were certain we would be hit later if we did not act now?

But the grossest aberration of all is one which assumes the success of such a monstrous venture. After we atom-bomb Moscow and Leningrad and Stalingrad and the other principal cities—what shall we do then? Even assuming we destroy Russia's capacity to retaliate with atomic weapons of her own, what shall we do about a Red Army that will almost automatically pour into Europe? Do we atom-bomb all Europe, killing perhaps hundreds of non-Russians for every Russian? And what do we do about those countries which have large internal Communist problems? Do we atom-bomb them too? What about France? And China? And India, Iran, Egypt, Africa? And those countries of South America with strong Communist parties?

Once we start acting out of atomic jitters, does anyone suppose that we can stop short of attempted domination of the world— or whatever portion of the world that will not be reduced to radioactive rubble? And what will such domination mean if it will be operated under the type of insanity that achieved it?

Fortunately, this trigger-happy Congressman represents a viewpoint with which the overwhelming majority of Americans have no sympathy. They realize that a preventive war against Russia is no answer. It would inevitably mean the destruction of everything America was meant to stand for; perhaps the destruction of America itself.

This does not mean that America must stand by idly while Russia attempts to pick off the intermediate nations, one by one. Moreover, it would be foolish to suppose that the same pressures which exist here for a preventive war do not exist elsewhere, and for the same reason. Russia, too, has its own belligerent mental dwarfs who, like the Congressman referred to a moment ago, believed in the stomach-to-stomach, chin-to-chin, toe-to-toe approach to its foreign policy. Russia has its own volatile blunderers who indiscriminately label any attempt to adjust differences as dangerous appeasement. Russia, too, is in the grip of incendiary atomic jitters.

To repeat: the primary disease from which the world is suffering is competitive and combustible nationalisms—the conflicting ideologies accelerating and intensifying the basic struggle. Each nation is unwilling to create or maintain an authority with compulsory jurisdiction and adequate power. Each nation wants to be left to its own devices to assure or insure its security.

One nation's security can be another nation's insecurity.

*   *   *

To return to our opening question—"What about Russia?"—it might be helpful to consider a related question: Would the basic problem in the world be changed if the earth opened up tomorrow and swallowed Soviet Russia, and Communist parties everywhere were dissolved? Would the threat of war or the causes of war disappear as well? If so, how are we to explain the fact that Europe has been chewed up by war continuously since there was a Europe to fight over—for centuries before anyone ever heard of Lenin or Stalin? How are we to account for the innumerable wars between England and France at such cost to both? How are we to account for World War I—or even World War II, for that matter? How are we to account for the long processions of revolutions, whatever the particular banner? How can we be certain that the same causes might not result in a Russia-less World War III?

The overnight disappearance or destruction of Russia would not change the fact that more than a billion of the world's peoples are shopping for a revolution. All across Asia, the Near East, and Africa, there is a vast upheaval. The sources of discontent are as varied as the peoples themselves who are involved. Communism did not create the conditions in the East that make for violent change; Communism has sought to exploit those conditions and turn them to Russia's advantage. The resentment against the West produced by 150 years of colonial imperialism; the bitterness created by the white versus color issues; the sharpened political consciousness caused by hunger, sickness, homelessness; the grievances over local and political abuses—all these and more would not vanish if the heartland of world Communism should cease to be a factor in world politics.

The Soviet has not hesitated to create false issues when it has served her purpose to do so; but she has found it far more convenient and effective to seize upon real issues where they exist and turn them to her advantage. Moreover, as long as revolutionary situations exist anywhere in the world, Russia will do everything possible to keep them from becoming independent and hence competitive forces. In the Far East especially is this true. Geographically, the Soviet's greatest danger is represented by her vast and sparsely populated Asian territory bordering on overpopulated states. All around her in Asia the pressure of peoples is building up. Meanwhile the arable land of these peoples continues to shrink. Russia fears that independent revolutions in Asia would inevitably move in the direction of open space, converting her far-flung Asian empire into giant spillways for overflowing populations. Along with this goes the acute threat of political penetration. Hence the determination to control Asia at any cost.

Yet, even if we were to discount the internal danger to Russia from independent revolutions in the East, there is another reason why the Soviet wants control of Asia. Such control would give Russia the majority of the world's people. And the ideological pulling power on the minority outside would be prodigious—whatever the military programs or coalitions of the minority bloc.

In any event, the basic situation in Asia would continue to exist and be a source of critical world unrest whether or not Soviet strategy sought to appropriate it for her own purposes.

No; Russian unilateralism today is not the disease; it is a product of the disease. Not *the* problem, but *part* of the problem. That problem is the centuries-old problem of competitive national sovereignties, as Mr. Emery Reves demonstrated so cogently in *The Anatomy of Peace.* That problem involves the race for security, each nation deciding for itself what is necessary for its own security, with the result that two or more nations would mark out the same areas as their exclusive security zones. That problem involves the setting up of military bases and the conversion of small nations into buffer states, with spheres of influence extending everywhere. That problem involves jockeying for position and power, with military alliances and blocs of states arrayed against each other. That problem involves reliance upon national military establishments, leading inevitably to an armaments race, and, equally inevitably, to the use of those armaments.

Either world problems will be settled through *real* world organization, meaning world law, or they will be settled by world war.

World law is not the end but the means. It is no distant goal, but a present and indispensable one. It is not merely a hope, but the *only* hope, the only chance. To whatever extent we delay, to whatever extent we move in other directions, by that much do we plan for chaos.

CHAPTER XXVI

TWO GUESSES ABOUT TOMORROW

What follows is pure guesswork. It is an attempt to guess about the next generation in human history.

Two sets of guesses are presented. The first is painfully pessimistic; the second is reasonably hopeful, even heartening.

The reason for two separate and conflicting sets of guesses is that the human community is at one of those rare pivotal points in history. A wrong turning could mean that nothing on the earth will become cheaper than human life, for nothing will be more easily expended or dispensed with. But a proper turning now could mark the beginning of a vast upward surge in human history, infusing life with enriched purpose and meaning. There is a precarious balance between terror and hope, both of which have their legions and their momentum.

The future historian or anthropologist, then, might be writing from one of two vantage points. He could be looking out at the scattered radioactive remnants of twentieth century civilization as he contemplates his notes for a book that might be called *The Repudiation of Man.* Or he could be surveying an age of surmounted crisis, as he gathers together his notes for a book on *The Age of Valor.*

Hence the following guesswork in the next thirty-seven pages—in the form of two separate and hypothetical accounts that the future historian might write about our time. We begin with excerpts from a post-World War III volume titled:—

The Repudiation of Man

Over everyone and everything today there is the giant shadow of a single word: "Why?" You see it in the taut and anxious faces of people, young and old; it jumps out at you from the spilled stones of tumbled towers and from the dismembered parts of once-great bridges. Why did it happen? Why is it that suddenly there should be so little where there was once so much? Why did man sanction these massive hammer blows against his own society and indeed against the conditions of his own existence?

People ask "why," but no one seriously expects an answer. And even if a full answer were found, it is doubtful that it could be put to any useful purpose. In this case, knowledge of error will not necessarily make for progress.

Here we come to what is perhaps the most significant fact about the effect of the atomic war on man in the post-atomic age. The fact is that the will to rebuild in man has been largely destroyed. No other damage he has suffered can compare with this. The decimation of life itself, the empty shells of the cities, the parching and the clotting of the land—all these are virtually unimportant alongside the crumbling of the will to create and restore. After endless years saturated with mass violence and the recurring assaults on his communities, man has lost the instinct or the desire to clear away the wreckage on which to reconstruct the city as the traditional unit for group living.

In this vital sense has man changed. Much had been written in the past about the inviolability of human nature. It was said and widely believed that the basic drives and instincts of man were beyond alteration. Not enough, however, was said about the conditions or circumstances which could affect and even alter man. It is strange that with all man's knowledge about other species and about nature in general he should have been so unperceptive about change in himself. He compiled bulky volumes about the mutability of life in other species. Then he reinforced these observations by producing new strains, thus becoming a biological interventionist. He was able, in short, to push back the frontiers of information and theory about changeability in life in all forms except one: man.

For he regarded himself as a constant in the universal equation—nature's favorite son.

The years of collapse, however, have provided a grim corrective to some of the old theories. The nature of man can change. The conditions surrounding human life determine such change. The present conditions not only have robbed man of the urge to rebuild, but, indeed, have separated him from the desire for progress. What for many centuries was a forward momentum in human development has now run down like the spring of a giant clock.

Man today knows that progress is not the law of life. The general feeling is comparable perhaps with that known in the eighth century before Christ, so clearly described by Hesiod in the *Works and Days:* "Would that I did not live in this time; would that I had died before, or were born much later." The passing of time, as Hesiod observed it, had brought, not growth, but decay. His was an aged and tired world, as is our own today.

The reason that man in the post-atomic-war world has separated himself from the idea of progress is easily comprehended. Progress—which is to say the advancing development of humanity—became too complicated and difficult for mere human beings to administer. Through progress man not only conquered the threats of a hostile natural environment but went beyond that to the virtual conquest of self. The means to create a more abundant life were perverted and directed against the human species. When progress is measured by the construction of rockets and space suits that would enable man to project himself like a cannon shot off the earth for the conquest of the moon—in order to use the moon as a launching platform for rocket attacks on himself—then progress becomes a monstrous liability.

Progress, however, is only another word for civilization. Can man live without civilization? The answer, of course, is Yes. Man preceded civilization and is now surviving it. Indeed, such survival is possible precisely because he has detached himself physically and intellectually from the complex of civilization.

Life today is primitive, but it is less precarious than it was under a nominally civilized society. True, the family groups that constitute the basic units frequently have to struggle against each other to sustain themselves. The safety factor for each individual, however, is much greater than it was before the atomic war, when every person enjoyed a reasonable amount of protection against attack from a predatory individual neighborhood but had no protection at all against annihilating attack from an all-powerful nation.

If the rational process rather than the nation had been sovereign in the world of man, science might have been able to create a truly abundant life for the human community. But advancing science, by its very nature, required an ordered world. Out of the same cyclotron that produced isotopes for the war against cancer came the fissionable materials for the war against life. The test tube that produced the antibodies for building up immunity against disease for thousands of people became the spawning ground for germs that were invincible in taking the lives of millions. The long-range plane that could speed the delivery of a miraculous new drug across continents could also speed the delivery of explosives for mass extermination.

What made civilization especially precarious, however, was that the people were grouped together under different and conflicting systems—political, religious, economic. These differences by themselves were not unhealthy. Under certain conditions they might have promoted self-appraisal and fertilized thought. Diversity within unity could have given vitality to the human family as long as fixed limits could be set to the competitive and explosive aspects of the differences. But here again it required wisdom of a very high order to create and maintain a higher unity. It required application both of the scientific method and of group conscience. But the scientific method went into technology—not into politics, human relations, and the operational arts of a complex civilization. And a group conscience never materialized—perhaps for want of stature in leadership that could mold it and release it, perhaps because men never learned to comprehend that they were interrelated parts of a single organism—the human organism.

Thus it was that civilization became inimical to man. It became contrary to his nature, or at least to that aspect of his nature which required some margin for error. When the war came, it furnished proof that man could survive only by purging himself of his civilization. All the attributes of that civilization—the advanced mechanization and industrialization, the turbines and the dynamos, the high-speed methods of mass communication and transportation, the cyclotrons and the synchrotons and the nuclear reactors, the laboratories and the research centers—all these were lifted from the human burden. For these were part of the man-made environment that turned out to be far more of a threat to man than anything nature could throw his way. And in the end man destroyed the challenge before the challenge destroyed him.

It may be thought that the abandonment of civilization is a small price to pay for human survival. If the supreme purpose of human existence is sheer survival, then that is true, and there need be no concern that man will vanish. However far the species may retreat or retrogress, it is likely that human life will be mustered in some form or other—even if only as Neanderthal Man—lest there be some shrinkage in nature's inventory.

But if the end of human existence is a purposeful life, creating ever higher levels of awareness and a fulfillment of the human potential, then survival by itself is little more than conscious vegetation. Those taut and anxious faces I mentioned earlier—faces asking questions to which there can be no useful answer—belong to minds and bodies that were deprived of a vital inner spark. The luminous sense of human dignity and purpose that inspired the poets; the nobility that animated great lives and great ideas; the depth of man's faculties that enabled him to extract secrets from the cosmos and to encompass the mysterious and wonderful experiences of others—all these magic qualities have been dimmed and deeply recessed. Survival on such a lowered threshold offers a sparse and grim consolation for the collective conceit.

It is possible, of course, that civilization and all its components could have been made to serve the ends of man. It is possible that wisdom and conscience might have been mobilized on a world scale to free the human community of world anarchy. Indeed, there is evidence that men everywhere hungered for the great ideas and ideals that could have averted the idiocy of continental devastation, while preserving these values without which peace would be attrition and stagnation. But the leadership for such a human crusade was nowhere in evidence. And since peoples were incarcerated in their national entities, it was difficult for leadership to develop around the idea of human destiny. Viewed from the present perspective, it now seems clear that the principal threat was to humanity at large and not merely to the individual nations. The central issue was man in his collective being rather than the nation-state. But where were the spokesmen for the human community? It was as though a large ocean liner had struck an iceberg, creating immediate danger for all on board. A large hole had been ripped open in the forward part of the ship. There was a possibility, however, that if all the forward compartments could be sealed off the ship might remain afloat. When this fact was made known to the passengers, general relief was felt. It soon became apparent, too, that nothing short of an immediate and complete cooperative effort by all the passengers could save the ship. In order to accomplish this purpose, it would have become essential for the passengers, rigidly kept apart in the three passenger classes, to forget their compartmentalization and work side by side.

The officers quickly discovered that they lacked the authority and the strength to compel the passengers to follow instructions.

In the midst of this increasing peril the second-class passengers decided to attack the first-class passengers. It seemed like a good time, apparently, to seize control of the ship. This threw the third-class passengers into confusion and indecision. They realized that neutrality would place them at a disadvantage with the victorious side; and they prepared to throw in their weight with what appeared to be the ultimate winner. The first-class passengers appealed to the crew for help, but the crew lacked cohesion, authority, or actual weapons. The crew became increasingly frantic and helpless, running around in large circles and pleading with the combatants to cease their warfare for the sake of mutual survival. But the hopelessness of their cajoleries soon dawned on them and they, too, began dividing among themselves and jumping in on the side that appeared to have the upper hand.

Meanwhile the hold kept filling with water and the prow of the ship began to sink. There were desperate cries as the water came rushing over the sides. After the ship went down, some heads could be seen bobbing up and down in the water. People clung with one arm to boards or life preservers. And with the other arm they continued to claw at each other. It continued this way until they became senseless or were separated by the waves. It was no particular triumph for human intelligence that eventually a few survivors were washed ashore.

To be sure, if the story of the sinking had been told by a survivor, an entirely different emphasis would have been presented. There would have been a long and involved and grisly tale of politics aboard ship; of strained relations between the classes and of slights and provocations and factionalisms long before the ship struck the iceberg; of specific acts which set the stage for the overt aggression. The record would clearly lay the blame with the aggressor, but being able to assess responsibility was now an academic matter. Indeed, all the minutiae pertaining to the tensions and the provocations were meaningless to an outsider who was confronted with the hideousness and idiocy of the tragedy. Viewed objectively, the factions aboard ship comprised a human entity, and the human entity had been in mortal peril.

No analogy is perfect, of course, but there are certain aspects of the preceding episode which have a painful relevance to the events leading up to the recent atomic war. The first and most important point of similarity is that a common danger existed for the human race as a whole, but the human race was divided and subdivided, its attentions being focused on the antagonisms and frictions among nations and systems. Each nation and system had forces at its command, but man in his collective sense was open and exposed, unarmed and unrepresented. An organization had been formed for the maintenance of peace, but it was an organization of nations rather than of peoples. It had tremendous promise, but the promise never matured because no state was willing to become subordinate to the whole. And when the danger did crystallize in the form of an attack, there was a flurry of support behind the idea of a powerful world body enjoying the machinery of government, but nothing came of it. Later, when the attack mushroomed into the world war that everyone feared, it was too late, though everyone then knew what should have been done.

In short, being a member of the human race was of lesser importance than being a member of this or that system or national unit. There was no party of humanity, no overriding allegiance to the family of man, no banner which represented the major similarities of man to be flown above the multiple banners which represented his minor differences.

No one could deny that individual man was capable of great deeds and works of art, of vast loyalty and integrity and courage. But there was a sharp and tragic distinction between traits that characterized the individual and traits that characterized the species as a whole. There could be no doubt that the individual, invested with dignity and wisdom and nobility, had justified his right to life in a purposeful world. But not enough such individuals could come together for the creation of a society that might reflect those values —for the greater good of all. Collective man had failed. For every symphony or work of art representing individual genius there was an instance of the collective evil of war, or of group injustice in the form of slavery, starvation, torture. Nor was there in operation anywhere in the world a group conscience—assuming conscience to be, if not the source, at least the filter, for the determination of right and wrong.

For questions of right and wrong were absorbed and indeed obliterated by the group ego. Thus it was always the group, right or wrong. While the group denied to the individual the right to prey upon or commit aggression against the rights of another individual, the individual had no choice but to join in the collective murder of war because society or the state arrogated to itself exemption from the moral code. Morality became weaker in direct proportion to the size of the collective unit. At the highest level of all, the world level, morality ceased to exist.

The group, of course, had the right to defend itself against evil. But even in that case, the evil was represented by other human beings who, collectively, had abandoned morality. When the group acted as a group, such action was more often selfish than altruistic, more often predatory than social.

Here we come to what is the dominant fact of this story. That fact, to repeat, is that the human race had throughout its history lived within a wide margin for error. Until the final war came, man could make mistakes but never on so large a scale as to threaten his own existence. He could indulge in wars, despoil the earth on which its subsistence depended, engage in massacres, invite disease and plague out of filth and ignorance; he could do all these things, make all these mistakes, again and again, and yet have an ample cushion against ultimate catastrophe. History was lush with the proliferation of error, but there was always room for recovery—and opportunity for further error.

But that margin for error was used up. Man, in repudiating himself, denied his capacity for presiding over experience, whether personal or historical. Thus his trouble was not that he was obsolescent but that he was adolescent. He was not outmoded but immature.

The fact of this repudiation is not surprising. Consider man's own limited intellectual experience. He has been working with organized knowledge for perhaps only a hundred generations. He has lived in almost total ignorance of what he is, how and why he thinks, and what the connection is between body and mind. Though he houses a vast universe inside his own body—billions of cells, an electrical system involving countless millions of connections, a supremely coordinated apparatus for receiving outside stimuli and impressions—he has been largely oblivious of its workings, its motivations, its purposes. He has resided in it without governing it. He has acted as though he were superimposed upon a highly differentiated clot of energy.

Not until three centuries ago did he even discover the fact that the dominant fluid of life actually circulated through him. He has mastered only the barest knowledge of the workings of his nervous system, of the reasons why at a certain point growth yields to the degenerative processes, or, indeed, what the degenerative processes actually are. He has been baffled by an activity that occupies almost one third of his lifetime—sleep—about which he has many theories but no knowledge. As for the phenomenon of ideas—which help to differentiate him from the four-legged mammals, birds, and fish— he has been as ignorant of their true operation and composition as he was back in the days when his most complicated idea centered in the fashioning of a club.

He has been brilliant and inventive—but precociously so. It is by now trite to observe that he possessed a fabulous gift for devising gadgets and launching enterprises which he promptly found himself unable to control. One aspect of this inventiveness, however, is perhaps relevant. In many nations, the real significance of the machine age was not that it replaced human labor but that it replaced human thought. No sooner did it become possible for the great mass of men to enjoy several hours of leisure each day than a dozen contrivances jumped into relieve them of creative thought. But the contrivance was to be invented that could make man's decisions for him.

If man was lacking in knowledge of himself, consider the lack as it concerned his knowledge of others. For nothing was more characteristic of his adolescence than his inability to understand adequately the society of which he was a part, or the techniques by which society could be changed to meet changing conditions.

Could anything be more immature than the acquiescence of the world's peoples to live within the unraveling fabric of the nation-state system? Surely no group should have hesitated for a second to discard the death-laden concept that peace was possible through the retention by individual nations of their absolute sovereignty. Yet such a conception dominated the thinking and the established structure of the national groups.

One might have supposed, after the Second World War, that there would have occurred a volcanic eruption of popular protest against the first sign that the same measures and methods which failed in the past years were again in use, starting up again the tragic cycle.

One might have supposed that those who were chosen to lead or who found themselves in positions of leadership in the building of the peace would have had some sense of destiny about them, some understanding of the sweep and the meaning of history, some conception of the long and grand jumps that have to be taken in order to realize the promise of tomorrow. One might have supposed that the instinct for survival alone would have caused these leaders to define necessary new goals with fervor and eloquence. One might have supposed that the sudden liberation of the greatest and potentially most cataclysmic force known on earth would have touched off a great awakening of the human will and conscience in the cause of survival. One might have supposed that the need for a world federation would have risen over the earth like the sun itself, for nothing short of a world federation could have kept expanding nations from colliding inside a shrinking world.

One might also have supposed that there would have been universal recognition that without world federation there could have been no control of science for destructive purposes. For out of that science came awesome but not inspiring improvements upon the original forms of atomic death. Scientific genius went beyond mastery of fission into fusion. It discovered the technique of fusing hydrogen atoms into helium, creating destruction that could convert matter into space. One hundred square miles of total destruction was the minimum performance expectancy of a hydrogen bomb. Science had also discovered the techniques for creating radioactive rain. It could make of the sky a dispensing unit for vast quantities of radioactive dust particles, which not only contaminated entire cities but prolonged the killing ability of atomic energy far beyond the comparatively limited time vouchsafed to the atomic bomb.

"The cheapness of man," said Emerson, "is everyday's tragedy." When he wrote that, he had no way of knowing that the time would come when more men could be killed in a minute than it once took generations of mass warfare to accomplish. But science itself was destroyed before it converted the earth into a planetary crematorium.

Man's immaturity was reflected, finally, in what might be called the Four Fascinations.

The First Fascination was the fascination of the mirror. Almost every people saw itself possessed of such virtues and skills as it was convinced to the death could exist nowhere else in the world— whether with respect to religion, politics, science, or invention. The Americans prided themselves on their skill at shattering the atom, confident that it would take others many years before they could do the same, and derived a false sense of security from this fact, though they themselves were the most vulnerable major nation of all because of the intensive concentration of their industries and population. The Russians boasted of their own atomic weapons and even more fiendish war-making devices, the meanwhile making of their corrupt absolutism a political religion, and attempting to spread that religion through violence and deceit.

The Second Fascination was the fascination of apparent reasonableness. In many places people permitted themselves to be hypnotized by what had all the charms of a seemingly logical approach to world problems. They succumbed to the apparent reason which held that a weak world organization could keep the peace. They were lured into investing all their hopes in international conferences, whether with respect to human rights or boundary arrangements, though each conference was fated to be an end unto itself, since nothing that infringed upon national rights need have been accepted by the individual nations. They became enamored of official declarations of intent, though not much was said about the machinery to translate intent into action.

Yet reasonable men said that all this represented progress—as much progress as one ought to expect at that particular stage of the game.

The shame and pity of it is that, to all intents and purposes, the statesmen were doing their best. They were doing their best on the traditional level on which nations have always been accustomed to carry on their affairs—the level of power politics, political and military coalitions, armament preparations, diplomatic maneuvers, treaties, conventions, conferences, pacts. They were doing their best within an outworn and dangerous framework—a framework of limitations rather than of possibilities, a framework which had as its continuing and general objective the winning of the next war rather than the avoidance of it.

What had to be done was to break through to a higher level—to replace conferences with legislative bodies, treaties with law, violations with duly constituted force; in short, the substance of justice and the machinery of justice.

The Third Fascination was closely related to the previous two. It was the fascination with difficulty. World federation, it was said, was too difficult to establish. Certainly world federation would not have been easy—either to achieve or to operate. But was it easier to undergo atomic war? It was thought less difficult to drain off the largest portion of man's resources and energies in preparation for atomic war; less difficult to build giant industrial plants underground; less difficult to subject democratic institutions to the heat and pressure of rising tensions; less difficult to operate vast research and production facilities pressing yet further into techniques for destroying life.

The Fourth Fascination was with the crisis daydream. The dream was a simple one: If America and Russia could agree, then all the world's ills would be cured. It was a daydream because there could be no basic agreement between Russia and America without a higher authority which had the right and power to enforce those agreements and to carry out its decisions through preponderant force if necessary.

The United Nations as constituted possessed no such powers; it was not a government but a voluntary association which had as its stated purpose the eradication of war, yet it also guaranteed the sovereignty of all nations, and formalized that guarantee both through the veto and the right of any nation to relinquish its voluntary membership at its pleasure.

There was nothing strange about this; what confronted the world was merely the standardized behavior of sovereign nations which, whether out of the sincere need for self-defense or out of the vicious need for predatory expansion, had to look out for their own. And looking out for one's own was a global project, since the entire earth became a single theater of potential military operations.

World federation could not possibly have eliminated the natural antagonisms between these two countries; it could not possibly have eliminated the differences between two contrasting and contradictory ways of life. All world federation could have done was to set limits to that natural antagonism between the two; it could have had the means to halt rigidly and abruptly whatever danger of war might proceed out of the highly volatile competition for military supremacy between the two, whether measured in terms of geographical expansion or the race to perfect and produce weapons of mass destruction. It could have limited the war-making ability. It could have forestalled aggression. It could have reduced the areas and circumstances of potential conflict. It could have established machinery by which the infringements of one upon the other could be forestalled or blocked. For the function of world government would have been to insert itself between the states— not to merge them—and to create and keep watch over the rules of the game.

There was a related daydream belonging to the Fourth Fascination. It gloried in the image of a Russia-less world. If only somehow the Soviet were to be shattered, it was felt that all the world's problems would automatically have been solved. But the question the daydreamers forgot was this: Expunging Russia would not necessarily have expunged war—or history itself. For Soviet Russia was but an actor in a recurrent play, acting out parts and lines that were as old as war itself.

If a Russia-less world lacked the machinery to make and enforce law on nations, the world would still have been ripe for war. The same would have held true even if Russia and America had had the same political systems, for the dynamics of a two-power world were such that neither nation could have afforded to be at a disadvantage vis-à-vis the other.

Only in a daydream could it be imagined that the way to have avoided the final error of war would have been by preserving the sanctity of the error itself after eliminating one error-maker in a situation saturated with error.

It must not be supposed that there were no advocates for world federation. Indeed, there was general sympathy for this program, but it was felt that the achievement of such an objective was beyond reach. The question most people asked was, How do you get it? Wasn't world federalism, like the word "peace" itself, a proposition which was easy to accept emotionally and even intellectually but which lacked practical expression?

In retrospect now, however, it can be seen that advocacy of world federation might have been a worth-while end in itself, even if not all nations agreed. There was little hope that Soviet Russia—jealous, fearful, insecure internally and externally—might have accepted. Moreover, Russia would probably have continued to resist going into a world government—unless, and this was the crux of the matter, she was convinced that the rest of the world was determined to set one up and that any isolation from a world society might have come at too high a price—morally, politically, economically. But Soviet Russia was never put in the position of having to take a stand on world government.

No; America, like Russia, indicated no unqualified willingness to give the U.N. specific and adequate powers to create or maintain the conditions of peace.

What was needed was a popular prodding action of mountainous dimensions which could have convinced the American government that the American people were ready for an open and clearly defined official policy in favor of developing the United Nations into a world federation. Then America's moral position in the world would have been clear. Then at least and at last, the American people could have had the peace of mind that came from knowing that on the biggest issue of their time, on the one cause without which no other cause is possible, their government had lived up to its responsibilities as the world's most powerful democracy.

America had been born in an idea—that the individual was sacred and precious and had natural rights even against the state—and that the purpose of the state was to serve the cause of men. Woodrow Wilson dramatized this idea when he said that America was established to vindicate the rights of man. "We did not name any differences between one race and another. We did not set up any barriers against any particular people. We said, 'This independence of ours is not a selfish thing for our own exclusive use. It is for everybody to whom we can find the means of extending it.' Nothing can make America great except her ideals. I hope we shall never forget that we created this nation not to serve ourselves but to serve mankind."

Yet Americans after 1945 did seem to forget. They apparently forgot that the nation's real security and strength lay not in superior stockpiles of weapons but in a vital identification with humanity at large. Her principal role in the world could have been as champion of those ideals to which men have always responded— justice under law and recognition of individual worth, a man's chance to own the land he tilled, an individual's security in his person and the protection of his private property, absolute non-interference with his spiritual development, access to information and the right of expression and protest; and in general, the opportunity to develop the human potential.

Ideals such as these, advanced and articulated in and through a powerful United Nations, might have served as a rallying point for the world's peoples. Certainly they would have been powerful factors in keeping the preponderance of the world's peoples, especially in Asia and the Near East, from being attracted to, or from passing under the control of, Soviet Russia.

I have attempted in this short survey to take an almost extra-planetary view of man. I have attempted, in general, to view him in his collective being, rather than as Americans or Russians or Englishmen or Frenchmen or Chinese or Indians or Africans, and so on. Looking back now, it is possible to recognize how dangerous it was to be caught up in the passions and pressures that grew out of national differentiations. The differences between East and West that split the world before the biggest of all wars seemed deep and real to those who were involved in them. But viewed from the outside today, those differences and differentiations seem idiotic to the point of insanity.

To the outsider there is only the entity of mankind. If he were to seek an objective and rational explanation for the authorized mass murder of war, or for the staggering lack of political and social justice in the world, or for the clustered misery and starvation that cursed man's existence, the outsider would find it inconceivable that only one species was involved. He would be certain that some competing species was preying upon man—and perhaps vice versa.

In the course of my observations I have also referred to the flaw in man's development which prevented him from creating an adequate basis for existence within the group, as well as between the groups. I have been concerned with his failure to invest the group with an essential moral code or conscience.

I have referred to his failure so far to recognize that only world government could have averted the conflict.

There was a direct connection between the two. World government offered a chance to break away from the inevitability of war. It offered a chance to gain the perspective and wisdom necessary for the attainment of the indispensable and ultimate objective.

That ultimate objective was the development and refinement of a collective conscience. In the long run lack of it would have destroyed even (or perhaps especially) a world government. But at least world government might have served as the germinating agency for a collective conscience. At least it might have provided the means through which a sense of community of the world's peoples could have been nurtured. It might have invested the term "world citizenship" with real meaning. Perhaps a world freed of war might have been able eventually to generate new habits of mutuality.

But all this is now part of a shattered past. When the war came, it marked not so much the end of an age as the repudiation of the human community by man himself.

*   *   *

So much for the negative hypothetical account of the next few years of human history, as it might be viewed by a future historian. There is a contrasting story—equally likely and equally hypothetical

—that might be written about our time. What follows for the rest of this chapter, then, is wishful thinking in the most literal sense of the term. It attempts to anticipate some of the principal problems that would arise in the creation of a world federation and the possible approaches to those problems. It is based on the assumption that peace will not usher in any Utopia but could at least provide the basic conditions for what a later historian might call—

The Age of Valor

The world is at peace. It is not a utopian peace, but at least the world has been made safe for its differences. It will be many years before the peoples of the world develop a true sense of world community or world citzenship, but at least they are moving in that direction.

Democracy and totalitarianism today vie with each other, as they have for many years. There is, however, this difference: the competition between the two is now kept within bounds. Totalitarianism, deprived of its traditional dynamic and aggressive drives, is changing from within and has not been in the ascendancy for a number of years. The world is still beset by economic ills and by the problems of population pressure and conservation of natural resources, but for the first time in human history a world organization is in being which is attacking these matters and is able to show progress. For the United Nations has undergone a vast development in the past two decades. Despite too frequent stumblings and failings, it has been able to operate effectively. What its long-range character will be, it is too early to tell.

What happened was simple: Enough people decided they didn't want to resign from the human race.

The faculty of anticipation in man was important. He was able to anticipate the hell of the transient survivors of an atomic war. He was able to anticipate his place among them—the things he would see and the things he would do. He anticipated the things he would think about—his sense of disbelief that all this organized insanity should have been allowed to come to pass; his later certainty that all this could have been averted; his need to live with his conscience.

He realized that it was fantastic that anyone anywhere should concern himself with anything except the drive to create a world government in time. He was sickened at the thought that the peoples should allow themselves to be persuaded by talk of difficulties and differences in the way of world government. He was appalled at the fact that the statesmen had for so long failed to make the proposal for world government, for he knew that even if some nations declined, at least all the others might have rallied around a moral principle in pooling their sovereignty—enjoying preponderance but keeping the door open and making it clear that the purpose of the common government was a common security under justice.

This was the type of anticipatory wisdom that unlocked within many people not only the essential intellectual and physical energies but the first real manifestations of collective conscience. They had nothing to lose but their adolescence.

In terms of specific action, the United Nations became the representative body of the human community. It crossed the Rubicon of national sovereignty.

It had its own actual and potential forces, large enough to prevent aggression or to cope with it instantly if it should occur. It was able to legislate effectively in the matter of national armaments, and for the first time peoples could have confidence in disarmament arrangements. It enjoyed the right of inspection to guard against secret manufacture of weapons adapted to mass destruction.

The individual nations retained, or rather recaptured, sovereignty over their own institutions and cultures. The word "recaptured" is used because sovereignty in domestic matters had been seriously weakened under the old world anarchy, with war or the fear of war determining the careers and destinies of millions of citizens, or the sizes of their taxes, or the pressures upon free institutions.

What was most important, of course, was that the nations were now freed for common action on the basic problems of the world's peoples.

Economic development, education, housing, health—these became the fields of effective joint action on behalf of the world's peoples.

Human freedom, as a consequence, received its greatest impetus.

It is difficult to single out the world leaders and statesmen who made the strongest contributions to the fashioning of this world body. Each continent was able to boast of its own vital role. Once the stage had been set for greatness, once a new level had been created for constructive achievement, there was no dearth of purposeful leadership. It might be mentioned, however, that two declarations from the United States were helpful in initiating and advancing the meetings that led to elevating and bolstering the United Nations.

The first declaration was in the form of a Presidential Address to a joint session of Congress. In it, the American President said:

"I come before Congress and the American people for the purpose of seeking authorization to issue new instructions to the American delegates to the United Nations.

"These instructions seek to explore the means by which the United Nations may be properly developed into an organization capable of law-making, law-enforcing, and law-interpretation. In short, they seek to give the United Nations the effective powers of government.

"In particular, these instructions direct our delegates to propose the calling and holding of a Revision Conference of the United Nations as provided under Articles 108 and 109 of the Charter. These articles specify that a conference may be called for the purpose of altering the structure of the United Nations if two-thirds of the nations wish to do so.

"Such a call is not subject to the veto.

"The American purpose in proposing such a Conference is to give the greatest possible strength to the United Nations in the shortest possible time. Our proposal takes into account the happenings in Korea. In a larger sense, they have also taken into account the events since the end of the Second World War, as well as our hopes and plans for the years ahead.

"We in America have been deeply shocked by the events in Korea. The struggle to put down aggression in that country was on a scale that hardly seemed possible only a few months before it started. We were deprived of the advantage we had in the first and second world wars, when allies held the field until we could mobilize and direct our strength.

"It is no secret that the aggressor in modern warfare possesses a tremendous advantage. He can choose the time and place of attack, counting on surprise to attain the objective before the victim can defend himself or rally support.

"I am asking the American delegates to make our proposal in all good faith. We seek nothing from a strengthened United Nations that would not be available to all nations, large and small.

"Here is a chance for the world to wipe the slate clean. The benefits of participation are equally available to all. And when I say 'all' I mean 'all.' Any nation sincerely interested in security and the common welfare of the world's peoples should have no hesitation in joining with the rest.

"But let there be no mistake about it. There are benefits, but there are also obligations and responsibilities. The durable, meaningful peace to which humanity is entitled cannot be obtained without sacrifice.

"Unlimited national sovereignty cannot be retained—if we sincerely want peace.

"No nation can expect to retain sole jurisdiction over the size and nature of its arsenals—if we sincerely want peace.

"These are some of the basic principles which must go into the making of a system of law and order. And, again I say, any nation sincerely interested in security, any nation that does not covet other territory, should have no hesitation in accepting these duties as a member of a world community.

"The aim of such a strengthened United Nations would be universal membership. The conditions for membership can be clearly stated: respect for the rules of the game, respect for the rights of the individual members, prompt fulfillment of obligations, recognition of the fact that the human community enjoys precedence over the national community in those specific matters related to a common world security.

"So much for the form of a workable world organization. The instructions to the American delegates to the United Nations are also concerned with the substance that would go into the making of such a body.

"In spirit, the United Nations must become the protector and spokesman for humanity at large. It must transform itself from a forum of the nations into a Congress of the peoples. It must serve a higher purpose than the mere projection of the foreign policies of the individual nations.

"Human interest must transcend the national interest.

"Because of this, the American delegates should be free to con-

sider every issue or question coming before the councils of the
United Nations according to this simple test: Does it help or harm
human welfare?

"I am sure all Americans will agree with me when I say that
our delegates can best represent the American people by regarding
themselves as representatives of the human community.

"It is inconceivable that there should ever be any real conflict
between the general welfare of humanity and the welfare of the
American people. If such a conflict does arise, then American democracy will have lost its meaning as we know it.

"We hope that in a revised and strengthened United Nations the
delegates of all nations will vote as individuals on each issue according to their consciences and best judgment, and not as members of
national blocs.

"Participation in the building of such a responsible world body
is the greatest challenge and privilege for statesmen in history. It is
a summons to greatness.

"We in America hereby make a complete commitment—moral,
physical, spiritual—to the cause of human progress and welfare.
We will oppose imperialism to no less an extent than aggression. We
will support and associate ourselves with the struggle for freedom
and human rights. Humanity is now one, and we propose to be at
one with humanity.

"No one knows whether this total commitment to the cause of
a strong and just United Nations and to a free world will succeed.
No one knows whether it can come in time to prevent world-wide
atomic war. But if this madness is to be; if there is nothing that
any of us, acting with heart and might, can do to stop it—then at
least we can answer to our consciences. At least it can be said we
spoke for man.

"Surely, there can be no greater purpose or mission than this,
to stand before the world as humanity's champion.

"And even if the war is averted, the years ahead will not be easy.
Charting an even course for human destiny will require anguish,
disappointment, sacrifice. But it will be known in history as the Age
of Valor. No struggle in history will have had a more towering
dedication."

World-wide support for such a conference was not long in forthcoming. Indeed, a number of leaders of other nations had previously

proposed such a meeting but were unable to attract necessary backing from either of the two largest states.

Not all nations endorsed the proposal, but a two-thirds majority was obtained. It was made clear to the hesitant nations that participation in the discussions presupposed no commitment to accept the final recommendations. Beyond the Conference was national ratification. All the Conference could do was to define the need and nature of revision. What happened after that was a matter of national determination.

The role of the United States at the Revision Conference had been defined in part by the President's message to Congress. It was supplemented by a second declaration by the President which was presented at one of the opening sessions of the Conference. At these opening sessions the various nations expressed their concepts of, and hopes for, the meeting. The American President's statement read in part:

"I am sure I need not tell the people of the United Nations that I come before them with the utmost humility. The crisis in which we find ourselves—a world crisis and a human crisis—is so large that no man or nation can pretend to have all the answers. The affairs of nations and of man himself have become so complicated that we in the United States would have to be superhuman if we could offer certain solutions and answers to all the problems that perplex and challenge us. What all of us can do, however, is to consider the nature of these big problems and attempt to think them through together.

"Let us begin by taking the problem at its largest.

"The problem at its largest is not the condition of world organization but the condition of man.

"This human community of ours is not an organized community but it is a community none the less. We reside on the same planet. That planet has now become a single neighborhood. We have common needs, common dangers, common hopes, common fears. This is the central meaning and challenge of our times; it is what distinguishes the twentieth century from all previous centuries. The human family, starting as a single unit and spreading into separate lands, has crossed the last frontier only to create a single unit of itself again. Is this unit, this neighborhood, to become a safe and proper place for man?

"The problem at its largest, to repeat, concerns human destiny. It is the problem of a human family that has made the world small without making it whole. We must not allow the political and ideological questions that absorb us and torment us to obscure that fact. We must not allow the pressures and tensions of international unrest to divert us from recognition of a common destiny.

"It is in this spirit that I speak to you today.

"Here are ten facts which pertain to the welfare and safety of the human community:

"The first fact is that we live in an age that is trying to find itself. If any description can be given to our generation—and here I am thinking of all men everywhere—it is that this is a generation in search of its soul. It is a generation looking for spiritual and intellectual anchorage at a time of uncertainty and upheaval.

"The second fact is that almost half the people in the world are hungry or sick or poorly housed.

"The third fact is that many of the world's peoples are in a revolutionary mood. These peoples do not have to be persuaded about the importance of freedom, but the longing for freedom takes different forms in different places. There is the longing for freedom from outside rule. There is the longing for freedom from indignity. People want the chance to prove their worth, a chance to prove that the color of their skin has nothing to do with their right to walk with a feeling of decency and self-respect among their fellow men. There is the longing for freedom from legalized abuse—whether economic, social, or political.

"The fourth fact is that every four years there are 100,000,000 more people in the world—which is the equivalent of the population of a new major nation.

"The fifth fact is that the good earth is shrinking. Each year billions of acres are abandoned because they are dry or devitalized and can no longer yield food.

"The sixth fact is that the world's mineral resources are not inexhaustible. Coal, oil, iron ore, timber—all these are being used up faster than new sources are being developed or discovered.

"The seventh fact is that a large portion of the resources and vital energies of the world's peoples are being poured into preparation for war. The reason for this is the lack of an adequate security system to protect the world's peoples against aggression and lawlessness.

"The eighth fact is that another war, if it comes, will be fought with whatever weapons are available. Those weapons now approach the ultimate in potential destruction. So far no adequate defense has been devised against those weapons. At the present time, it can only be said that counter-attack constitutes a possible deterrent. In any event, all cities are now vulnerable. A single bomb can now destroy a major city. The area of destruction for a single bomb has now been increased to 100 square miles.

"The ninth fact, related to the eighth, is that another major war may not necessarily alter the conditions that make human life possible on this planet, but it could destroy industrial society, decimate the world's population, enfeeble peoples everywhere, and deprive them of such means as are now available for attacking hunger, disease, homelessness.

"The tenth and final fact is that the human race today is without representation in those matters of common concern to all peoples. Such representation as the individual does possess is largely nominal and is not concerned with the basic threats to his existence. A nation may attempt to provide justice for dealings between its own citizens, but it cannot protect its citizens any longer against injustice between nations—and the consequences of injustice between nations are far more dangerous to the individual today than injustice between citizens within a nation. In fact, the nation is no longer able to fulfill its historical role: to protect the lives and property of its citizens. War is no longer between armies but between populations, and the question of war and peace is no longer within the determination of any single state.

"These ten facts, I believe, represent the central questions of our time. Food, peace, freedom. These are the main challenges to humankind today. No nation, no people can exempt themselves from the need to ponder these challenges and the facts behind them.

"As we think about these ten facts or questions, certain things do come to mind. We know, for example, that there is an answer to the shrinkage of the world's arable land. In the agricultural laboratories today we stand on the threshold of astounding discoveries that can reclaim vast lands now given up for dust. Already there have been developed rejuvenating chemicals that have substantially increased the food yield, or that have compensated for loss of rain. New types and sources of food are being developed. Chemical gardening and farming is a rich and fast-growing new prospect.

"We know, too, that vast new sources of energy are opening up. Much more research needs to be done in tapping and utilizing the boundless energy of the sun, but even now the scientists have been able to develop solar heat traps on a modest scale. These traps can be used for small energy requirements, for heating, or for refrigeration. The promise and potential usefulness of such sun traps for countries of large agricultural population near the equator excites the imagination.

"Another highly promising development concerns the utilization of the vast resources of the oceans. We have yet to make an intensive and full-scale exploration of all the possibilities. Already, however, magnesium and other resources yielded up by the ocean give us bright and reasonable expectations concerning the shape of things to come.

"All this even before we mention atomic energy. So far, the overwhelming bulk of the efforts of science has gone into the use of atomic energy for purposes of war. But even the comparatively modest efforts made thus far for purposes of power and medicine have been enormously productive and promising. We have only to attach the same importance to atomic energy for creative ends that we do for destructive ends in order to bring about incalculable benefits in terms of increased power, improved standard of living, longer life expectancy.

"All these mind-stretching new developments—in agricultural and chemical research, in mining the ocean's wealth, in solar and atomic energy—make it theoretically possible for us to solve the present critical dwindling food supply and resources at a time of increasing population. In fact, there is now the distinct possibility that we can bring about a Golden Age of Man. Up to now, only certain peoples at certain times have been favored by a golden age. But we know today that a golden age of the human community is a distinct promise. We have the skill, we have the knowledge, we have the means.

"How can we fulfill such a promise? Obviously, little or nothing can be done so long as the world's peoples live under war or the fear of war. Our energies, our ingenuity, our imagination—no less than our resources and our wealth—are poured into the means of physical protection against violence in a lawless world. We are arming ourselves, but we know that armaments are not the final answer. We arm, but we are not deceiving ourselves about the cost —in the expenditure of human effort and money, in the increasing strain upon our economy, in the pressures and tensions it creates within the nation, and finally, in delaying or blocking the release of our energies in the making of a better world.

"Yes, we arm, but there must be some other and better way to protect peoples against lawlessness. Surely the destiny of the human community must be something finer and more meaningful than a precarious existence under the shadow of guns and bombs. I cannot bring myself to believe that the human mind, capable of almost infinite comprehension and inventiveness, cannot devise the means of enforceable peace. Nor can I bring myself to believe that a few predatory states could effectively block the firmly expressed will of the overwhelming majority of the world's peoples to establish the rule of law among nations.

"Let us help the U.N. dedicate itself to the cause of the human community. Let us rise above secondary quarrels and issues and assert the moral stature that befits us as human beings. Let us not be timid about what the United Nations needs or what it must become if it is to eliminate anarchy from the world neighborhood. Let us not shrink from the concept of government on a world scale.

"This is what the human race needs. This is what it deserves.

"The response of certain leaders of certain nations to such a proposal should not trouble us. I know that it will be impossible for such rulers to keep from their people the fact that there is a mighty movement in the world in behalf of peace, food, and freedom and that this movement has behind it the integrity, sincerity, and resoluteness of countless millions of human beings.

"Our proposal is made in good faith. It does not seek to exclude any nation. It does not ask any nation to give up anything more than any other nation and it offers no special rights or privileges to any nations that are not obtainable by all. It seeks a pooling of sovereignty in those matters concerned with the common security. It seeks adequate enforcement of disarmament. It seeks a workable method for protecting and preserving the diversity of peoples—

diversity in religions, cultures, philosophies, and ways of life. It seeks an effective attack on the basic problems that relate to man's estate midway in the twentieth century.

"In short, it seeks the greater good of man.

"It seeks to represent man.

"These objectives are necessary, therefore they are possible. They are possible, that is, if we believe in human destiny. The great forward thrusts of history have not always been the product of universal assent but of courageous and persistent leadership behind a great idea. Let us not undervalue the striking power—even in supposedly impregnable places—of the idea and hope that purposeful peace is possible and that the golden age of man can be a reality."

* * *

In the early days of the Revision Conference, the majority of the statesmen recognized that the aims and needs of the world community might not all be resolved at a single session of the conference. It would take several years at least before the numberless questions that were certain to come up could be adequately examined and resolved. For this was to be not merely a political meeting; it was to be a Congress of history and hope, studying man's efforts to govern himself in units of increasing size and complexity. It would require the most painstaking scrutiny of the historical record; it would have to add wisdom to knowledge, insight to information, vision to comprehension. Three or four years or more would not be too long a time for such a service to the world community. The Philadelphia Convention of the American States, it was recalled, took the better part of two years.

Widespread support for this enlarged conception of the Conference's task was readily forthcoming. The plan of the Conference, in the long-range organization of its work, was fairly simple. Following the initial session of the Conference, which would be concerned with a general discussion of problems and objectives and which might last a month or so, the group would be narrowed down to a working committee of not more than seventy-five delegates, with every nation having at least a single representative. The group would meet regularly, with no fixed date for concluding its labors. At least twice a year, the full Revision Conference would be reconvened for the purpose of receiving an interim report of the working committee and for advising the committee on the general pattern of its work.

This plan was accepted and followed. The working committee was in almost continuous session for four years. And every six months the full Revision Conference was assembled for several weeks. Recurrently, it would appear that the working committee would have to be dissolved, all its efforts wasted when it became deadlocked over various issues, the most controversial of which was on the question of representation—whether based on population or national states or other factors. But it was recognized that world public opinion would not countenance failure, and the delegates stayed with their task.

The most difficult yet most important achievement of the working committee in the first months of its meetings was its plan for giving the United Nations interim police powers until such time as the working committee might complete its efforts to equip the U.N. with the general powers of world law, and until such time as the nations would ratify the proposals of the working committee. The need for such a plan was dramatized by the steady and progressive worsening of world conditions. It seemed ludicrous to suppose that the world crisis would stand still pending completion by the working committee of its labors. Hence a timetable was devised for the execution of a four-phase plan for interim world security.

In the first phase of this timetable, the United Nations was to be given command of military forces of at least three times the size of the forces it maintained in Korea. This would amount to approximately one million men under arms—a small figure as modern armies go but enough to serve symbolic purposes as well as to act as a deterrent for the type of aggression that, as in Korea, would try to capitalize on weak spots which might otherwise seem attainable at low cost. The U.N. Army would be completely up-to-date. It would have an air arm of its own. It would have access to such weapons as would be required to cope with the arsenal of any possible lawbreaker.

The precedent for the establishment of such a force was Korea itself, with two significant differences. One was that the U.N. would not have to wait until the aggression was actually committed before recruiting a force of its own. The force would now be preventive rather than combative in purpose. The second difference was that the U.N. would no longer have to rely on the nation most vitally concerned to furnish the bulk of men and material. Surely the common cause of an enforceable peace was compelling enough, it was argued, for a just and compulsory sharing of obligations. No question of good or bad faith was involved. Rather it was essential that there be a complete understanding by all nations concerning their world obligations and fixed responsibilities. No nation now need fear that its own contribution might be out of proportion to the total effort.

* * *

In the second phase of the timetable for interim security, the plan for enforceable disarmament would come up. On the assumption that the U.N. force would have served its purpose—namely, to act as a shield behind which the U.N. could develop a sound basis for a workable peace—the next step would be control over national armaments. A bona fide offer would be made to *all* nations. In return for participation in the plan for enforceable disarmament, each nation would have its security underwritten by the U.N., which by now would have substantial military authority, plus a call on immediate additional strength as needed.

The strength of this proposal lay in the fact that the question of disarmament could now be considered inside an entirely different framework from the one that history had discredited. The new framework had nothing to do with treaties or conventions—history was littered with the wreckage of such treaties and conventions. The new framework was concerned with workable machinery, with enforcement measures; in short, with disarmament under law. No talk of disarmament made sense, no proposed quotas for reduction of armaments was possible, unless the world's peoples could be confident that the success of any plan rested on something firmer than the good intentions of the agreeing parties.

In particular, the disarmament plan brought before the nations called for control of all weapons adapted to mass destruction. Inspections and sanctions were mandatory to keep nations from engaging in such manufacture. Atomic energy, for example, would be developed under proper safeguards, with each nation participating as its own resources and industrial establishments would permit, and deriving benefits in proportion to the individual contribution to the over-all effort. This would not exclude other states from atomic benefits, particularly where health and economic development were concerned, but it did leave to those states with atomic-energy installations the primary rights of development and use for peaceful purposes. The U.N. inspectors would maintain careful safeguards against diversion of such facilities for military purposes. The U.N. would cease to manufacture atomic weapons once universal membership was achieved in U.N. and the means for preventing war established.

The principal difference between this plan for control of atomic armaments and the Baruch Plan was to be found in the fact that the U.N. would now be given powers against war itself. Formerly, atomic disarmament was sought without any comparable machinery for dealing with the circumstances which might dictate the use of atomic weapons. No state under the proposed plan could justifiably argue that control of atomic energy was not being pursued in a vacuum, or that there was no agency strong enough to protect it against war and to ensure its rights.

*   *   *

The third phase of the work of the Revision Conference grew out of the previous two. Just as investing the U.N. with appropriate forces of its own was the precondition for any plan for enforceable disarmament, so the need to create a durable structure for carrying out disarmament led to the plan for a federalization of the U.N.

Disarmament, it was held, was the vital factor in any attempt to equip the United Nations with law-making and law-enforcing powers. Law begins with the conquest of force. Law consists of a clear definition of the rules of the game, or the requirements of justice, backed by the fact that it is strong enough to keep excessive strength from passing into the hands of potential violators. And it is in the implementation of this idea that government takes shape. Whether that government is good or bad, whether it is a government in which all men are subject to the laws, including the leaders, or whether it is a government in which the laws serve the purposes of a few men or a man bent on capturing the state and its people, depends upon the wisdom and courage of the founders and the continuing faith in it of the people themselves.

The proposal for federalism came after long and careful consideration of the alternatives—league, confederation, central government.

A league—which is to say a loose organization of states held together by treaty with the individual nations retaining ultimate authority in armaments or other matters related to the common security—was dismissed in the light of the experience of the League of Nations and of the United Nations itself.

The idea of confederation was rejected for many of the same reasons. Though the relations between the nations were much more clearly defined than in a league, a confederation would lack a central authority transcending the nations in those matters clearly concerned with common dangers and common needs.

The idea of a strong central government was rejected because it was felt that the basic requirements of such a government were lacking. The easiest way to kill such a government, in fact, was to impose upon it functions and powers far beyond its capacity. A central government taking upon itself all the powers exercised by the individual nations—powers in the fields of taxation, currency, immigration, trade, economic development, mutual security and defense, general welfare, and so forth—would be dealing with such complexities and imponderables as would bring about its possible early collapse. Moreover, the differences in national institutions and cultures might create an almost insurmountable barrier for any government which attempted to maintain jurisdiction over the individual.

Hence the strength of the proposal for federation with limited powers. In a federation each nation would retain jurisdiction over its people and institutions in all matters except those clearly related to the common security and common development. There would be clear-cut distinctions between world jurisdiction and national jurisdiction, between the sovereignty that would be pooled in the federation and the sovereignty retained by the national states. The powers of a federated U.N. would be specifically confined to common needs and common dangers.

So far as jurisdiction over the individual was concerned, it would be restricted to those matters affecting the security of all peoples. The Nuremberg trials, it was pointed out, had proceeded on the principle of individual responsibility and guilt for acts leading to war. What was now proposed was exactly the same principle, except that this time the guilty parties could be apprehended in time to avert war rather than after the damage had been done and the dead counted.

Economic development, especially in the case of Asia and Africa, was to be regarded as a signal opportunity for the federated U.N. It was recognized, however, that many of the nations of Asia and Africa were just extricating themselves from a century or more of outside rule and that nothing should be done which would be regarded by those states as interference with their problems of internal development and control. Hence, it was to be made clear that any requests for economic, technological, or scientific assistance to individual nations were to originate from the nations themselves. The greatest care would be taken to see that each development project would operate in a way consistent with each nation's own culture and institutions and that its own facilities with human resources would be fully utilized.

As for the specific commissions that would be concerned with non-military assistance, it was pointed out that the U.N. already had within it many excellent agencies—in the fields of world health, food, refugee problems, education, science, and so forth. But two things were in the way of their effective operation. The first was that these groups lacked any real authority or the means of carrying out the necessary programs. The second was that the dominant energies and resources of most of the nations were being diverted to military purposes. The combination of authority and means could enable the special agencies of the U.N. to demonstrate high usefulness in improving the conditions of human existence.

These agencies, of course, would be directly responsible to, and established by, the legislative branch of the U.N.

Concerning the actual form of a federated U.N. with limited

powers, it was made clear that the structure of the U.N. as then constituted was actually a bar to effective operation. It was doubtful that the big states would like to see important powers given to the General Assembly in its present form in view of the fact that they were on even footing with states with only a fraction of their own populations. Meanwhile, the Security Council, run by the big states, was bound by the unanimity principle. This meant that no issue of consequence involving the major nations could be settled on the basis of strict adherence to law, for a major nation could negate the law through the veto.

Any attempt to redefine the authority of the General Assembly and Security Council, however, squarely opened up the entire question both of representation and of division of powers.

If a purely democratic basis were used as the basis of representation, then two or three populous nations might be able to dominate the voting. If a one-vote-for-one-state basis were used, then a few small states with perhaps an aggregate population of twenty million might be able to outvote nations with an aggregate population of 750,000,000 or more. This was the thorniest problem to come before the group. There could be no authority without representation, but representation under existing circumstances seemed impossible. Wasn't it therefore futile to talk of world federation? Perhaps the nations ought to resolve to do the best they could with the U.N. as it was.

This dilemma was resolved through a plan for *dual federalism* based on a regional approach inside the United Nations. Under this arrangement the General Assembly would be divided into its component regional parts, each of which would receive a total of one hundred votes or less, depending upon population, size, resources, and other vital factors. Each region was to determine for itself the voting procedures for its own members in arriving at decisions concerning the vote that would be taken by the unit as a whole. A regional unit consisting of, say, ten members, two of which had a combined population larger than the combined total of the remaining eight members, might wish to give proportionate weight to the larger members in working out an equitable system of representation within itself. A regional unit might wish to split its hundred votes in the General Assembly, if it so wished, in order to reflect the mixed voting within itself on any question.

The advantage of the regional arrangement, it was argued, went far beyond the possible solution it offered to the impasse of representation by population as against representation by nation. It recognized a certain grouping of interests on the regional level—economic, cultural, political—and provided the means by which these natural interests might be protected and advanced.

The only questions on which the regional units would be called upon to vote as units in the General Assembly were on questions involving the common security, or on relations of units to each other, or the relations of members of one unit to members of another.

The over-all approach, then, was to be *dual federalism:* federalism of nations within regional units, and federalism of nations as members of regional units on the world level. The nation, the regional unit, and the federated U.N. would each exercise such sovereignty as was natural to it. The individual nations would have authority and jurisdiction in all matters pertaining to their own institutions and internal affairs. The regional units would have authority and jurisdiction in all matters pertaining to the regional needs and interests of the members. Finally, the federated U.N. would have authority and jurisdiction in those matters directly affecting the safety and vital needs of the world community.

As part of this general proposal, the Security Council was to be reconstituted as the Executive Council. Its primary function was to carry out the wishes and enforce the decisions of the General Assembly. The Executive Council would elect its own chairman and vice chairman, subject to ratification by the General Assembly. All the special agencies of disarmament—atomic controls, world health, food, economic development, refugees, and so forth—of the U.N. would come within the administration of the Council. The operating budget of the Council and its agencies would have to come before the General Assembly, which would have powers of appropriation and review.

The Executive Council, unlike its predecessor, the Security Council, would not be concerned with votes or vetoes within itself. It was not a legislative agency but the principal enforcement arm of the United Nations. As such, it could make recommendations but it could not enact legislation or review it.

Judicial review of legislation enacted by the General Assembly, and of the enforcement activities of the Executive Council, would be vested in a World Court.

In general outline, then, the proposals looked to world federation with powers adequate to enact, enforce, and interpret world law, and with all other powers guaranteed to the nations.

* * *

The fourth and final phase of the creation of the world federation was the world debate that preceded ratification.

The most articulate objection to the federation came from those who were opposed to any strengthening of the U.N. if there was any danger that not all nations would accept. Another group declared it would oppose the U.N. if all nations *were* given the opportunity to accept.

In a sense, both groups had much in common. Neither recognized the essential nature and purpose of government under law. Federal government is not organized for the purpose of distributing favors for those who accept membership. Nor is its primary purpose the imposition of penalties for those who fail to accept. The purpose of federal government is to provide a rational, just, and workable method for the definition and enforcement of valid obligations among nations in the interests of common safety. The question of desirability of membership comes up only if the organization is a league or a confederation. Lacking authority of its own, a league or confederation could be dominated by recalcitrant or obstructive members. But federation is not without means and resources of its own to deal with obstructive members. Indeed, its very reason for being is that it assumes that there will always be natural or unnatural controversy among its members and that its main function is to keep such controversy from erupting in war.

Opponents of world federalism, however, pressed their arguments. Those who feared that it would result in a formal split of the world if Russia and China refused to accept called for recognition and restoration of the unanimity principle. They believed that no fundamental strengthening of the U.N. should be attempted on the grounds that additional strength was impossible without unity and that if unity could be achieved no formal strengthening would be necessary.

The reply to this was that the unanimity principle was based on the dangerous fallacy that the will of a nation should be supreme. It was important to face up to the central challenge of the times—to place law and the machinery of law above nations. The principle here was the same as good government had to face in placing even the lawmaker under law. This did not mean that there were no obstacles in the way of achieving this with nations, but at least one had to begin with an acceptance of certain basic principles pertaining to the creation of a workable world organization.

The federalists argued further that the widest possible latitude should be given to all nations for the fullest possible consideration of membership and that no fixed deadline be set for acceptance. In the event that some nations wished to see the federated U.N. in action over a period of time before deciding finally on the advantages or disadvantages of membership, it was proposed that such protracted consideration was not to be regarded by the others as being unfriendly. Even allowing for the many striking differences between the U.N. Revision Conference and the American Constitutional Convention, it could be pointed out that there might have been no United States if the Philadelphia Convention had insisted upon immediate and universal ratification before proceeding with federation. New York, Rhode Island, Virginia (including Kentucky), and North Carolina (claiming Tennessee) were in organized opposition to membership in the United States following the Philadelphia Convention. It was the better part of two years before all the original thirteen states recognized the tremendous advantages of an integrated federal government.

Convincing arguments were offered in the U.N. to support the view that while universal federation was the goal, perhaps the only way to achieve it would be to make a start with the majority. The member nations would make it clear that they were not proceeding on any principle of exclusion. Indeed, the only justification for proceeding on a less than universal basis was to demonstrate the workability and equity for those nations that wanted to wait and see.

There remained, however, the persistent arguments of those who objected to universal federation under any circumstances. Totalitarian governments should not be invited to join, they contended.

It was argued by one group that Russia, China, and the satellite countries should not be recognized by the federated U.N., since such recognition would give those nations status. And it was argued by another group that Spain and Argentina should be excluded because of the authoritarian form of their governments. If such nations were to be admitted, wouldn't their weight affect the functioning of the federation? Wouldn't this weight, in fact, affect the very life of the federation?

Here, again, it had to be pointed out that what was being created was not an exclusive club dispensing privileges but an organization of the nations exacting obligations. The greater the menace to the peace a nation might be, the greater the need to have that nation within a workable system of security. The established method of dealing with a lawbreaker, it was pointed out, was not to exempt him from the laws but to use the full machinery of the law to keep him within reach.

The main problem, however, was not to devise means to keep some nations out but to get them all to come in. Related to this was the need to recognize that if the free world waited too long to propose federation they might be confronted by a totalitarian bloc enjoying a majority which would attempt to set up a world government of its own.

Such a world government would not be federal in form. It would not rest upon principles of justice; it would not provide for equitable representation; it would not be one which, in the final analysis, would look for its ultimate power to the world's peoples. No nation acting in good faith would feel justified in accepting. The source of its authority would be force. But a federal government built around concepts of world justice could resolve at least that aspect of the danger to world peace resulting from competitive insecurity.

*   *   *

It was five years from the original convening of the Revision Conference to the ratification of the federalized United Nations by enough nations to get it started. Once launched, it had a powerful effect on the thinking of the world's peoples—especially those who belonged to the non-member nations. The good sense and good will behind it, the historic nature of the federation, the hopes that were wrapped up inside it, the promise it held for the human community —all these created tremendous groundswells inside even the totalitarian nations. No amount of counter-propaganda was enough to offset the fact that sanity and conscience had come together in a mighty attempt to keep civilization from becoming inimical to man.

The fact of world federation, as was mentioned at the outset, has not by itself solved all the world's problems. But at least it has conquered the fear of war by conquering war itself. And it has released resources to man for higher ends—the pursuit of justice and a purposeful life. And if nothing else was achieved, at least for the first time in history the human community had its own voice; it had a spokesman; it was represented.

*   *   *

This, then, completes the "optimistic" account of our time, as a future historian might see it.

CHAPTER XXVII

THE SUMMING-UP

This book grew out of the conviction that human history has never known so many hopes and so many fears so delicately balanced. Our time is almost like a summing-up of man himself, so frequently poised between affirmation and negation, promise and despair, altruism and selfishness, clarity and confusion.

But far more powerful than supposedly inexorable forces is the human will. It is confidence in that free will that is primarily responsible for the writing of this book.

In that sense, this book intends to be an argument for the cause of man. But it recognizes that the cause of man in our time is hurt because man is unrepresented. Partial man is represented. That is to say, the part of him that is national man is represented. The part of him that is fraternal, social, and cultural man is represented. But the whole man, or world man, lacks representation. In the sum total of everything he is; in his oneness with all men everywhere; in the basic matters that involve his personal safety, his subsistence, his values; in his station as the dominant occupant of the planet Earth; in his stark need to direct and control his ingenuity and inventiveness for the common good—in all these respects the cause of the whole man today is without effective representation.

The principal significance of the industrial revolution is that it catapulted man into world anarchy. It made the world one without making it whole. It gave potential aggressors mighty engines for surprise destruction and conquest. It pulverized the old concepts of national sovereignty. It demolished the nation as the ultimate protective ring for society. In sum, it converted man's total environment into a jungle. All the towering differences throughout the ages that divided man were suddenly brought together within a single compressed area. These differences—ideological, religious, racial, cultural—all have their spokesmen and legions, ready to act or react as a group, ready to claim, charge, contend, or defend. But the community of which the differences are a part has no specific form; it cannot summon legions in its behalf; it lacks even a vote. And the differences have been allowed to overshadow the infinitely larger problem of man himself.

Therefore the question, Who speaks for man?

The obvious answer is that man must speak for himself. He can make of the human community a group having a specific form and structure, one that offers adequate protection and representation in those matters of common concern to all peoples everywhere, one that is sensitive to the needs and meaning of human destiny. Far from having to discard his nations, his cultures, and his other institutions, man can now create a framework large and strong enough to embrace them all. He can make the world safe for diversity.

In short, he is called upon to create a government of the whole.

But this book does not intend merely to present an argument for world government. Such a book is unnecessary. World government is coming; in fact, it is inevitable. No arguments for it or against it can change that fact.

World government is inevitable because the world has become a geographic unit and the means and the power are at hand to give it organization. There remain only these questions: What are the circumstances under which it will come about? Will it come in time to avert a new war? Will it come about as the result of a war? In either case, what kind of government will it be? Will it be a government of clearly defined and limited powers? Or will it be a world totalitarian system? Will it be truly representative of the human community or will it reflect the wishes of a small group intent on using its vast and unprecedented power to stay in power and enlarge its power? Will it ennoble man or diminish him, inspire him or degrade him? Will it be congenial to his inner growth?

The world unit at present is in a condition of near anarchy. Sooner or later the anarchy will give way to organization. Such organization could be brought about by force or by the threat of force, in which case it would require force to hold it together. Or it could be brought about by the determination and decision of the over-whelming majority of the world's peoples to make this planet a proper place for man, in which case it would rely on law and justice to hold it together.

This book, then, is not an argument for world government per se but for a *certain kind* of world government. It calls for action leading to government responsive to the needs and the nature of man. It believes that a federated United Nations is potentially man's best hope for achieving such a government. It believes the United Nations has within itself the capacity to grow into a body capable of creating and enforcing world law.

This development of the U.N. requires much more than altering a few phrases on a document or devising a shiny new outer covering to conceal basic weaknesses. What it requires is a new approach to the problems of the peace based on historical experience and the principles of workable organization, backed by the will and determination of enough people to invest their hopes, energies, and common destiny in an organized community under law.

And it is in their leadership towards such a goal that the American people have such a glittering opportunity. In this sense can America speak for man.

But this book does not believe that world federation will automatically produce a better man or a nobler one. All it can do is to open up an arena in which man may have a better chance to prove himself.

If freedom from war and the fear of war has been emphasized in this book, it is not because I believe that peace, by itself and of itself, is the ultimate goal of human existence. Peace that is merely non-war would be stagnant and without purpose. Government can only provide a field for progress or decay; the making of world law is not the end but the beginning.

The end is the supreme development and release of conscience, manifesting itself not only as a brake on conduct, but as a source of majestic inspiration in human affairs—on individual and group.

Whatever man's limitations may have been in the past, what has to be done now is well within his capacity. For what is needed is not superhuman attributes. Man is not called upon to rearrange the planets or alter the composition of the sun. He is not asked to scoop out the seas or raise the plains. He does not have to work miracles.

He is called upon to make decisions affecting his own welfare. The only price he has to pay for purposeful survival is decision.

Man is not imprisoned by habit. Great changes in him can be wrought by crisis—once that crisis can be recognized and understood.

He has at his command such resources of courage and intelligence as he himself hardly dares imagine. "The human individual," William James once wrote, "lives far within his limits; he possesses powers of various sorts which he habitually fails to use. He energizes below his maximum, and he behaves below his optimum. His life is contracted like the field of vision of an hysteric subject—but with less excuse, for the poor hysteric is diseased, while in the rest of us it is only an inveterate habit—the habit of inferiority to our full self." But once there is the challenge of necessity, he can be "carried over the dam."

Man can recognize this "challenge of necessity." The average individual possesses at least four or five times more brain power than he puts to use. There are no arbitrary limits to this capacity for expansion. Only man's own needs and his understanding of those needs can govern that growth.

The panorama of man's history is not even or flat, but heavily patterned and marked with peaks and valleys. On top of those peaks we find forcing houses of genius; in the valleys we find huts of ignorance and servility. Were the men who lived on the peaks structurally different from those who lived in the valleys? Did they possess different senses, different organs? Hardly. The same group that lived on the peaks during one century might find itself in the valley the next. Why did a golden age in one corner of the globe coincide with an iron age in another? Why did China enjoy the greatest flowering of its civilization at precisely the time Europe was stumbling through the Dark Ages? Why did America come to life so brilliantly in the late eighteenth century?

The answer is largely to be found in two of the greatest forces in history, to which Aristotle, Darwin, Spencer, Lamarck and, more recently, Toynbee, have called frequent attention. These two forces are challenge and response. And this is what can enable man to release and summon those vast reserves of intelligence and courage for the vital decisions and action that can surmount crisis.

War is an invention of the human mind. The human mind can invent peace with justice.

". . . there are no men so dull and stupid, not even idiots, as to be incapable of joining together different words, and thereby constructing a declaration by which to make their thoughts understood; and that on the other hand, there is no other animal, however perfect or happily circumstanced, which can do the like."

RENÉ DESCARTES

*   *   *

"God grant, that not only the love of liberty, but a thorough knowledge of the Rights of Man, may pervade all the nations of the Earth, so that a philosopher may set his foot anywhere on its surface, and say, 'This is my country.' "

—BENJAMIN FRANKLIN

*   *   *

"I believe that man will not merely endure; he will prevail. He is immortal, not because he alone among creatures has an inexhaustible voice but because he has a soul, a spirit capable of compassion and sacrifice and endurance. The poet's, the writer's duty is to write about these things. It is his privilege to help man endure by lifting his heart, by reminding him of the courage and honor and hope and pride and conscience and pity and sacrifice which have been the glory of the past."

—WILLIAM FAULKNER